Poet on Demand

Celia Thaxter in the 1860s. (ML)

Poet on Demand

The Life, Letters, and Works of
Celia Thaxter

by
Jane E. Vallier

Peter E. Randall Publisher
Portsmouth, New Hampshire
1994

Photographs are reproduced courtesy of the Isles of Shoals Collection of the Department of Instructional Services, University of New Hampshire (UNH), the Portsmouth Public Library (PPL), the Miller Library at Colby College (ML), and the Thaxter family.

"A Memorable Murder" is reprinted from the *Atlantic Monthly*, vol. 35, pp. 602-15, May 1875.

Library of Congress Cataloging-in-Publication Data
Vallier, Jane E.
  Poet on Demand : the life, letters, and works of Celia Thaxter / by Jane E. Vallier.
    p. cm.
  Originally published; Camden, Me. : Down East Books, 1982
  Includes biographical references (p.) and indexes
  ISBN 0-914339-47-8
  1. Thaxter, Celia, 1835-1894. 2. Women poets, American--19th century--Biography.   I. Title.
PS3013.V3 1994
811' .4--dc20
[B]
                                                        94-13822
                                                            CIP

This is a reprint of the original 1982 edition published by Down East Books, with the addition of a new introduction, bibliography, and photographs.

Peter E. Randall Publisher
Box 4726, Portsmouth, New Hampshire

for
Dorothy Seward Anderson,
Teacher

There is no frigate like a book
To take us lands away,
Nor any coursers like a page
Of prancing poetry

This traverse may the poorest take
Without oppress of toil;
How frugal is the chariot
That bears a human soul!

– Emily Dickinson

Celia Thaxter reading in her parlor. PPL.

Introduction to the Second Edition

A book is like a life: it cannot be rewritten, it can only be re-introduced and re-interpreted. Like the human subject of the book, a biography such as *Poet On Demand: The Life, Letters and Works of Celia Thaxter* (1982) belongs to a time and a place; it has its own literary family, its own generation. The author conceives the thesis of the book and, after a period of gestation and labor, gives birth to a publication which takes on a life of its own.

After a flurry of reviews and best wishes from the community which will nurture and help raise this new life, the author is left to watch her off-spring grow, behave and misbehave, endure the seasons, and take on an independent life. Most authors watch this process with wistfulness, hoping for the best, yet prepared for heart-break. Accidents do happen in the world of books where many are casualties of critical wars and publishing battles; sometimes a genetic flaw, present at conception but undetected until years later, claims the life of the book, and thus the rich and full life the author has envisioned for her fledgling may never develop.

Happily, when a book has endured the growing pains and tests of its early years, the author may have the opportunity to re-introduce her literary off-spring to the world again. This time the book is full-grown, and although affectionately aware of its weaknesses, the author smiles humbly and says, "This is my book, *Poet On Demand*. She won't be able to stay, but I'd like to tell you about her. She's a little thin, and everyone said she looked just like me when she was born. But we have our differences—she's disorganized, hard as I tried to make her otherwise. I wish she'd go out more, maybe have more male friends—but her women friends are such a joy. I wish she'd travel more—she's spent most of her life in New England and the Midwest. Like me, she seems happiest in the library or

Celia at the time of her marriage, c. 1851. (ML)

garden, so what can I expect? She has a tendency to get lost in history, reads too much, but she's wonderful company, always affectionately welcomed at home. I'm pleased with the way she's turned out."

In 1994, the centenary of the death of Celia Leighton Thaxter, this literary biography is being reissued—on demand. The first edition from 1982 has been completely sold out, and

Levi at the time of his marriage, c. 1851. (ML)

because of the dynamic growth of the research on women's lives and literature, there appears to be a need for a new edition and an update on the last twelve years of Thaxter studies. Celia emerges today in three increasingly important ways: 1) As a member of the literary and art community of her day; 2) As an environmentalist of the first generation, or as we say today, an ecofeminist; 3) As herself—a remarkable human being who left an extraordinary record of her life and her mind.

Thaxter Literary Studies

The recognition of Celia Thaxter's more than 300 poems has risen and fallen with the cycles of literary fashion. One hundred years ago, lyric poems played a similar role to that which popular music does today in American culture: lyrical verse, no matter what the times, still has the social function of organizing human emotions—taking the extremes of joy and sorrow, love and pain, life and death, and articulating the readers' or listeners' overwhelming, yet non-verbalized physiological responses to life's ecstasy or desolation. Lyric poetry translates into words the physical agony of longing and grief, the orgasmic release of joy and beauty, the visceral tension of terror or despair. All people seek to discharge such emotions through the arts: poetry, music, dance, theater.

Because lyric poems often use ritual language and highly rhythmic structure, they are prone to charges of being intellectually shallow or of sacrificing content to rhyme and meter. Thaxter's poems have been vulnerable to this approach over the years. The criticism, however, misses the point of the genre: lyric poetry fills the often terrifying void between human feelings and our human inability to articulate those feelings. Celia Thaxter knew this in her bones; therefore her lyrical poetry belongs to all times and places. The following update on Thaxter scholarship will demonstrate her appeal to a variety of readers in 1994, one hundred years after her death.

Since *Poet On Demand* was published in 1982, five scholarly discussions of Thaxter's poetry have appeared in professional journals and studies. "Hardy, Thaxter, and History as Coincidence in 'The Convergence of the Twain'" (1989) explores the similarities between Thomas Hardy's famous poem written after the sinking of the *Titanic* in 1912 and Thaxter's poem, "The Tryst" written in 1874. The article focuses more on Hardy's theory of history than his literary style, but the comparison suggests that Hardy was familiar with Thaxter's poem.

Barbara White's "Legacy Profile: Celia Thaxter" (1989) in which White claims that Thaxter's real profession was "the creation of beauty from chaos to please those around her," also addresses Thaxter's verse primarily as a source of biographical information. Yet another feminist reading of Thaxter's poetry can be found in Pauline Woodward's "Celia Thaxter's Love Poems," (1987) a mythic interpretation of Celia's love poems to her mother based on a reversal of the Demeter/Kore myth where grieving mother and daughter are separated.

The Thaxter poem I find most satisfying, "In Kittery Churchyard," is described as a "haunting meditation" by Lawrence Buell in *New England Literary Culture* (1986). Buell uses Thaxter as the classic example of historical literature and the literature of place in New England. Finally, my own recent essay, "Spiritualism as a Path for Female Rhetorical Development in 19th Century America" which will be published in 1994 contains a discussion of the development of Thaxter's literary voice.

In the area of literary biography, new information and interpretation has emerged in the last decade. First is Judith Roman's *Annie Adams Fields: The Spirit of Charles Street* (1990) which recounts the deep friendship between Fields and Thaxter. Roman emphasizes Annie's loathing of Levi Thaxter whom Fields thought suppressed Celia's substantial talent. Roman's study presents detailed evidence of the extensive network of women writers who supported one another and thus is required reading for all Thaxter scholarship.

Emily Dickinson and Sarah Orne Jewett scholarship has continued to burgeon, and many of the studies contain references to Thaxter. The Dickinson scholarship, often mentioning Thaxter as the most successful contemporary female poet, emphasizes the irony that Dickinson is now so much alive, while Thaxter has been neglected. Thaxter is cited in most of the Dickinson studies, the most useful being Karl Keller's *The Only Kangaroo Among the Beauty: Emily Dickinson and America* (1979).

In virtually all of the Jewett studies, Celia Thaxter is

Celia, age 17, and Lucy Titcomb, her sister-in-law, c. 1852. (ML)

included as part of a New England literary community and a sister regionalist writer. Most interesting from the perspective of Thaxter studies is the effect of Celia on Jewett's imagination. That Celia might have been at least part of the inspiration for the mythic Mrs. Todd in *The Country of the Pointed Firs* suggests the powerful effect Thaxter had on her contemporary writers. In Jewett's short story, "A White Heron," Celia Thaxter might have been the model for young Sylvia, and Levi Thaxter, amateur ornithologist and hunter that he was, might have been the model for the hunter.

Always an entree into Thaxter studies is scholarship on John Greenleaf Whittier, supporter of so many women writers such as Thaxter, Lucy Larcom, Gail Hamilton, Elizabeth Stuart Phelps, Alice and Phoebe Cary, Annie Fields, and Sarah Orne Jewett. The most important research in this area can be found in Shirley Marchalonis's *Patrons and Protegees: Gender, Friendship and Writing in Nineteenth Century America* (1988). Furthermore, Marchalonis's *The Worlds of Lucy Larcom* (1989), contains more biographical information on Thaxter and her circle. Susan Coultrap-McQuin's *Doing Literary Business: American Women Writers in the Nineteenth Century* (1990) analyzes the publishing world in which Celia Thaxter managed to succeed.

It is my opinion that literary studies alone will not be the key to her survival into the 21st century. The literary and academic world tends to clean house at the turn of the century in order to make room for new assessments. Such was the fate of Thaxter and many of her contemporaries at the turn of the last century; it took the feminist literary revolution of the 1960s and 70s to rediscover Thaxter and her circle. (Of course I hope that I am wrong on this matter.) However, there is now hope that Thaxter and her contemporaries will survive into the next century in anthologies, those blueprints of the various literary canons.

Several important anthologies have appeared in the last decade. Foremost is Cheryl Walker's *American Women Poets of the Nineteenth Century* (1992), one of 18 volumes in the Rutgers University Press American Women Writer Series.

Celia in 1880, Florence, Italy. (ML)

Here Thaxter can be compared to her sister poets, and although I question Walker's choice of selections from Thaxter's works as well as her critical assessment, I am pleased to have this important volume available. A new Norton anthology, *American Women Regionalists 1850-1919* (1992), edited by Judith Fetterley and Marjorie Pryse, includes Thaxter's prose. The introduction, an outstanding summary and analysis of period, delineates the connections, influences, and common themes among the American women regionalists.

Questions of the literary canons remain problematic in American literature; women are now being anthologized separately, reminiscent of the "women's sphere" a century ago. Elaine Showalter addresses these issues brilliantly in *Sister's Choice; Tradition and Change in American Women's Writing* (1991). Her discussion of Harriet Beecher Stowe's *The Pearl of Orr's Island* (1861) is central to the understanding of Thaxter's role as an inspiration for her sister writers: Thaxter was the model for Mara in Stowe's novel as well as the inspiration for at least two Jewett characters mentioned above. It is important that anthologies allow readers to pull together from lost and forgotten sources these literary connections that weave together the fabric of 19th century American women's writing.

Celia Thaxter and the World of Art

Nothing would have pleased Celia Thaxter more than to have known that her life story would perhaps be more fully celebrated in the world of art than in literature. While Thaxter seemed to view her literary output with skepticism—"my poor poems"—she called them, she approached the worlds of art and music with much more confidence. Although the musical qualities of her poetry have never been fully investigated, her contributions to the visual arts have received strong attention recently.

First, in the area of biography, there have been major scholarly works on William Morris Hunt and Childe Hassam in the last decade, both Hassam and Hunt being central figures in Thaxter's life. Turning first to William Morris Hunt, the brightest light in American painting in the 1860s and 70s, we find a man whose life affected Celia's at the deepest possible level. Not only did she study painting with Hunt, but William Morris Hunt became, in the early 1870s, Levi Thaxter's soul mate and closest companion, living with Levi at the Newtonville house from time to time. During that period, not only were Hunt and his wife divorcing, but Celia and Levi Thaxter made the decision to live separately, he in Newtonville and she at the Shoals. An important diary which belongs to the Hunt family records these painful marriage break-ups; sadly, this diary is unavailable to scholars. However, a fine new scholarly biography, *William Morris Hunt* (1991) by Sally Webster, presents a balanced view of Hunt's life and a detailed description of his tragic death by drowning at the Isles of Shoals in 1879. Webster gives an accurate account of the role of Levi and Celia Thaxter in Hunt's life.

Shortly after Hunt's death, a young American Impressionist, Childe Hassam, became a central force in Celia Thaxter's life. They met when Celia took painting lessons from Hassam in Boston, and then developed a glorious friendship in which each inspired the other to express their maximum artistic capacity. Their dramatic story is recounted by David Park Curry in *Childe Hassam: An Island Garden Revisited* (1990), the book which accompanied Park's exhibition of Hassam's Shoals paintings. The best of the four hundred Shoals paintings were exhibited at Yale University Art Gallery (1990), The Denver Art Museum (1990), and The National Museum of American Art: The Smithsonian Institution (1990-91). Many favorable reviews and the well- attended exhibition made thousands aware of Hassam, Thaxter, and the Appledore Salon which inspired the visual arts in America during the last two decades of the 19th century. *Time* magazine recognized "An Island Garden Revisited" as the best exhibition of 1990.

Celia Thaxter's garden was an inspiration not only for Hassam but several other prominent American painters of the day. Art historian William H. Gerdts' *Down Garden Paths: The Floral Environment in American Art* (1983) discusses Hassam in addition to J. Appleton Brown, Arthur Quartley, Ross

Celia, c. 1888. (ML)

Turner, John La Farge, and Ellen Robbins, all of whom took inspiration from Celia Thaxter and her garden. Thaxter's ability to mentor, to inspire and to facilitate the development of so many artists testifies to her broad intellectual capabilities.

Celia Thaxter demonstrated remarkable artistic talent of her own as illustrated in the 1986 Metropolitan Museum of Art exhibition, "In Pursuit of Beauty: American and the Aesthetic Movement." Celia Thaxter is presented as one of the premier china painters in America, producing several hundred exquisite pieces during the 1870s and 80s. The exhibition book, *In Pursuit of Beauty* (1987), gives a detailed interpretation of Thaxter's talent and work, emphasizing the domestic beauty at which Thaxter excelled.

Celia in her garden, 1890s. (ML)

Poetry, art, and music were Celia Thaxter's aesthetic trinity, and as stated earlier, the musical qualities of Thaxter's poetry have been noted but not thoroughly explored. Her sonnets to Beethoven, Mozart, Schubert, and Chopin, and the singer, Helena Mojeska, reveal her musical taste, but the fact that 20 poems are simply entitled "Song" suggests that Thaxter may have had musical performance in mind for these lyrics as well. Ballads such as "Wreck of the *Pocahontas*," "The Watch of Boon Island," "The Cruise of the *Mystery*," and *"The White Rover"* could all be performed with the accompaniment of standard guitar chording. Two hymns, "Love Shall Save Us All" and "My Lighthouse," are still sung. "Good-By, Sweet Day" with music by Kate Vannah is occasionally performed as an art song. Finally, "The Spaniard's Graves" has been developed into a contemporary progressive rock performance piece with four parts: The Farewell, The Lament, The Elegy, and The Reprieve.

In 1992, *The Isles of Shoals Remembered: A Legacy from America's First Musicians' and Artists' Colony* with introduction and text by Caleb Mason was published, and it may open a new chapter in the musical history of Appledore. Based on musician and composer William Mason's 1901 daybook, *The Isles of Shoals Remembered* is an electronically enhanced facsimile of an important document in the history of American music. Celia Thaxter's salon on Appledore at the Isles of Shoals was a center not only for musical appreciation but also musical innovation. It was there that William Mason introduced Edward MacDowell's "Tragica" sonata; that Margaret Lang, one of the first women to compose large orchestral works, performed her compositions; and that composer John Knowles Payne wrote and performed. Thaxter's musical roots run deep and deserve further attention.

Celia Thaxter, Environmentalist and Ecofeminist

In the 1980s, saving the environment—and the planet—became a strong movement within American feminism, and who better than Celia Thaxter could be considered a fore-

Oscar Laighton as a young man, c. 1870. (UNH)

mother of environmentalism. In 1994, Celia Thaxter is widely
discussed in nature and in environmental writing by both sci-
entists and historians. Perhaps the most dramatic example of
Thaxter's resurgence is found in Vera Norwood's *Made From
This Earth: American Women and Nature* (1993) where
Thaxter is compared to Rachel Carson and Lady Bird Johnson
as active preservers of the natural landscape. Norwood makes
an extensive analysis of Thaxter's *An Island Garden* (1894)
and observes that Thaxter, like Carson, saw women's modes of

interacting with nature as being passive rather than active. Norwood's extensive bibliography would be a good starting point for any study of Thaxter and the environment. Concurrently, Daphne Spain's *Gendered Spaces* (1992) opens Thaxter's poetry to new interpretations with its discussion of the unique ways women perceive space. Expect to hear more from ecofeminists such as Spain and Norwood in the next few years.

Thaxter is included in Lorraine Anderson's *Sisters of the Earth: Women's Prose and Poetry About Nature* (1991) not only for her natural history *Among the Isles of Shoals* (1874), but also for her work for the Audubon Society in bird preservation. Deborah Strom's *Birdwatching with American Women* (1986) details Thaxter's contributions to the bird preservation movement. Like Thaxter, Sarah Orne Jewett has been cited for her concern with the environment, especially in "A White Heron," written in 1886, the same year that Thaxter wrote for the Audubon Society "Woman's Heartlessness," an impassioned plea to persuade women to stop using plumage in their hats. Michael Poulan was inspired by Thaxter in his *Second Nature: A Gardener's Education* (1991) where she is once again compared with Thoreau in her attempt to seek harmony with rather than mastery of nature.

The environmental movement of the 1980s led to a renewed interest in gardening across America, and that trend, supported by the Cornell University Marine Biology Research Station's efforts to re-establish Celia Thaxter's garden on Appledore Island, and Houghton Mifflin's 1988 facsimile reproduction of *An Island Garden,* may account for the wide popularity of articles on the Thaxter garden in recent popular travel, home decorating, and gardening magazines. (See bibliography below.) Furthermore, *An Island Garden Daybook* (1990) contains excerpts of Thaxter's writing and illustrations and pictures by Hassam. A miniature version of *An Island Garden* by Heartland Samplers, Inc., sells in gift shops across the country. The lush beauty of Hassam's Appledore paintings on the cover of any book or magazine is enough to guarantee sales to people who have never heard of Celia Thaxter. Finally, a children's book which contains Loretta Krupinskis' illustrations of *Celia's Island Journal* (1992) captures Celia's girlhood relationship to the natural world.

In 1994, Celia Thaxter remains the guardian spirit of the history and culture of Portsmouth, New Hampshire, and the Isles of Shoals. For example, John Bardwell's *The Isles of Shoals: A Visual History* (1989) and Captain Whittaker's *Land of Lost Content* (1993) are two recent books on the history of the Shoals. Thaxter's prose and poetry still sell at local bookstores; her life story was dramatized in a Theatre-By-The Sea production of "Sandpiper" in the early 1980s; historical readings and presentations in the New Hampshire schools have kept Thaxter's remarkable story alive locally. A public love affair with the Victoriana so elegantly pictured in Celia's parlor and garden testifies to Americans' hunger for an aesthetic balance we like to imagine having prevailed a century ago—a beautiful woman writing romantic poems with a quill pen, the scent of old roses, the song of a bird, the murmur of the sea. Such a scene did, in fact, occur occasionally in the life of Celia Thaxter.

The Life of an Archetypal Woman

The remarkable story of Celia Thaxter is available to readers one hundred years after her death because of one other remarkable woman: the late Miss Rosamond Thaxter of Kittery Point, Maine, Celia's granddaughter and the Thaxter family historian. Upon Rosamond's recent death, more family pictures and memorabilia were given to the Miller Library, Colby College, Waterville, Maine. Several of the pictures have been included in this new edition, thanks to the cooperation of the Thaxter family and Colby College. Literary historians will always be grateful to Rosamond Thaxter for maintaining the primary research materials which make up this portrait of an artist as a woman.

In *Among the Isles of Shoals,* Celia writes about the development of her own artistic voice:

Ever I longed to speak the wind, the cloud, the bird's

flight, the sea's murmur...the manifold aspects of Nature held me and swayed all my thoughts until it was impossible to be silent any longer, and I was fain to mingle my voice with her myriad voices, only aspiring to be in accord with the Infinite harmony, however feeble and broken the notes might be. (141)

The ritual modesty with which all women writers of Thaxter's day were expected to present themselves can distract us today, we whose presentation rituals include academic degrees and lists of publications. Although some of us may feel, like Celia that our notes are feeble and broken, we are unlikely to claim that we are mingling our voices with nature or allowing nature to speak through us. Like the nineteenth century spiritualist mediums and trance speakers who thought they were the passive instruments through which the spirits of the dead would speak, we contemporary literary historians and feminist critics might think that it is the voice of feminism, or justice, or the voices of those writers outside of the canon that are speaking through us.

I must admit that I often feel that I speak through Celia Thaxter, and that she, in turn, speaks through me. Our shared experiences seem to take on a life of their own through writing, lecturing, and publishing. When my children were younger, they wondered if Celia Thaxter were a relative: her pictures hung on our wall, our summer vacations took us the Isles of Shoals, and we told them the stories of her childhood. I would have to say also that I am related to Celia Thaxter, through my mother, who taught me "The Little Sandpiper" as she had memorized it in country school. When I was an impressionable adolescent, my mother brought "The Little Sandpiper" to life again by telling me of a romantic walk on the beach in California she had taken with a young man who recited the poem to her. Celia Thaxter, my mother, my children, myself—all four generations speak through one another.

Would I do anything differently if I were starting over on a Thaxter biography in 1994? I would probably make less of a distinction between the prose and the poetry because of their rhythmic and imagistic similarities, but I would not change any of the interpretations of her character. None of the newly surfaced research contradicts my first reading of Celia Thaxter as a person. It would be much easier now than it was fifteen years ago to fill in the details of Thaxter's literary and artistic circle, but then the reader might lose sight of the original purpose: to focus on the development of Celia Thaxter's unique literary voice which arose first in poetry, then in prose. Thaxter's prose is the "solidification" of her poetic voice; all of her major themes are introduced first as poems, then later as prose. And of course, everything she wrote was ultimately autobiography: it was Thaxter's only genre.

Jane E. Vallier
Iowa State University
Ames, Iowa
1994

Bibliography

Anderson, Lorraine (ed). *Sisters of the Earth: Women's Prose and Poetry About Nature*. New York: Vintage, 1991.

Armstrong, Tim. "Hardy, Thaxter, and History as Coincidence in 'The Convergence of the Twain'." Victorian Poetry, Spring 1992, 30:1, 29.

Bardwell, John D. *The Isles of Shoals: A Visual History*. Portsmouth (NH) Marine Society: Peter Randall Publisher 1989.

Boyle, Richard J. *American Impressionism*. Boston: Little, Brown and Company, 1982.

Brooks, Paul. *Speaking for Nature: How Literary Naturalists from Henry Thoreau to Rachel Carson have Shaped America*. Boston: Houghton Mifflin, 1980.

Buell, Lawrence. *New England Literary Culture: From Revolution To Renaissance*. Cambridge: Cambridge University Press, 1986.

Coultrap-McQuin, Susan. *Doing Literary Business: American Women Writers in the 19th Century*. Chapel Hill: University of North Carolina Press, 1990.

Curry, David Park. *Childe Hassam: An Island Garden Revisited*. New York: Norton, 1990.

Edgerly, Lois Styles (ed). *Give Her This Day: A Daybook of Women's Words*. Gardiner, ME: Tillbury House Press, 1990.

Fetterley, Judith and Marjorie Pryse (eds). *American Women Regionalists, 1850-1910*. New York: Norton, 1992.

Gerdts, William. *Down Garden Paths: The Floral Environment In American Art*. Cranbury, NJ: Associated University Presses, Inc., 1983.

Griffen, Susan. *Women and Nature: The Roaring Inside Her*. New York: The Women's Press, 1984.

Griswold, Mac and Eleanor Weller. *The Golden Age of American Gardens: Proud Owners, Private Estates 1890-1940*. New York: Harry N. Abrams, Inc. 1991.

In Pursuit of Beauty: Americans and the Aesthetic Movement.

New York: Metropolitan Museum of Art, 1987.

Jesup, Paul Peter and John Bowdren. *The Lady Ghost of the Isles of Shoals*. [For children 4-10] Portsmouth, NH: Seacoast Publications, 1992.

Keller, Karl. *The Only Kangaroo Among the Beauty: Emily Dickinson and America*. Baltimore: Johns Hopkins University Press, 1979.

Marchalonis, Shirley. *Patrons and Protegees: Gender, Friendship and Writing in 19th Century America*. New Brunswick: Rutgers University Press, 1988.

—*The Worlds of Lucy Larcom 1824-1893*. Athens, GA: The University of Georgia Press, 1989.

Mason, Caleb. *The Isles of Shoals Remembered: A Legacy from America's First Musicians' and Artists' Colony*. Boston: Charles E. Tuttle Company, Inc., 1992.

McGill, Frederick T., and Virginia F. *Something Lika A Star.* Star Island Corporation, 1889

Norwood, Vera. *Made From This Earth: American Women and Nature*. Chapel Hill: University of North Carolina Press, 1993.

Poulan, Michael. *Second Nature: A Gardener's Education*. New York: Atlantic Monthly Press, 1991.

Roman, Judith. *Annie Adams Fields: The Spirit of Charles Street*. Bloomington: University of Indiana Press, 1990.

Roman, Margaret. *Sarah Orne Jewett: Reconstructing Gender.* Tuscaloosa: University of Alabama Press, 1992.

Showalter, Elaine. *Sister's Choice: Tradition and Change in American Women's Writing*. Oxford: Clarendon Press, 1991.

Smith-Rosenberg, Carroll. *Disorderly Conduct: Visions of Gender in Victorian America*. New York: Alfred A. Knopf, 1985.

Spain, Daphne. *Gendered Spaces*. Chapel Hill: University of North Carolina Press, 1992.

Strom, Deborah (ed). *Birdwatching with American Women: A Selection of Nature Writings*. New York: Norton, 1986.

Thaxter, Celia. *Celia's Island Journal*, illustrated by Loretta Krupinski. [For children 4-8] Boston: Little, Brown, 1992.

Titus, Donna Marion. *Celia Thaxter Coloring Book*. [For children 4-10] Goffstown, NH: QPS Enterprises, 1992.

Vallier, Jeff, Robb Vallier, Eric Fawcett. "The Spaniards' Graves," Ames, IA: Outrageous Music, 1988.

Walker, Cheryl (ed). *American Women Poets of the 19th Century: An Anthology*. New Brunswick: Rutgers University Press, 1992.

—*The Nightengale's Burden: Women Poets and American Culture before 1900*. Bloomington: Indiana University Press, 1982.

Webster, Sally. *William Morris Hunt*. Cambridge: Cambridge University Press, 1991.

White, Barbara A. "Legacy Profile: Celia Thaxter (1835-1894)," *Legacy: A Journal of American Women Writers*. 7:1, 1990.

Whittaker, Robert H. *Land of Lost Content*. Dover, NH: Allen Sutton, 1993.

Woodward, Pauline. "Celia Thaxter's Love Poems," *Colby Library Quarterly* 23, (1987) 144-53.

Popular Magazine Articles

Burris, Bill. "The Isles of Shoals," *Oceans,* June 1988, 21:3, 28.

Deitz, Paula. "A Cultivated Coast," *House and Garden*, 163, Sept. 1992, 126-131.

Jacobs, Katharine L. "Celia Thaxter and Her Island Garden," *Landscape,* 24, 1980, 12-17.

Logan, William Bryant. "Impressions of an Island," *House and Garden*, 162, June 1990, 42.

May, Stephen. "An Island Garden, A Poet's Passion, A Painter's Muse," *Smithsonian,* 21, Dec. 1990, 68-76.

Nevins, Deborah. "The Triumph of Flora: Women and the American Landscape, 1890-1935," *The Magazine Antiques*, 127, April 1985, 904-19.

Rayfield, Susan. "Blossoms by a Summer Sea," *Americana,* 18, May/June 1990, 28-34.

Thorpe, Patricia. "Garden Plots," *House and Garden*, 161, May 1989, 90-91.

Tozer, Eliot. "The Phoenix Garden," *Modern Maturity*, April/May, 1992.

O were I loved as I desire to be!
    What is there in the great sphere of the earth
Or range of evil between death and birth
    That I should fear, if I were loved by thee?
All the inner, all the outer world of pain
    Clear love would pierce and cleave, if thou wast
        mine;
As I have heard that somewhere in the main
    Fresh water springs come up through bitter brine.
'Twere joy, not fear, clasped hand in hand with thee,
    To wait for death,—mute, careless of all ills
Apart upon a mountain, tho' the surge
    Of some new deluge from a thousand hills
Flung leagues of roaring foam into the gorge
    Below us, as far as eye could see!

Contents

List of Poems   ix

List of Illustrations   xi

Chronology of Celia Thaxter's life and publications   xii

Foreword   xiii

Acknowledgments   xvii

Introduction: The Role of Celia Thaxter in American Literary History: An Overview   1

1   In Childhood's Fair Season, 1835–1851   27

2   Land-locked, 1851–1872   47

3   Drifting, 1872–1884   73

4   On Quiet Waters, 1884–1894   101

5   Farewells Fond and Brief   123

Poems   137

A Memorable Murder   217

Chapter Notes   245

Bibliography   254

Index   261

Poems

From *The Poems of Celia Thaxter,* Appledore Edition, 1896

Land-locked	138
Off Shore	139
Expectation	140
The Wreck of the Pocahontus	141
Rock Weeds	145
The Sandpiper	147
Twilight	148
The Swallow	149
The Spaniards' Graves	150
Watching	152
In May	153
A Summer Day	154
Before Sunrise	157
Sorrow	159
Courage	160
Remembrance	161
A Tryst	162
Imprisoned	164
Heartbreak Hill	165
In Kittery Churchyard	167
At the Breakers' Edge	169
Wherefore	170
The Watch of Boon Island	172
Beethoven (Sonnets I, II, III)	174
The White Rover	176
Contrast	178
A Faded Glove	179
Two Sonnets	181
Lars	182

Beethoven   185
The Sunrise Never Failed Us Yet   185
Sonnet   186
Mutation   186
Love Shall Save Us All   187
The Cruise of the Mystery   188
Good-By Sweet Day   193
Impatience   194
Love, Dost Thou Wait For Me   195
Oh Tell Me Not Of Heavenly Halls   196
Questions   197
From *The Heavenly Guest*
The Heavenly Guest   198
Lift Up Thy Light, O Soul   202
O Were I Loved As I Desired to Be   VI
If God Speaks Anywhere In Any Voice   203
On The Beach   203
From *Verses,* 1891
Lost   204
The Dream Pedler   205
On Quiet Waters   206
From *Stories and Poems for Children,* 1878
The Burgomaster Gull   206
The Butcher-Bird   209
Jack Frost   211
The Kingfisher   212
Inhospitality   214

Illustrations

Celia Thaxter in her parlor — Frontispiece

Celia Thaxter, *circa* 1860 — xx

Celia Laighton at age fifteen — 26

Map of the Isles of Shoals — 30

White Island lighthouse — 30

Cedric Laighton — 34

Oscar Laighton — 36

Celia Thaxter with John and Karl, *circa* 1856 — 40

Levi Thaxter and Roland — 42

Celia Thaxter at age twenty-one — 46

Celia Thaxter, *circa* 1873 — 72

The Appledore Hotel — 80

Eliza Laighton — 83

Celia Thaxter, *circa* 1880 — 100

Celia Thaxter's parlor — 104

Annie Fields — 110

Celia Thaxter's cottage and garden — 116

Celia Thaxter, *circa* 1890 — 122

Celia Thaxter with grandson Charles Eliot Thaxter — 126

Chronology

1835	Birth of Celia Laighton, Portsmouth, N.H.
1839	Thomas Laighton and family move to White Island Lighthouse.
1846	Levi Thaxter visits the White Island Lighthouse.
1848	Thaxter asks Laighton for permission to marry Celia.
1851	Marriage of Celia Laighton and Levi Thaxter.
1852	Birth of Karl Thaxter.
1854	Birth of John Thaxter.
1856	Thaxter family moves to Newtonville, Mass.
1858	Birth of Roland Thaxter.
1861	"Land-locked" appears in March issue of *Atlantic Monthly*.
1867	Death of Thomas B. Laighton.
1872	*Poems*
1873	*Among the Isles of Shoals*
1874	*Poems*, an enlarged edition.
1875	*A Memorable Murder*
1877	Death of Eliza Rymes Laighton.
1878	*Driftweed*
1881	Thaxter family moves to Champernowne Farm, Kittery Point, Me.
1883	*Stories and Poems for Children*
1884	Death of Levi Thaxter.
1886	*Cruise of the Mystery and Other Poems*
1888	*Pastorals and Idylls*
1891	*Verses*
1894	*An Island Garden*
	Death of Celia Thaxter

Foreword

When I first came to New Hampshire, I had barely heard of Celia Thaxter. I knew her only as a name listed in articles on forgotten women writers whose lives and works were worth exploring as part of the new feminist criticism. But in the seacoast region of New Hampshire and southern Maine, Thaxter had never been forgotten. Her poems and essays were read and are still read, mainly because of the continuing fascination of area residents and tourists with the Isles of Shoals.

I was soon made acquainted with the Thaxter legend, which is usually expressed as a series of vignettes: first, we see Celia as a child on Star Island, a solitary sea sprite who is "cradled" among the waves and soothed by the "lullaby" of the ocean; next she is transformed into an island "goddess" or "queen" gathering flowers from her garden and then making her way into the parlor where she conducts a salon for distinguished guests. She is now gregarious and cheerful, and Whittier, Jewett, Annie Fields, William Morris Hunt, Childe Hassam, etc., are delighted with her paintings, books, and conversation. Celia is always dressed in white (even in the child picture she is surrounded by white foam and mist)—she is a sort of Little Eva of the Islands.

In its bare outline the Thaxter legend is true, and certainly the romantic heightening of the facts was done not by today's readers but by Celia and her contemporaries themselves. Yet I find it hard to forget my first sight of the Isles of Shoals when I recovered from violent seasickness long enough to wonder how anyone could make flowers grow from rock or survive a winter storm at the Shoals. Thaxter spent some winters, as well as summers, on Appledore Island and wrote of her "white, stark desolation here in the howling Atlantic." In her poems the lullaby of the ocean is usually a roar, and the waves serve not as cradles but as graves. Thaxter even extended the favorite image of our Puritan ancestors, the howling wilderness, to her family life. While it is true that she was often surrounded by admiring friends and guests, part of her life was spent catering to the demands of what she called a "howling wilderness of men."

In her *Poet on Demand: The Life, Letters and Works of Celia Thaxter*, Jane Vallier moves beyond the Thaxter myths to make a serious and scholarly examination of the reality of Celia Thaxter's life and work. Professor Vallier is primarily concerned with the story behind Thaxter's life of "cheerful dissimulation." Like most critics who are engaged in the reinterpretation of female authors, Vallier uncovers a great deal of new information by going back to the writer herself—her published work, manuscripts, and letters—and asking, "What does this writer have to say about her life as a woman, about her career as an author?" In Thaxter's case it is particularly revealing when she is approached not simply as a personality, as she has always been viewed, but as an artist attempting to pursue a career.

Vallier quotes an intriguing letter to Thaxter from her friend John Greenleaf Whittier wherein he warns her not to become "strong-minded" or "blue" and praises her for fulfilling her duties as wife and mother. Whittier, lest we forget, does not represent organized hostility to female authors; he was the friend and mentor of many nineteenth-century women and probably did more to help them with their writing careers than any other man. Whittier proceeds to tell Thaxter that a recent poem of hers is "liked by everybody, and all the more that its author is not a writer by profession."

Certainly Thaxter was not a writer (or a painter or a naturalist) by profession, and that was part of the problem. If she had a profession, it was the creation of beauty, especially the creation of beauty from chaos, to please those around her. Her production of a lush garden from barren rock is the most powerful symbol, but one also recalls her constantly more elaborate hand-illustration of her books, as though the print weren't enough, and her endless housekeeping (most of it necessary, no doubt, but there is an element of compulsiveness in her account). This continual beautification was what her friends and readers wanted from her and praised her for—what could be more admirable in the nineteenth century than the domestication of a wild island?—but it was not the way of growth and development for that part of Celia which Vallier claims was a serious and self-conscious artist. Interestingly, Celia Thaxter referred to her poems as "weeds that sprang out of the rock and never knew cultivation."

The point is not that Thaxter should somehow have acted otherwise. Her unfortunate financial situation (she did make money by illustrating her books) and the very attitude toward female writers Whittier is transmitting were only two of several deterrents. Vallier shows us that Thaxter was very much a woman of her time. Although the Thaxter legend encourages a view of Celia as a solitary phenomenon, as apart from the mainstream as the Isles of Shoals from the mainland, Vallier finds patterns in Thaxter's career and family life which are very similar to those of other nineteenth-century female writers; she even makes a convincing comparison with Margaret Fuller, that romantic intellectual who seems on the surface so different from Thaxter. Perhaps the most significant contribution of *Poet on Demand: The Life, Letters and Works of Celia Thaxter* is the placing of Thaxter's life and work in context within American women's literary tradition. As the author states in her introduction, Celia Thaxter's "literary life stands a sign and symbol for all that women in the nineteenth century could—and could not—accomplish."

Barbara A. White
Assistant Professor
University of New Hampshire
Durham, N.H.

Acknowledgments

In bringing together this study of Celia Thaxter, I have had the support, advice and good will of many scholars, colleagues and friends. My first debt of appreciation goes to Miss Rosamond Thaxter of Kittery Point, Maine for her encouragement in the writing of this book, as well as the sharing with me of Thaxter family letters, scrapbooks, pictures, paintings and personal reminiscences. The initial stage of the study was built upon the thorough and professional bibliography on Celia Thaxter compiled at the University of Minnesota by Patricia M. Loving, the person who brought Celia Thaxter to my attention.

Since the book has been written in Ames, Iowa, I was fortunate to have efficient and kindly help in New England. Susan Mansfield, Executive Secretary of the Star Island Corporation in Boston, assisted me in making plans to do the research I needed at the Isles of Shoals. The history of the islands came alive for me in Lyman Rutledge's *The Isles of Shoals in Lore and Legend* and in Frederick T. McGill's *Letters to Celia.* Alice N. Downey shared with me her transcriptions of some Thaxter letters that she had used in her own research. To the United States Coast Guard I am indebted for the tour of the White Island Lighthouse.

Librarians are a researcher's primary asset, and for their assistance I would like to recognize Jessica Owaroff of the Houghton Library, Harvard University, and Patience Anne Lenk of Miller Library, Colby College. From the Dimond Library, University of New Hampshire, Professor Barbara White contributed a sound critique of the manuscript as well as the introduction to the book.

Several professors at the Department of English,

University of Colorado served on the committee that supervised the doctoral dissertation from which this book evolved. Professor James K. Folsom deserves my deepest appreciation for support and scholarly advice in the early stages of the research, while Professor Philip F. Gura served as advisor during the final stages. Professors Suzanne Juhasz, Arthur Boardman and Martin Bickman were readers who gave expert advice. At the Department of English, Iowa State University, my colleagues Keith Huntress and Kathy Hickok critiqued the manuscript. Special appreciation goes to Judith Conlin Johnston from the Iowa Commission on the Status of Women who edited the final manuscript.

I am indebted to John Bardwell, Director, Media Services, University of New Hampshire and Sherman Pridham, Librarian, Portsmouth Public Library, for the use of photographs from their Isles of Shoals collections.

To my own family goes the last word of gratitude. My husband, Fred J. Vallier, supported this project joyfully at every step, and in so doing served as the ideal role model—a role model of love in action—for our two sons, Jeff and Robb. Finally, to my mother, Mabel Little Sigwalt, I publicly acknowledge my appreciation for her life-long gift to me—a love of poetry and a respect for literary accomplishment.

POET
ON DEMAND

Celia Thaxter, *circa* 1860. UNH.

Introduction

The Role of Celia Thaxter in American Literary History: An Overview

There are two stories to tell about the lives of many women writers in nineteenth-century America. The first story, whether it be told about Margaret Fuller, Emily Dickinson or Celia Thaxter, is a rather conventional melodrama about a talented woman who stole time from her domestic duties to write an amazing quantity of literature, some of it a recognizable variation on the "standard" literature written by Emerson, Longfellow and Whittier. The superficial "first story" has been chronicled in American literary history by generations of critics and historians who concluded that women in nineteenth-century America—with the exception of Emily Dickinson, perhaps—wrote an enormous pile of second-rate literature, the imputed inferiority of which was based in the erroneous but widespread belief that female experience was in itself an inferior form of human experience.

Typical of the muddled judgment women's writing has received is this statement made by Robert Spiller in *The Cycle of American Literature*, 1955: "There is something about the way women lived in the nineteenth century that encouraged repression."[1] Spiller, like most of the literary historians of his and earlier generations, was content to leave that "something" a vague and unsolvable mystery; "something" was not worth in-

1

vestigating. There was, he assumed, neither rhyme nor reason to women's literary expression. The question of what was repressed or why anything was repressed did not seem worth pursuing; rather, the critic-historian threw up his hands in despair and sighed, "Women! *We*'ll never understand them!"

The repression of which Spiller speaks has become one source of entry into the "second story"—the real story—of the lives of female writers in America. Today, when the literary profession appears to be flooded with information—all that eager graduate students and tireless computers can compile—we still know precious little about the lives and works of women writing in nineteenth-century America. Thanks to the language of modern psychology and to the social revolution which calls for a total re-evaluation of female experience, one dimension of which is literary expression, the labor and the pleasure of telling these "second" stories is now before us.

No study of female literary experience in the nineteenth century would be complete without reference to Sandra Gilbert and Susan Gubar's *The Madwoman in the Attic: The Woman Writer and the Nineteenth Century Literary Imagination*,[2] a comprehensive study which covers not only the popular canon of such writers as Jane Austen, Charlotte and Emily Brontë, George Eliot, Elizabeth Barrett Browning, and Emily Dickinson, but takes the reader into the lesser known texts of these famous authors wherein can be found unmistakably the "second story." Gilbert and Gubar devise a revolutionary method which affords entry into the turbulent and enlightening "second stories," filled as they are with the images of entrapment, metaphors of physical and mental illness, and the reality of madness. That is what Spiller's mysterious "repression" is all about.

Much of that which nineteenth-century female writers repressed comes to life in the letters, the diaries, the unpublished fragments of poems and the autobiographies that these women wrote. Thus it becomes imperative that the full canon of each writer be available before literary and historical judgments be made on their work. The "second story" cannot be told until the texts upon which the "first story" is based are clearly and accurately established. As Thomas Johnson provided this scholarly material in establishing the case for Emily Dickinson, and as Paula Blanchard has done in assembling the facts of the case for Margaret Fuller, so this study will begin to compile the facts of the case for Celia Thaxter, a poet whose work represents the popular taste of her day, and even more importantly, whose literary life stands as sign and symbol for all that women in the nineteenth century could—and could not—accomplish.

A rewriting of the female literary history is perhaps the major academic and aesthetic responsibility of our generation of literary scholarship. The study of Celia Thaxter is part of the vast amount of work to be done, work that includes the establishment of accurate texts, the recasting of biographies, and the re-evaluation of literary traditions. In the case of Celia Thaxter, perhaps the most widely published woman writing poetry in America the last half of the nineteenth century,[3] the establishment of an accurate text is not a problem, although the assembling of the canon into a complete and usable volume remains to be done.

The challenge for today's student of Celia Thaxter's poetry lies in transcending the conventional reading of the poems, a reading which too often ends in dismissal of Thaxter as a serious poet. A serious and self-conscious artist she was, and so the "first story" of her life and art must be written accurately so that the "second story" can be read. It will be found that many of the difficulties other female writers such as Dickinson and Fuller met will also be found in Celia Thaxter's literary life. The themes and patterns that Gilbert and Gubar find hidden in works of Austen, the Brontës, Eliot, Barrett Browning and Dickinson will be found in works of Thaxter, acutely aware as she was of literary traditions and conventions of her time.

The external events of Celia Thaxter's life are in themselves so dramatic that readers might be content with just the recounting of the "first story": Her childhood at the White Island Lighthouse, her arranged marriage to Levi Thaxter, her experiences as wife and mother, her widespread popularity as a poet, her friendships with Whittier and Annie Fields, her later years which alternated from the depths of illness and poverty to the heights of public adoration as a Cult of the Beautiful centered around her poetry, her garden, and her life.

Telling the "second story" of Thaxter's life requires not only the complete rereading of her prose and poetry, but also the assembling of all extant correspondence, and an investigation into the domestic realities of her everyday life. For example, one of the central facts which emerges in Thaxter's letters is the exhaustion caused by the daily domestic labor. Illness seemed to be the normal state of affairs in the Thaxter family life, leaving Celia the only vigorous and healthy one. The burden of caring for her brain-damaged child, Karl, and an invalid husband, Levi, must have weighed heavily, given the fact that there was no medical treatment from which either the child or the husband could benefit. Just this one example of the difficulties with which she struggled on a daily basis would be enough to discourage any writer. The recounting of some of these burdens, then, becomes a method of measuring how fully committed Thaxter was to her role as a poet. Finally, her story illustrates how strong, how invincible was the tradition of the female literary imagination in nineteenth-century America.

*   *   *   *   *

The cross-currents of the mid-nineteenth-century American culture flowed through the life of Celia Thaxter. A third generation Transcendentalist, Celia began her public career as a lyric poet, and then progressed through successive stages of development as a folklorist, a juvenile author, a free lance journalist, a dramatic actress who wrote her own material, and finally a highly respected naturalist who won the admiration of John Burroughs. The variety of Thaxter's talents, abilities and interests can be accounted for only in terms of genius.

In 1851 Nathaniel Hawthorne spoke for literary New England when he referred to sixteen-year-old Celia Thaxter as the "Island Miranda," thus identifying Celia with two important literary sources: First, the obedient daughter of King Prospero in *The Tempest*, and second, the learned daughter of a wise father who saw the necessity of his daughter's education.[4] The second "Miranda," who serves as an ideal example in Fuller's *Women in the Nineteenth Century*, was raised somewhat as Celia was, outside of the constraints of a traditional female education.[5] Uncomfortable as Hawthorne was with Margaret Fuller herself, he recognized in young Celia many qualities Fuller had hoped women might cultivate in the nineteenth century. The unusual combination of intelligence, common sense and natural beauty that Hawthorne saw in Levi Thaxter's young bride was recorded in his *American Notebooks*; furthermore, he commented that she was unspoiled and unaffected by the models of femininity that Boston had to offer.[6]

Ten years before Hawthorne's visit to the Isles of Shoals, he and Levi Thaxter had joined James Russell Lowell, Maria White, Thomas Wentworth Higginson and other young Boston intellectuals in Elizabeth Peabody's bookstore perhaps to hear Margaret Fuller's brilliant conversations, not the least of which were about the role of women in American life.[7] Margaret Fuller's discussions on education for American women must have fallen on receptive ears, for from this group called "the Brothers and Sisters" were to come several men whose social and intellectual relationships with women were to break away from traditional norms. It is probable that Levi Thaxter heard Fuller elaborate on the importance of education for women:

> The position I early was enabled to take was one
> of self-reliance. And were all women as sure of
> their wants as I was, the results would be the
> same. . . . The difficulty is to get them to the point
> from which they shall naturally develop self-
> respect and learn self-help.[8]

That education was the road to self-reliance and self-respect for women Levi knew in his heart, but time would reveal that he was a man who could seldom match ideals with actions. He did, however, place Celia in a social position where her talents would be appreciated—notwithstanding the fact that she was a woman. First as Celia's tutor, and later as her husband, Levi Thaxter was to introduce the "Island Miranda" to Boston Brahmin society where she would win the affection and the interest of Emerson, Longfellow, Lowell, Howells, Dickens and Browning.

Quite by accident, young Celia Laighton had received somewhat the same education that Bronson Alcott was trying to achieve in his experimental school and that Margaret Fuller was trying to prescribe in *Women in the Nineteenth Century*. Celia was educated by her father at the White Island Lighthouse during the long winters of her early childhood. Thomas Laighton taught Celia not only her reading and arithmetic, but he taught her at a very young age to think for herself—just as Margaret Fuller hoped that all women would someday be able to do. Margaret Fuller's description of Miranda's education serves as a prophecy for Celia:

> Her father was a man who cherished no sentimen-
> tal reverence for Woman, but a firm belief in the
> equality of the sexes. She was his eldest child, and
> came to him at an age when he needed a compan-
> ion. From the time she could speak and go alone,
> he addressed her not as a plaything, but as a
> living mind. Among the few verses he ever wrote

was a copy addressed to this child, when the first
locks were cut from her head; and the reverence
expressed on this occasion for that cherished head,
he never belied. It was to him the temple of im-
mortal intellect. He respected his child, however,
too much to be an indulgent parent. He called on
her for clear judgment, for courage, for honor and
fidelity; for such virtue as he knew. In so far as he
possessed the keys to the wonders of this uni-
verse, he allowed free use of them to her, and by
the incentive of a high expectation, he forbade, so
far as possible, that she should let the privilege
lie.[9]

Whether or not her head was a "temple of immortal
intellect," Celia was recognized by her father as having
an uncommon mind. Celia's childhood play was spent in
imitation of her father's activities; that is, she launched
little purple boats of mussel shells and orated to the
gulls, the rocks, and the waves. What a thrill of power
the child must have felt as she climbed the lighthouse
stairs to light the mirrored lamps which then shone for
miles into the darkness. As she surveyed the rolling sea,
little Celia must have felt like a princess in a tower. What
a sense of drama must have seized her imagina-
tion—indeed the island was her stage in the vast ocean!

But all of her childhood moments were not so
carefree, and she recalls that during a storm in 1839,
while she and her family were living at the lighthouse:

We were startled by the heavy booming of guns
through the roar of the tempest—a sound that
drew nearer and nearer, till at last, through a sud-
den break in the mist and spray we saw the heavi-
ly rolling hull of a large vessel driving by, to her
sure destruction, toward the coast . . . and well I
remember that hand on my shoulder which held
me firmly, shuddering child that I was, and forced
me to look in spite of myself.[10]

Celia learned later that day that it was the brig *Pocahon-
tus*, homeward bound from Spain, and that the vessel
and all her crew were lost. The "firm hand" that Celia

recalled was that of her father, introducing her to the
world outside the domestic sphere—a new world which
Margaret Fuller herself saw as the domain of women in
the nineteenth century.

Little Celia Laighton was not a pampered child hid-
den away from the harsh world by her father, nor did any
stale classroom confine her. Fuller's description of
Miranda's education again applies equally to the White
Island child:

> This child was early led to feel herself a child of
> the spirit. She took her place easily, not only in
> the world of organized being, but in the world of
> mind. A dignified sense of self-dependence was
> given as all her portion, and she found it a sure
> anchor. Herself securely anchored, her relations
> with others were established with equal security.
> She was fortunate in a total absence of those
> charms which might have drawn her bewildering
> flatteries, and in a strong electric nature, which
> repelled those who did not belong to her and at-
> tracted those who did.[11]

Hawthorne had observed that Celia was easy-mannered
and unaffected, but his opinion was contradicted by
Thomas Wentworth Higginson, the only intimate who
ever wrote an unflattering remark about young Celia.
Higginson had been Levi Thaxter's college roommate
and intimate friend. Furthermore, he might have felt a
bit rejected when Levi turned his attention and affection
toward Celia. Higginson wrote that she was silly and
prone to exaggeration;[12] nonetheless, Higginson was
willing to defer judgment until Celia was older—she was
only fifteen at the time, and perhaps too high spirited for
his taste.

Margaret Fuller's Miranda, however, was completely
winsome. Stressing the importance of friendship, Fuller
wrote of Miranda words that were often used to describe
Celia:

> With men and women her relations were
> noble,—affectionate, without passion, intellectual
> without coldness. The world was free to her, and

> she lived freely in it. Outward adversity came, and
> inward conflict; but that faith and self-respect had
> early been awakened which must always lead, at
> last, to an outward serenity and an inward peace.[13]

The ideal that Fuller held for her Miranda was to be echoed in the words of Celia Thaxter's friends throughout her life.

When in 1847, Levi Thaxter took over the tutorial duties of Thomas Laighton, he was still in regular contact with the young Transcendentalists who had grouped a few years earlier around Margaret Fuller. Levi Thaxter was just the man to experiment with Fuller's ideals, for he was a model of the Transcendental spirit, sustained, as so many of the serious Transcendentalists were, by private income. Thus Levi Thaxter, trained professionally as both lawyer and actor, could proceed to complete the education of Celia Laighton with leisurely strolls along the beach, dramatic storytelling around the family hearth, and occasional investigations into the scientific lore of seaweeds and mosses.

Like the formal education of most women in her day—including Margaret Fuller's a generation earlier—Celia Thaxter's education was uneven and unsystematic. Fuller had written that if a woman knows too much, "she will never find a husband; a superior woman hardly ever can."[14] Levi Thaxter recognized early that his young pupil was a genius and that she would probably outdistance him, but that realization did not cause him to direct her education in any manner except by haphazard conversations about whatever was on his mind . . . or whatever was blowing in the wind.

Although both Mr. Laighton and Mr. Thaxter had begun their pedagogical tasks with enthusiasm and idealism, neither man was capable of carrying on Celia's education with systematic rigor. The press of business in Mr. Laighton's life and the absence of structure in Mr. Thaxter's life pulled the two men in opposite directions. After about the age of ten, Celia was left to educate herself.

The neglect of Celia Thaxter's formal education, seen in retrospect, was a sin of omission on the part of both her father and her husband. Lacking a traditional, Latinate education, Celia was reluctant to acknowledge her own talent and her own genius. In one of her letters she asks her editor, James T. Fields, "Don't you know I never went to school? I can fancy you smiling and saying to yourself that there is little need of telling you that."[15] Thaxter's letters abound with such self-deprecating comments and apologies. The lack of a formal education so undermined her self-confidence that she could seldom free herself from an editor long enough to experiment and grow artistically. Thus little development is found in either her prose or her poetry. Rather, Thaxter skipped from one genre to another—from lyric to ballad to mystery tale, from local history to juvenile fiction to hymns and greeting card verse.

Where could a talented woman turn for support? Speaking of the mythical "Judith Shakespeare" whose story she so convincingly wrote, Virginia Woolf posed the classic problem of the female poet:

> It seemed to me, reviewing the story of Shakespeare's sister as I had made it . . . that any woman born with a great gift in the sixteenth century would probably have gone crazed. . . . For it needs little skill in psychology to be sure that a highly gifted girl who had tried to use her gift for poetry would have been so thwarted and hindered . . . that she must have lost her health and sanity to a certainty.[16]

Both Fuller and Thaxter would have undoubtedly testified that a woman in the nineteenth century might also go crazed, limited as she was not only in expression but also education.

The lack of systematic formal education might also have been a factor in Celia Thaxter's preference for oral rather than written literature. It could be said that Thaxter wrote poetry "by ear" much in the same way an untrained person with some musical talent might play the piano "by ear." A generation earlier Margaret Fuller had seen that most American women were in fact educated "by ear," and she set about in her conversations to induce active thinking rather than passive listening in the minds of the Boston women whom she hoped to liberate from male intellectual domination. But Thaxter, like Margaret Fuller herself, continued to seek advice and inspiration from the public lectures and private conversations of such men as Ralph Waldo Emerson and Theodore Parker. The pulpit and the lecture hall demanded the masculine voice, and there was little that the idealism of Fuller or the wide-ranging intellectual curiosity of Celia Thaxter could do to change that fact.

The Transcendental ideals of education were, unfortunately, not to serve Celia Thaxter very well. Although self-reliant, individualistic, sensitive to the intimations of nature around her, Celia was not possessed of the additional resources that it would take for a woman in the late nineteenth century to succeed at a serious literary career. From today's perspective it can be seen that there were some stringent requirements for a woman's becoming a writer whose reputation was more than ephemeral. Seen in retrospect, economic issues lay at the root of these requirements:

1. A formal Latinate education, either public or private. Only the wealthy could afford to educate their daughters. It was difficult to compete with the popular poets of the day—Longfellow, Lowell, Holmes—without some classical studies.

2. Freedom from the daily press of domestic chores. Cooking, cleaning, child-care, and invalid nursing were the economic as well as the moral responsibilities of women. (Neither Thaxter nor Fuller had a "Lavinia" to care for her as Emily Dickinson did.)

The economic straits of most nineteenth century American women were all but inescapable, and Celia won a degree of financial independence too late to do her career any good. Levi's high-minded Transcendentalism didn't include such mundane considerations as allowing his wife household help, and thus Celia was forced to write most of her poetry in a state of mental, physical and emotional exhaustion.

In the earlier days at the lighthouse Celia's mind had been allowed to range freely, but at the Thaxter household in Newtonville she was a prisoner, a slave to Levi's wishes. Margaret Fuller predicted a generation earlier what would happen in this type of marriage:

> For the weak and immature man will often admire
> a superior woman, but he will not be able to abide
> by a feeling which is too severe a tax on his
> habitual existence . . . he loves, but cannot follow
> her; yet is the association not without an enduring
> influence. Poetry has been domesticated in his life;
> and though he strives to bind down her heaven-
> ward impulses, as art of apothegm, these are only
> the tents beneath which he may sojourn for a
> while, but which may be easily struck, and carried
> on limitless wanderings.[17]

Levi's own failures as a man and as an artist eventually made it impossible for him to live with his wife's success. Celia's letters of the 1870's sound much the same note as those written by Margaret Fuller a generation earlier when Margaret was forced by necessity to assume the financial burden of her family, educate her younger brothers and sisters, and still manage to steal time for her own writing.

In theory, the Transcendentalists should have been leading the way for women's education and women's rights. In practice, it was quite the opposite. Emerson gave lip-service to the idea of a woman's developing her individual talents, but he was uncomfortable around women, such as Fuller, who did. The most positive con-tribution to women's rights was made by Thomas Went-worth Higginson, who supported not only women's political rights, but also their artistic rights. His willingness to encourage the poetic genius of Emily Dickinson along with that of several other writers such as Helen Hunt Jackson and Harriet Spofford must be applauded. Likewise, Levi Thaxter played a supportive role from time to time in young Celia's education, but he could not possibly provide psychological support and he refused to provide financial support once her promising career was established. He undermined her career at every turn. The youthful idealism of the "Brothers and Sisters" was difficult, if not impossible, to sustain when the responsibilities of maturity came.

On the other hand, Margaret Fuller was a Transcendentalist who lived out her idealism to the end. Unlike her high-minded Boston brethren who were content with small scale experiments such as Brook Farm and Walden Pond, Margaret put her words into action and transcended the provincial life of New England. Fuller could hardly be called "popular" in her own day; rather, she was highly respected by a few intellectuals whose opinion in fact, did matter: Emerson, Guiseppe Mazzini, Adam Mickiewicz, and the Brownings recognized Fuller's genius and paid her the homage that was due.

Fuller's dream was to redeem American womanhood, and from today's perspective it can be recognized that in her maturity she did have the intellectual power to have done so. The opportunities that Margaret Fuller found for personal growth in New York and later in Rome were denied Celia Thaxter. Fuller was tested in the crucible of the Italian Revolution, and she herself tested the Transcendental philosophy beyond the imagination of even Emerson. Celia Thaxter never sought to develop the international reputation that Fuller achieved, Thaxter's reputation being for the most part regional. As in the case with many popular artists, Thaxter was to outlive her own reputation.

It was the inner life, the psychological dimension of Celia Thaxter's life, that Margaret Fuller was able to predict with such remarkable accuracy. Writing of the paucity of educational opportunities for women in 1844, Fuller stated: "Women have a tendency to repress their impulses and make them doubt their instincts, thus often paralyzing their action during the best years."[18] Repression, self-doubt, and emotional paralysis are the story of Celia's adulthood. Thaxter's letters to Annie Fields reveal a ritual which sustained her for thirty years. The letters would begin with an anguished account of her daily heartbreaks: Levi's irresponsibility, her son, Karl's, mental instability, her parent's prolonged illnesses; then after the frustration was expressed, Thaxter would pull herself together with some consolation. In a letter dated March 22, 1876, Thaxter writes:

> I am so blue (let me whisper in your kind ear!)
> that I feel as if I bore the scar of Juggernaut upon
> my back day after day. I totally disbelieve in any
> sunrise to follow this pitch-black night. I believe I
> am going to see everything of a funereal purple
> color from this time forth and forever! But nobody
> guesses it. I don't tell anybody but you.[19]

Her letters follow much the same pattern as many of her poems. Occasionally Celia was able to break free, as in the two years after she left Levi in 1872, and the two years after his death in 1884, but the weight of her energy was always to be expended on the welfare of her children, her brothers and her parents. Ironically, when Celia was no longer needed by her family, she literally had no place to go. Financially and artistically denied, Celia was homeless and hence dependent upon the charity of friends.

At the end of *Women in the Nineteenth Century* Fuller wrote an observation which might be elevated to a prophecy:

> The lot of Woman is sad. She is constituted to ex-
> pect and need a happiness that cannot exist on
> earth. She must stifle such aspirations within her
> secret heart, and fit herself as well as she can, for
> a life of resignations and consolations. The life of
> Woman must be outwardly a well intentioned
> cheerful dissimulation of her real life.[20]

Celia Thaxter led that outwardly cheerful life Fuller had predicted, and only by remarkably good luck did Thaxter's letters survive to reveal the dissimulations. She poured out her heart to Annie Fields through the ritual of the daily letter while no one else ever spoke of the details of her suffering which were known only to Annie Fields. The hopes that Margaret Fuller had voiced in her description of "Miranda" were not to be fulfilled for the "Island Miranda" whom Hawthorne had christened into the literary world.

Heartbreak aside, Margaret Fuller and Celia Thaxter represent succeeding generations of feminine achievement. There are remarkable similarities in patterns of their professional lives as well as in their personal lives. Both women were known as brilliant conversationalists, further evidence of their education "by ear," and each woman had an admiring group of followers: Fuller for her conversations and teaching in the Boston area, and Thaxter for her poetry readings at the Appledore Hotel where hundreds of New Englanders spent their summers. Bearing sometimes the entire financial responsibility for their families, both women turned to journalism, one of the professions open to them since they had dependent families and had to remain in their homes. Their experiences in journalism, although separated by twenty years, led both writers away from romantic themes and toward realism. Each ended her career with a manuscript for publication which was grounded in the experience of the outside world rather than the inside world of the domestic imagination. Unfortunately Fuller's manuscript of the Roman Revolution was lost in her fatal shipwreck, but Thaxter's *An Island Garden*, the work of an amateur naturalist in the tradition of Thoreau, has survived and has recently been reprinted (Peter E. Randall, Publisher, Hampton, N.H.)

Although their talents were not similar—Fuller's gift was analytical and historical whereas Thaxter's was narrative and lyrical—their psychological patterns are

surprisingly similar. Margaret Fuller warned "Let it not
be said that wherever there is energy or creative genius,
"She was a masculine mind!"[21] Because both Fuller and
Thaxter possessed vigorous problem solving skills and
physical stamina, they were often described as
"masculine." Self-possessed and self-reliant, neither
woman could afford the luxury of being dependent on
anyone for long. Thaxter's physical vitality, her shun-
ning of the sentimental, her vigorous problem solving
skills—all were prompted by her early childhood training
and tested in the daily round of activities in which she
took charge of the lives of so many people. She, like
Margaret Fuller, was not afraid of responsibility,
although they both yearned for a strong spiritual com-
panion with whom they could share their unusually
heavy family burdens. Each woman was ultimately
responsible for herself.

In order to escape the domestic quagmires in which
they found themselves, both Fuller and Thaxter
developed self-concepts as stage personalities or
actresses. In 1844 Fuller wrote that it was not winning
an admiring audience that was so difficult, it was attain-
ing the "platform" in the first place.[22] Fuller and Thax-
ter both enjoyed playing the role of the public personali-
ty. It was often said that Fuller played at being "Mar-
garet." Aware of her stage presence and how she looked
in public, Margaret took pains to dress beautifully,
elegantly, and tastefully.[23]

After learning the arts of "self-culture," Margaret
took on a regal appearance.[24] Like Thaxter, she had fan-
tasized that she was a queen, a royal foundling left on
her parent's dreary doorstep. Celia used this same image
in her autobiographical fragment, only she is a royal
foundling left in the care of ignoble fishermen. Thaxter
may well have borrowed the theme from her favorite
poem, "Aurora Leigh," Elizabeth Barrett Browning's
story of the abandoned female artist. Clearly Fuller and
Thaxter, as well as Browning, saw themselves as set
apart from even their own families by those superior in-

tellectual qualities which in turn separated them from their culture at large.

The feeling of not belonging even to their own families may have led Fuller and Thaxter and other talented women to form strong supportive relationships with men who were established successfully in their respective fields: Fuller with Emerson, Thaxter with Whittier—even Dickinson with Higginson. As mentors to these women, Emerson, Whittier and Higginson were probably flattered and somewhat bewildered. The relationships were safe ones for the women: Friendships were free to grow on an idealized plane that was totally acceptable in New England society. Perhaps to evade the issue of their sexual lives it was said that both Fuller and Thaxter had great talents for "friendship."[25] The fact that each of these female artists chose a strong, culturally powerful male to authenticate, verify or support their work ties the women's reputations securely to the men who were their mentors.

*   *   *   *   *

To Appledore Island, less than a mile square, came New England and then the world, first in the form of the aesthetic and scholarly Levi Thaxter, and later in the form of Celia's friends—James and Annie Fields, William Dean Howells, Nathaniel Hawthorne, Horace Greeley, Thomas Wentworth Higginson, Sarah Orne Jewett, Lucy Larcom, William Morris Hunt, Childe Hassam, Julius Eichberg, Ole Bulle and John Greenleaf Whittier. The painters and musicians who came for the summer seasons provided entertainment for the wealthy guests of the Appledore Hotel, many of whom were women recovering from bad cases of "nerves," or so they were diagnosed by the famous Dr. S. Weir Mitchell of Philadelphia. The resort hotels on the Atlantic coast welcomed the rich and the sick, victims of both urban blight and medical quackery. By the 1880's science and medicine were rumored to be related, but exactly how the general public didn't know. Rest and fresh air were still the treatment for everything from tuberculosis to insanity, while hypnotism and seances served simultaneously as religion, science and entertainment. The Appledore Hotel was definitely middle-class America: Someone like Henry James would have preferred to have stayed in Boston.

It was Levi Thaxter, however, who in the 1840's set the tone for what the summer life on the islands was to become. He himself had been sent to the White Island Lighthouse to recover from nervous depression, and it was to support his sinking spirits that his artist friends—Hawthorne among them—first came to the islands. Even before the hotel was built in 1848, Levi had begun a tradition of poetry readings for his friends and family in his cottage on Appledore Island.

Levi's friends were a motley group, many of whom had been participants in the Brook Farm experiment of the early 1840's. Levi himself might have been tempted to join Hawthorne, John Weiss and the others at Brook Farm had he not had such an aversion to manual labor. (In fact, Levi required the presence of a servant even while he lived in a fisherman's cottage.) The remote Isles of Shoals gave the second generation Transcendentalists a place to contemplate the glories of nature and escape the growing pressures of urban American life. Unitarian ministers such as Weiss and Higginson met on Appledore to talk long into the night about the issues of slavery and of church government. Out on the islands there always seemed to be endless time and respite from the clamor of Boston life. Hawthorne notes in his journal a convivial evening in Mr. Thaxter's cottage, an evening filled with laughter and singing:

> At about 10 o'clock Mr. Titcomb and myself took leave and emerging into the open air, out of that room of song, and pretty youthfulness of women, and gay young men, there was the sky and the three-quarters waning moon, and the old sea moaning all around the island.[26]

It was this haunting beauty as well as the spirit of friendship that brought people to the islands, and it was on this night, only two years after Margaret Fuller's tragic death in a shipwreck that Hawthorne christened Celia Thaxter the "Island Miranda."

The second-generation Transcendentalists who had gathered around Margaret Fuller for enlightenment on the social issues of the early 1840's had turned enthusiastically to the poetry of Robert and Elizabeth Barrett Browning long before the Brownings had reached the height of their popularity in England and Europe. An enthusiasm for Browning was in the wind in Boston by 1842 and Levi Thaxter quickly gained the distinction of being best reader and interpreter of Robert Browning in Boston. Not only did Levi read Browning to the "Brothers and Sisters," the romance of whose leaders, James Russell Lowell and Maria White, seemed to parallel the heroic love story of the Brownings; Levi had also read Browning to his young pupils—little Celia Laighton and her two brothers—at the White Island lighthouse.

The effects of the Brownings on the early poetry of Celia Thaxter should not be underestimated. Several of Thaxter's sonnets will be seen as comparable in style and quality to those of Mrs. Browning, the best example being "O were I loved as I desire to be."[27] Thaxter was to become proud of her own sonnets, although she readily admitted that her attempts to treat the subject of idealized love in lyric and narrative verse were unsatisfactory.

Most important to the poetic development of Celia Thaxter, however, were the dramatic monologues of Browning which she must have heard Levi read with great mastery. Her own dramatic monologues, "In Kittery Churchyard" and "The Spaniards' Graves" were Thaxter's most successful poems.

From the mid 1860's until her death in 1894, Celia Thaxter gave poetry readings daily throughout the summer season at the Appledore and Oceanic Hotels on the

Isles of Shoals. She read her own poetry first and
foremost, and that is perhaps one reason why she did not
polish the written versions of all of her poems, especially
the later ones. They came to life in oral performance, not
on the written page. Some of her poems go flat in the
same way Margaret Fuller's recorded bits of conversa-
tion do since part of their meaning is implicit in the per-
sonality and reputation of the speaker.

The reputation of the poet and the tradition of oral
performance bring to mind a major cultural cross-
current in mid-to late-nineteenth-century America: The
institution of the fireside poets. These poets, Bryant,
Whittier, Longfellow, Holmes and Lowell with their
formidable literary powers as critics, editors and an-
thologizers, shaped the literature of their day by their
examples—both negative and positive. They dominated
New England literary life until the last quarter of the
century when Howells, Twain and the realists divided
and conquered new literary territory.

Being both poet and journalist, Celia Thaxter had
friends in each camp. The poetry of Thaxter belonged at
the fireside, but her prose like Mark Twain's was pre-
cisely realistic. The poet James Russell Lowell admired
her poetry while the novelist William Dean Howells, ad-
mired her prose. The influence of the fireside poets can
be seen in Thaxter's conventional prosody and her
dogged optimism. "The sunrise never failed us yet" is
the closing line of a hymn that Thaxter wrote during one
of her darkest personal moments, and predictably the
words struck a responsive chord in the hearts of hard-
working and uneducated New Englanders, people who
probably needed a good dose of daily optimism.

Celia Thaxter could not accurately be called a
fireside poet: That title was reserved for men only, men
who wrote what might be called secular sermons in
poetry or verse. Entertaining and edifying, fireside
poetry was written for family reading which often meant
that the father read to his wife and children. The au-
dience for fireside poetry included men, even well

educated men, who would have found "feminine sensibility" in poetry inappropriate for themselves to read aloud. The fireside poets depended on a tradition of male authority in their verse.

From the firesides of Boston and New England homes came an ever increasing demand for the poetry of Longfellow, Holmes, Whittier and Lowell. The coals for those flames were kept constantly stirred by the ingenious publisher, James T. Fields, whose unusual combination of literary judgment and business sense made the publishing house of Ticknor and Fields largely responsible for the financial prosperity of these fireside poets. At least financially speaking, James T. Fields was the ideal editor to direct the early career of Celia Thaxter, sharing as they did their native Portsmouth, an informed and intelligent optimism, and the didactic legacy of Enlightenment poetry. Testimony to their deep friendship is the story of how Celia Thaxter was with Fields the moment he died—listening to Annie Fields read Thomas Gray's *Letters*.[28]

As partner in the firm of Ticknor and Fields and as editor of the *Atlantic* from 1861 to 1871, James T. Fields virtually controlled the popular poetry market in America. He created the market for fireside poetry by keeping the social and intellectual lives of the poets in the public eye. With his genius for publicity, Fields tantalized the curiosity of hard-working readers with exotic visions of the poets striving toward the peak of Parnassus. The Ticknor and Fields imprint was the guarantee of good literature, the best that America and England had to offer; however, Fields was not prepared to deal with the innovators in American literature— Whitman, Dickinson, even Henry James. Fields could tolerate neither Whitman's sensuality nor Henry James's irreverence toward America. (Henry James thought Fields bore an extraordinary resemblance to his wire-haired fox terrier.)[29] Although Fields himself wrote reams of lighthearted humorous verse which he read on public occasions such as his high school class reunion, he preferred to publish only the moral, the earnest, the genteel.

From James and Annie Fields, then, Celia Thaxter absorbed many of the literary standards and opinions that made her popular. Thaxter's earliest poems were remarkable for their freedom from moralizing and their sensuality, but as the influence of James and Annie Fields grew, so did the didacticism of Celia's poems. Before she was drawn into the Fields' social and literary life, Celia had only Levi Thaxter and his tastes for Browning and the Pre-Raphaelites to guide her. If Celia's first poem "Land-locked" had marked the beginning, not the height, which her poetry would reach, one can only speculate where her talent might have taken her.

But speculation is pointless: the fact was that James and Annie Fields were virtually to control Celia's literary life. Their friends were her friends, and their opinions seemed to become hers. Having neither the education nor the aesthetic confidence to go very far beyond the Fields' literary horizons, Celia became dependent on them, and thus limited by them. Furthermore, Fields's enthusiasm for Longfellow served as a criterion against which he measured all poets. Unfortunately, it was that same enthusiasm—specifically for Longfellow's "Hiawatha"—which became the turning point in Field's magnificent publishing career. His defense of the literary merit of "Hiawatha" weakened his reputation for discriminating editorial taste, and when he tried to persuade the Boston newspapers to "puff" the reviews of "Hiawatha" he was accused of letting financial profit dictate his literary judgments. Fields's dedication to genteel poetry helped pave the way for Celia Thaxter's success as a popular poet in the 1870's.

With the fireside poets, however, Celia Thaxter did share a belief in the moral responsibility of a poet. Although she could never espouse a traditional Christian view of the world, she did believe in the virtues of love, loyalty, friendship and truth. Had she succumbed to

Elizabeth Stuart Phelps's efforts to convert her to Christianity, Thaxter might have been an even more popular poet. "The consolations of religion I cannot bear,"[30] Thaxter wrote in 1877, and that one statement differentiates her from many of her sister New England writers—Phelps, Lucy Larcom, Harriet Beecher Stowe, even Annie Fields.

The female counterparts to the fireside poets were the writers of Sunday School fiction and verse, women such as Elizabeth Stuart Phelps and Lucy Larcom who wrote the stories and verses for the popular juvenile magazines, *Our Young Folks, St. Nicholas*, and the *Youth's Companion*. Their authority seemed best exercised upon children or upon other women. Although Celia Thaxter enjoyed the friendship of both Phelps and Larcom, she could never adhere to their religious tenets. Thaxter wrote a number of excellent poems and stories for children, but the theme was always the inexorable laws of nature rather than the laws of God: a canary is killed by a butcher bird, or a hunter shoots a burgomaster gull only after the merciless burgomaster has ravaged a flock of gulls. One historian of children's literature lauds Thaxter as being "sane and hale," not a sentimentalist.[31]

Religion, however, played a role in Thaxter's life; her fascination with spiritualism and eastern religions harks back to the earlier generation of New England Transcendentalists. She approached spiritualism from a scientific point of view, and when a significant number of experiments in which she participated failed, she was able to discard her interest entirely. After Mrs. Thaxter suffered two heart attacks, however, her attitude toward Christianity softened, and she was able to tell her solicitous Christian friends that she had begun to see the light.

Thaxter's unorthodox religious beliefs prohibited her from being included in a recent study of nineteenth-century American popular culture which developed the thesis that New England ministers and women "ex-

ploited the feminine image and idealized the very
qualities that kept them powerless: timidity, piety, nar-
cissim, and a disdain for competition."[32] Although Celia
Thaxter was a popular writer in every sense of the word,
she was not a "feminizer." Her literary topic was
"reason," and her approach was seldom sentimental. She
used several of the topics of sentimental litera-
ture—graveyard scenes, morbid isolation, nature's
soothing powers—but she seldom reduced herself to be-
ing the victim of adversity: she was rather the opponent
of adversity, the problem solver. She was not what
Albert Gelpi called "a lady poet."[33]

An admiring neighbor of Thaxter's and a fellow
poet, John Albee, wrote a tribute to Celia Thaxter that
reveals her to have fit the ideal expressed in the cult of
true womanhood.

> She knew how to play all the parts belonging to
> woman. She could make a musician play his best,
> the poets and scholars say their best—bring for-
> ward the modest, shut the door on the vulgar, and
> disengage one talent from another and give to
> each its opportunity . . . a poet with poets, an
> artist with artists . . . (she was) equally at home in
> the kitchen, . . . or with spade and trowel in her
> island gardens, or with fishermen and their wives
> and children, or as a nurse to the sick.[34]

Because she was a good woman, she had the potential, or
so her admirers thought, to be a good writer.

So talented, so resourceful, so individualistic was
Celia Thaxter that her life resists easy generalizations.
It can be said that she was a local color author like Sarah
Orne Jewett, a children's author like Lucy Larcom, a
journalist like Margaret Fuller, a romantic lyric poet like
Elizabeth Barrett Browning. Perhaps she was too many
things, and that is why she is so often included in lists,
as she was in the premiere article in the first issue of
Women's Studies, 1972, where she was not clearly dif-
ferentiated from other female local color writers. Even in
that journal dedicated to a more judicious view of
women's accomplishment Thaxter's individuality
escaped the researcher.

Had Thaxter written several local histories rather than one, *Among the Isles of Shoals*, or several books on horticulture rather than just one, *An Island Garden*, or several collections of juvenile literature rather than one—in addition to over three hundred lyric and narrative poems—Celia Thaxter might have been easy to classify. The case for her literary survival rests, like that of Margaret Fuller, not so much on what she wrote as *that* she wrote, and that she dared to live out her singular life with a self-awareness and personal integrity rarely seen in the fragments that survive as records of the lives of nineteenth-century American women.

In the end, Celia Thaxter, the "Island Miranda," might have said along with Margaret Fuller:

> I stand in the sunny noon of life. Objects no
> longer glitter in the dews of morning, neither are
> yet softened by the shadows of evening. Every
> spot is seen, every chasm revealed. Climbing the
> dusty hill, some fair effigies that once stood for
> symbols of human destiny have been broken;
> those I still have with me show defects in this
> broad light. Yet enough is left, even by experience,
> to point distinctly to the glories of that destiny;
> faint, but not to be mistaken streaks of future
> day. I can say with the bard, "Though many have
> suffered shipwreck, still beat noble hearts."[35]

Celia Thaxter would have found in the voice of Margaret Fuller's *Women in the Nineteenth Century* a kindred spirit and a thinking woman's consolation. Both women struggled against convention and prejudice in order to unburden themselves of the truth of life as they knew it. In the twentieth century Adrienne Rich speaks for those of us who have continued that very struggle:

> Today when I see "truthful"
> written somewhere, it flares
>
> like a white orchid in wet woods,
>   rare and grief-delighting, up from the page.
> Sometimes, unwittingly even,
>   we have been truthful.
> In a random universe, what more
>
> exact and starry consolation?[36]

Celia Laighton at age fifteen. UNH.

1

In Childhood's Fair Season
1835–1851

Books are for the scholar's idle times.[1]
Emerson

When in 1839 Thomas Laighton moved his small family to the White Island lighthouse ten miles off Portsmouth, people on the New Hampshire mainland said that he was crazy. They thought that he was carelessly throwing away a promising political career, and taking his family with him to the barren island was proof that he had abandoned all judgement. Lighthouse keepers in those days left their families on shore because the slippery rocks were no place for children. The education of young Celia Laighton, only four years old at the time of her family's removal, was accomplished on that six acre island according to Emerson's ideal.

Books were for this child's idle times. Young Celia was isolated at the remote White Island lighthouse from the time she was four until she was ten. With her two younger brothers, Oscar and Cedric, as her only playmates, the little girl learned to see each tiny flower and each lonely bird as her fellow creature. Her imagination was constantly exercised to invent a hospitable world on that barren rock.

Celia's father, Thomas B. Laighton, was the man in charge of her singular education. Born in 1805, young Thomas was left lame by an attack of typhus fever and

was thus unsuited for the strenuous activities of a sail-
ing life. Perhaps because of his disability, Thomas
Laighton was able to finish his high school education
and win honors in mathematics. Laighton followed a
number of successive careers, those experiences often
outweighing the value of a college education.

Mr. Laighton might have served as a model of Emer-
sonian self-reliance. Unable to depend on the security of
his family's business, young Laighton mapped out a
course of continuing education. He took the initiative in
starting a workingman's reading club and library so that
even the sailors, fishermen and dock workers could pur-
sue, as he did, higher goals. Thomas prided himself in
having chosen all of the books for this library which was
available to those who could not afford the membership
fees of the Portsmouth Athenaeum. Continuing his in-
terest in education, Thomas was elected to the local
school board, and was particularly responsible for the
quality of the high school.

The variety of Laighton's talents continued to sur-
face. He and some friends organized the Portsmouth
Whaling Company in 1832, and within a few years their
$25,000 investment had quadrupled. In 1833 Thomas
was appointed assistant postmaster and in 1836 he
became editor of the *New Hampshire Gazette*. The next
year he was elected to a two year term in the State
Senate perhaps because of his oratorical eloquence. He
had hoped to be appointed postmaster of Portsmouth
when his friend Abner Greenleaf retired in two years,
and for the interim period he accepted the position of
keeper of the White Island Light. Earlier in 1839
Thomas had purchased four of the islands: Cedar,
Malaga, Smuttynose and Hog (later named Appledore).

Little did the people of Portsmouth know that when
Thomas Laighton left the mainland he had plans of
rebuilding the fishing industry at the Shoals, and
perhaps dreams of building a resort hotel, the first of its
kind in New England. How, they would have wondered,
could any fool hope to build a large enough hotel on

those small, treeless islands to even begin to make a living?

Laighton was possessed of an unusual combination of information: 1) He knew the lumber and shipping industries well enough that he could figure out how to get the building materials to the remote islands; 2) He knew, from his family's import business, the habits and the manners of the rich whom he hoped to attract to the hotels; 3) His mathematical skills made him a precise accountant; and 4) He knew from his political and publishing experience how to advertise and promote the venture. It was from the Laighton Hotels that a Mr. Statler, later in the century, derived his ideas of modern hotel management.

A rehearsal of Thomas Laighton's numerous and varied accomplishments is important because the talented and intelligent man chose to educate his own children. For Celia, he was the model of public life, a life she eventually chose for herself. Celia recalled that he was a demanding taskmaster,[2] leading all three children through the basics of mathematics, reading and composition. Evidently Celia was his best and favorite pupil; her strong identification with her father and his world of action was to benefit her always. In contrast to the father, Celia's mother was a woman of great warmth, good nature, and patience who was scarcely able to read.

A "public man," Mr. Laighton gave Celia a practical education. Her father taught by both word and example how to be imaginative and self-confident. Most important, his vigorous example left Celia ill-suited to be satisfied with housekeeping. Four years older than her brothers, Celia grew quickly to become the third adult in her family, and by the age of twelve she worked in the hotel and had complete charge of her brothers while her mother served as cook. Over the years Celia's brothers were, sadly enough, to remain psychologically dependent on their sister.

Always able to recall vividly her childhood experience, Celia used the early days on White Island as

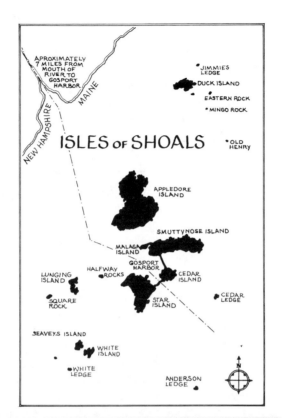

White Island lighthouse as it looked when the Laighton family arrived in 1839. From Samuel Adams Drake's *Nooks and Corners of the New England Coast*, 1876. PPL.

the basis for numerous poems and stories. A shipwreck
she witnessed the first winter on the island, 1839, later
became "The Wreck of the Pocahontus," a poem which
the editor of the *Boston Transcript* said was one of the
best contributions ever made to the *Atlantic Monthly*.[3]
Another of the early narratives is "Watching," in which
the little girl holding a lantern waits in the misty
darkness, and listens for her father's voice. The poem
begins:

> In childhood's season fair,
> On many a balmy, moonless summer night,
> While wheeled the lighthouse arms of dark
>   and bright
> Far through the humid air;
>
> How patient have I been,
> Sitting alone, a happy little maid,
> Waiting to see, careless and unafraid,
>   My father's boat come in;

Clearly it is Celia's observations of her father's life
and experience that furnish the material for the early
poems, but later in her life, however, the focal point
shifted to her mother.

Memory served young Celia in another useful way.
Books must have been scarce at the White Island
lighthouse, and so Celia memorized the poems that were
dear to her, only to recite them again to the rocks, and
waves, and her brothers. Oscar recalled her dramatic
rendering of Poe's "The Raven,"[4] and both brothers
heard her rendition of Longfellow's "Wreck of the
Hesperus." Years later Celia was to tell Longfellow that
she grew marigolds and planted flax to see the color of
the eyes of the captain's daughter in "Wreck of the
Hesperus."[5] What an impression Longfellow's dread
story must have made on this child of the sea.

Thomas Laighton shaped his daughter's mind in yet
another fashion. For him, the past instructed and the
future invited; consequently he was always trying to im-
prove upon his own financial success. Fortunately for

Celia, who was eventually to be burdened with the financial problems of her husband and sons, Mr. Laighton taught her how to make money.

In 1847 while Mr. Laighton was mulling over the prospects of financing the Appledore Hotel, along came an indolent dreamer and failed actor by the name of Levi Thaxter who had sought out the islands as a place to recover from a fit of nervous depression. Levi's family, bankers in Watertown, Massachusetts, would have supported any gesture Levi made toward establishing himself and thus earning a living. Anything to discourage his career on the stage! Levi was attracted to Mr. Laighton's plans: with Thaxter money and Laighton enterprise, anything seemed possible.

After Thaxter and Laighton had signed the agreement to become partners in the Appledore hotel venture, Levi was invited to move in with the Laighton family and become the children's tutor. For twelve year old Celia and her brothers, no more highly qualified tutor could have been found. In addition to his bachelor's degree from Harvard, Levi had acquired a law degree, probably at his father's insistence. The Watertown banker had evidently tried to urge his son away from the impracticality of literary studies, and toward a law degree around which he might structure his life, but Levi's life resisted external structure. He was well suited to be the tutor of three bright and unspoiled children—their play became his own—and he was unfortunately to remain somewhat the child all of his life.

By 1848 Mr. Laighton and Mr. Thaxter had dissolved their business partnership—their incompatibility seems obvious—but another relationship, equally doomed, was taking its place. Levi had fallen in love with his oldest pupil when she was only twelve, and furthermore had had the audacity to ask for her hand in marriage. It can only be imagined what the irascible Thomas Laighton's reaction to this request was! One story persists that Laighton ordered Levi off the island; but in fact, Levi quietly moved to bachelors quarters in the

North Cottage, and after a few weeks resumed cordial relations with the Laighton family.

Celia, recalling her engagement to Levi some thirty years later in a letter to Longfellow, spoke wistfully of her early days with Levi:

> April 3, 1878
>
> The first poems I read were yours. I had nothing but the "Pilgrim's Progress" and the "Arabian Nights," shut up in my island and somebody sailed into my world with your poems and "Hyperion" in his hand—Can you imagine what it was to me? You *spoke* my world—I was betrothed at twelve, and I learned to recite to my lover the "Wreck of the Hesperus" and all those enchanting old poems.[6]

That Levi brought enchantment to Celia's world is easy to understand, but Thomas Laighton was not a man who would allow himself to be bedazzled by poetry.

Mr. Laighton, however, did not deny Levi's request, and the paternal motives can only be speculated upon. At worst, he may have wanted to retain access to the Thaxter bank account. At best, he simply thought his daughter was too young. Wisely he insisted that the young couple be parted for a year, so in 1849 he sent Celia for her one term of formal education to Mt. Washington Female Seminary in South Boston. During the time when Celia was away from home she visited with Levi's family and made friends with his sister, Lucy. The marriage became inevitable.

Celia's feelings about the engagement can only be inferred. She wrote with no apparent enthusiasm to a young friend while she was still at the Seminary that there was a Mr. Thaxter whose wife she was to become the next year.[7] Young Celia must have imagined that life with Mr. Thaxter, the kindly tutor, would be an extension of her home life. When some twenty years later John Greenleaf Whittier urged Celia to write her autobiography she began with the love affair.[8] The only infor-

Cedric Laighton. PPL.

mation revealed in the fragment of the autobiography that remains is Celia and her tutor's shared enthusiasm for the beauties of nature.[9] Clearly Celia thought she was marrying someone of a more refined and sensitive nature than those rugged fishermen whose friendship she had known. In the autobiography she is both surprised and flattered at her teacher's interest in her . . . and then the story stops.

The autobiographical fragment reveals that Celia had a strong sense of her own individuality even in those early years. She portrays herself as an orphan raised by kindly fishermen until the dreamy eyed tutor rescues her from a vulgar, mundane life of stinking fish and endless housework. Celia characterizes herself as someone set apart from the ordinary run of mortals, someone whose life is marked by some mystical bond with nature, her true mother. She chose to call her self "Hjelma" a name familiar to the Scandinavian fishermen whom she loved.

> Hjelma gazed over the sea and laughed a long low laugh of joy as she felt the spirit of the morning salute her. She did not realize the details of the picture before her nor recognize the dim sense of beauty within her that so rejoiced at what she saw. She laughed and was glad it was morning, it was spring, the sun shone, the waves, sang, and that was enough, she was happy.

The tutor, in this fragment, reveals what must have been her memory of Levi.

> Farther up the beach stood the tall figure of a gentleman who held his straw hat in his hand as if to let the fresh breeze blow over his pale face and closely cut black hair, wherein threads of silver were shining. His shoulders stooped a little, as if from studious habit, his face was fine and high, his deep-set eyes burned with keen fires of intelligence and purpose, but his expression was a little weary, as if he were ill at ease beneath some burden of ill health either of mind or body. But the listless look gave place to a wonderful brightness of expression as he spoke to Hjelma with a smile.

Oscar Laighton. PPL.

Later, after the tutor has asked the shy pupil to come
and sit close to him, he says to her: "Tell me some more
things that make you glad. Only I think you are glad
enough to furnish cheerfullness for the whole town of
Seaport [Gosport]. If you could teach me to be as cheer-
ful I would give you in exchange all the knowledge I
have been able to gather in forty years' hard work."
Little Hjelma came to him reluctantly, but "as one ac-
customed to obey," and sat down at a little distance.

These passages, the only remaining clues to Celia's
understanding of the courtship and marriage, are viewed
from a painful distance of twenty years when all of her
worst fears about the tutor's "mental health" had
materialized.

Only one poem of Celia's hints at their early
romance. In the poem "Off Shore" the waves whisper
sweetly:

> They call to me,—incessantly they beat
> Along the boat from stern to curved prow.
>
> Comes the careening wind, blows back my hair,
> All damp with dew, to kiss me unaware,
> Murmur "Thee I love," and passes on.
>
> Sweet sounds on rocky shores the distant rote;
> Oh could we float forever, little boat,
> Under the blissful sky drifting alone!

Clearly the "we" in the poem referred to the girl and the
boat, but some readers have thought "we" included
Levi, and that the wistful tone of the poem was based on
Celia's mature recognition of what their relationship
might have been.[10] In most of her letters, Celia would
refer to her husband as "Mr. Thaxter," and speak of him
as one might speak of a kindly but difficult parent.

The other record of this romance was kept by Levi's
college roommate, Thomas Wentworth Higginson, who
noted in his diary that he saw no decided advantage in
the match, but would defer judgment.[11] He must have
known Celia's Boston schoolmistress, Mrs. Burrill, for
he reports that she "thought [Celia] most mature with an
uncommon mind, for a girl not yet fifteen."[12] Levi's fami-

ly was disappointed with their son's choice, although later Celia was to win their hearts.

The wedding of Levi and Celia took place without announcement on September 30, 1851, shortly after Celia's sixteenth birthday. The bride must have entered the marriage expecting that she and her husband would continue to live on the island near her family as Levi had for the last few years. It is hard to believe that this young girl or her family would have consented beforehand to the kind of nomadic life the young couple were to lead.

The first five years of the young Thaxters' married life was spent traveling from one house to another; first a few months with Levi's family in Watertown; then a summer on the island; then some months at Curzon's Mill on the Artichoke River in West Newbury; and then to the parsonage on Star Island. It fast became apparent that Levi Thaxter had no intention of employment in order to support his growing young family. The charity of family and friends supported Levi and Celia those first years. Finally Levi's father bought them a house in Newtonville in 1855, and how Levi paid the bills for the next fifteen years remains a mystery—to which some clues must have been in the Watertown bank.

As Levi whiled away the early hours and years of the marriage reading poetry, strolling in the woods, and visiting with his college friends Lowell, Higginson and Weiss, Celia was beset with problems which ended her exuberant girlhood much too soon. On July 24, 1852 while Levi and Celia were spending the summer at Appledore, their first child, Karl, was born. Celia had just turned seventeen, and there were problems with Karl's birth. No medical attention was available on the islands, and it seems today a lack of responsibility of all concerned that this negligence led to a tragedy which would dominate Celia's life. Brain-damaged at birth, Karl's mental, emotional, and physical handicap was evident by the end of his first year. Levi chose to ignore the problems with Karl, leaving all of his care to Celia. Mr. Thaxter was reluctant to acknowledge his son's handicap, and this neglecting of responsibility by Levi eventually was to break the marriage and the family.

While all of this heartbreak was going on behind the scenes, Celia seemed to blossom with the beauty of young womanhood. Hawthorne records in his *American Notebooks* a scene from the Isles of Shoals in August of 1852, just a couple weeks after Karl's birth.

> We found Mrs. Thaxter sitting in a neat little parlor, very simply furnished, but in good taste. She is not now more than eighteen years old, very pretty, and with the manners of a lady—not prim and precise, but with enough freedom and ease.[13]

Hawthorne reports that earlier in the visit Levi had confided to him that his dream of becoming an actor was fading. Hawthorne's sense of foreboding was right: the moments of joy for the young couple were doomed. They did spend a happy year on Star Island in 1853 where Levi had accepted a missionary appointment from the *Society for Propagating the Gospel Among the Indians and Others in North America.* Levi was probably welcomed by rude families of the Gosport fishing village as a cultural emissary from an exotic world called Boston. No testimony survives as to the degree to which Levi did, indeed, propagate the Gospel.

After the Star Island interval, Levi, age 29, retired from the world of action. Shortly after a second son, John, was born, Celia began to feel the strain of everyday living, with two babies and a hopeless husband to care for. The house in Newtonville that Levi's father bought for them had become a center of lively entertainment for Levi's Harvard pals. Later Celia was to refer bitterly to this house as a "Bachelor's Hall."

Now a gentleman of leisure, Levi Thaxter expected Celia to work like a drudge. The money his father provided was evidently not enough to cover the services of household help, and the energetic and lively Celia was as much housemaid as wife. Ten years later Celia would be using the money she earned from her poems to employ a maid, but for the time being, she had to suffer.

Celia Thaxter with John and Karl, *circa* 1856. UNH.

On January 18, 1857, Celia sounded her cry of frustration in a letter to Elizabeth Hoxie, a friend from the days at Curzon's Mill:

> Oh, these exemplary housekeepers, how much they have to do! I feel as if I were sinning against my conscience when I write a letter on any day but Sunday, because it is inevitable that I should neglect some important duty to do it, and I never do it except in a case of vital importance. It is a good thing to have your husband pronounce you "virtuous" when you are doing your best, but sometimes it's a great bore being exemplary.[14]

Celia was just twenty-one years old, with five years of grinding housework to her credit, when she wrote this weary letter. Two years later nothing much had changed, and she wrote to the same friend, "Patience at my household tasks leaves me forlorn, ugly, and horrid."[15] Later that same year Levi allowed Celia to have a washerwoman, probably because of his young wife's third pregnancy, and Celia wrote to Elizabeth that "the ironing is still hideous, ungrateful that I am!"[16]

By 1858 the cares of motherhood, including a third child, Roland, had become oppressive. While Celia coped with the two difficult children—Karl and John had already begun a lifelong habit of physical violence—Levi sauntered in the woods collecting dead birds and mosses, rowed on the Charles River, and read poetry with his college chums.

The older boys, John and Karl, were a trial of endurance. Karl, mentally retarded, made an unsuitable playmate for his younger brother. Probably because of Karl's difficulty and frustration with everyday life, he took his aggressions out on John, two years younger. Their violent and bitter fighting began in infancy and continued through their adulthood.[17] Celia kept intervening in the fights, in order to protect Karl and save him from the fate of an insane asylum. The young mother knew nothing of family life and child raising except for her own tranquil girlhood on White Island, and she was totally unprepared for her dreadful experience with motherhood. One photograph of Celia, Karl and John taken around 1856 reveals the young mother with a tense, rigid posture, restraining a belligerent John while Karl stares vacuously.[18] The fact that the two boys had to be separated for their mutual safety was as much the cause of the marriage breakdown as was Levi's indolence.

Trapped in Newtonville, Celia endured with the two difficult older boys and the one lovable infant. In 1859 she again poured out her heart to Elizabeth Hoxie: "Somehow 'Crude' is the word that expresses this place. It seems to me at the world's end—lonely un-get-at-able, uninteresting, not one beloved, friendly face within reach, no children for ours to play with."[19] She went on in the same letter to express delight in the baby, Roland, whom she said she wished had been a girl.[20] Sadly, this baby's infancy was the only time in her life when Celia could derive any pleasure from motherhood.

Levi Thaxter and Roland. UNH.

The impossible children and the meager funds were not Celia's only burdens. There was also Levi. In 1855 while the Thaxter family was spending the summer on Appledore Island, Levi and Oscar Laighton were caught in a terrific storm as they rowed from Portsmouth to the islands with household supplies. Celia watched through a spy glass as both the storm and the boat approached the island. The boat could not sail fast enough and was caught in the squall, whereupon Celia saw the men dumped from the boat into the boiling ocean near the treacherous north edge of the island. When the storm had passed, it was discovered that the two men had been washed upon the rocks—and had survived. Not until 1879 would Levi make the trip to the islands again. Although Celia was able to turn that dreadful experience into a poem—"All's Well"—Levi could never again enjoy Celia's beloved Isles of Shoals.

During the next five years in the dreary house in Newtonville, Celia slowly had to make a painful choice between her husband and children and her own family out on Appledore. In the end the bonds established long ago at the White Island lighthouse emerged the stronger, and the Thaxter family separated. Celia's first poem, "Land-locked," sums up ten years of frustration, homesickness, and despair for the young woman:

> O Earth! thy summer song of joy may soar
> >Ringing to heaven in triumph. I but crave
> >The sad, caressing murmur of the wave
> That breaks in tender music on the shore.

The tender music Celia longed to hear could never be found in Newtonville.

Despite his failure as a husband and a father, Levi Thaxter did contribute to the making of a poet. During the long evenings of those years in Newtonville he often read to Celia as she did her mending or rocked a sleepy child. He introduced his wife to some of the best writing of the day—Browning, Ruskin, Arnold, the Brontës. And he read widely—from the Arctic Expedition of Dr. Kane to Dante to the Greek tragedies. Celia listened, and

tuned her ear to the music of Levi's voice, but she heard
no love song.

When Celia's first poem was published anonymously
in the *Atlantic Monthly*, it must have been Levi who
sent the poem to James Russell Lowell, who in turn may
have thought that Levi had written "Land-locked." In
1872 when the first collection of *Poems* was published,
Levi managed all of the details and took out the
copyright in his name. Levi prided himself in handling
his wife's business affairs; it was his only opportunity to
practice the law for which he had studied.

The role of Levi Thaxter in the education of the poet
can never be fully understood. Certainly he enhanced
Celia's love of drama and dramatic poetry, and certainly
he must have instructed her in the art of reading poetry
which was later to play such an important part in her
success. Having studied elocution with Charles Keen in
New York, Levi might well have had one of the best
drama coaches of his day. The rave reviews of his Brown-
ing readings describe something of his style: "Thaxter
made each line graphic, picturing the passions it por-
trayed. The selections were made with discrimination
and he rendered them with all the power or pathos, the
verve and tenderness which each required, and his finely
modulated voice gave the true dramatic effect."[21]
Another critic wrote: "Mr. Thaxter's quick modulation
of voice from firm, fine appeal to the tenderness of eter-
nity, is a perfect bit of nature. Each poem read, has been
a faultless gem set in a few explanatory words."

Levi's career as a Browning reader, successful as it
was, spanned only two short seasons in 1881 and 1882.
Just as Levi made his debut, his terminal illness struck
him. But Levi's most brilliant moment was really many
years earlier, back on White Island, when he saw the
talent and the potential for growth in twelve year old
Celia Laighton. As his old friend Higginson wrote in his
diary, "Levi sees a great deal in her."[22]

Celia Thaxter at age twenty-one. PPL.

2

Land-locked
1851–1872

Ourself, behind ourself concealed—
Should startle most—[1]
Emily Dickinson

What Levi Thaxter saw in young Celia Laighton was raw talent, or to use a more nineteenth-century term, native genius. In the ten years between their marriage and the publication of her first poem, Celia spent most of her evenings listening to Levi read Browning, Tennyson, Keats and Shakespeare. As she mended ragged trousers, Celia received an education "by ear." Levi chose widely from the literature of the day: Ruskin, DeQuincey, Carlyle and Byron are mentioned in Celia's letters where she enthusiastically recounts the happy hours spent listening to Levi read.[2] It was in this decade that Celia grew from child to woman and began to live the life of cheerful dissimulation that Margaret Fuller had predicted all talented and intelligent women would lead.

In 1861, at the age of 26, Celia Thaxter cracked the mirror of domestic tranquility with her first poem, "Land-locked." Where the poem came from is not a mystery: it came forth from the hours of listening to Levi read, and it came forth from her psychological maturity as a woman. Celia had absorbed the iambic pentameter of English lyric poetry, and she had trained her eyes to see nature in its romantic glory. All of this came

47

together in "Land-locked," an amazing production for a
first poem, a poem that could have been written by any
number of educated Victorian women who were attempt-
ing to write up to the standards of Tennyson, Browning
and Longfellow.

The poem found its way to J.R. Lowell, editor of the
Atlantic, probably through Levi Thaxter whose literary
taste had been finely trained. Perhaps Lowell thought
his old Harvard pal, Levi, had written the poem;
moreover, the *Atlantic* was a struggling young magazine
only five years old and he may have needed filler. Never-
theless, it was a momentous beginning for young Celia
Thaxter's career when she opened the March 1861 issue
of *Atlantic*, and found to her surprise, "Land-locked."

Levi was undoubtedly amused, and maybe even
pleased, but he withheld any praise for his former pupil's
work. Celia told of her frustration in an unpublished
letter, the main subject of which is the ten dollars she re-
ceived for the poem:

> When I came home I showed it [the check] to him
> (the first mention of the existence of the "poem"
> which we had made to each other.) "Well," he
> said, "didn't you expect it?" "It never occurred to
> me," I replied—and that was all. But he called to
> me after I had gone into the bedroom to say that
> a lady had congratulated him on the subject that
> day. I know very well what he would say if I
> asked him if he liked it. Yet I think he is pleased.
> I would rather so much that he would like it than
> anybody else—but if nothing else prevented, the
> fact of his Landlocking me himself would prevent.[3]

Written February 25, 1861, this letter reveals the
estrangement that was already taking place between
Celia and Levi. Unable to live happily together, they con-
tinued to share literary interests. If the letter and the
poem are read separately, they both appear to be rather
insignificant, but when they are read together—as a
literary biographer must read them—an archetypal
story flares:

like a white orchid in wet woods,
> rare and grief-delighting, up from the page.
Sometimes, unwittingly even,
> we have been truthful.[4]

To press Adrienne Rich's simile even further, the poem and the letter serve as a "Double Monologue" spoken perhaps even unwittingly by Celia Thaxter. Behind the euphonic lines of this seemingly artless Victorian lyric lies a terror: "The fact of his Landlocking me himself." Imagine this poem being spoken by a madwoman in the attic, a woman who has just come to the full realization that she is a prisoner:

Black lie the hills; swiftly doth daylight flee;
> And, catching gleams of sunset's dying smile,
> Through the dusk land for many a changing
> > mile
The river runneth softly to the sea.

O happy river, could I follow thee!
> O yearning heart, that never can be still!
> O wistful eyes, that watch the steadfast hill,
Longing for level line of solemn sea!

Have patience; here are flowers of songs of birds,
> Beauty and fragrance, wealth and sound and
> > sight,
> All summer's glory thine from morn till night,
And life too full of joy for uttered words.

Neither am I ungrateful; but I dream
> Deliciously how twilight falls to-night
> Over the glimmering water, how the light
Dies blissfully away, until I seem

To feel the wind, sea-scented, on my cheek,
> To catch the sound of dusky flapping sail
> And dip of oars, and voices on the gale
Afar off, calling low,—my name they speak!

O Earth! thy summer song of joy may soar
> Ringing to heaven in triumph. I but crave
> The sad, caressing murmur of the wave
That breaks in tender music on the shore.[5]

Clearly this is a poem which invites the reader to hear a double monologue: a song about the beauties of nature, and the tale of a woman trapped literally in her marriage and home, and psychologically in a patriarchal system which denied her free expression of the truth as she knew it. Through the imagery she reveals that it is a living death. The poem moves quietly and swiftly as "the river runneth softly to the sea," and voices on the gale call her name. It is a poem spoken in silences, the silences of a life not lived, of dreams not uttered, of yearnings recognized only dimly by the self. Silence is both the theme and the mood of many Thaxter poems as her various speakers stand mute, inarticulate or terrified. It is the familiar silence of which Tillie Olsen speaks: "the unnatural thwarting of what struggles come into being, but cannot."[6] Young Celia Thaxter's dreams for her own autonomy were stillborn.

"Land-locked" has the hypnotic quality of a lullaby. As the somber mood of the first stanza lifts, the yearning, wistful heart is admonished to be patient: to repress, to deny itself, not to respond to the mystic calling of its own name. In anticipation of that call, the language and the meter of stanzas five and six become animated and sensual. In the melodious final stanza, the poet remains unmoved by Earth's joys, and rejects emphatically all with which that Earth and its domestic cares can tempt her: she will not be seduced. Sadly, there were no love songs in Newtonville.

"Land-locked" goes beyond autobiography and into archetype. One is reminded of Keats's "Ode to a Nightingale" where the speaker hears his name being called, and wishes, for the moment, to "die blissfully away." Weary and forlorn, the speaker in Keats's "Ode" says:

> I cannot see what flowers are at my feet,
>   Nor what soft incense hangs upon the boughs,
> But, in embalmed darkness, guess each sweet
>   Wherewith the seasonable month endows
> The grass, the thicket, and the fruit-tree wild;

> White hawthorn, and the pastoral eglantine,
>   Fast fading violets cover'd up in leaves;
>   And mid-May's eldest child,
> The coming musk-rose, full of dewy wine,
>   The murmurous haunt of flies on summer
>   eves.[7]

Surely Celia must have had this stanza in mind when she wrote the third stanza of "Land-locked."

> Have patience; here are flowers and songs of birds,
>   Beauty and fragrance, wealth of sound and
>   sight,
>   All summer's glory thine from morn till night,
> And life too full of joy for uttered words.

For anyone else summer's beauties would have been enough to bind her to the earth, but the call of the sea goes beyond reason. Long an admirer of Keats, Celia must have heard Levi read the "Odes" aloud. It is amazing that in her first poem, she could adapt the diction and arguments of "Ode to a Nightingale" so effectively to her own needs.

The death imagery that pervades "Land-locked" reveals the speaker's frustration. In the first stanza the imagery of the black hills, the sunset's dying smile, the dusk land, and the flight of daylight all suggest death. No wonder the speaker wants to escape such a sinister place. But escape where? Over the glimmering water, light still "dies," but this death is blissful. The dusky sail, the dip of oars, the voices—they are at once ominous and enticing. This paradox is central to the poem.

Finally, the bond between the speaker and the sea is mystical, past all of summer's "reasonable" attractions. Why would the speaker crave the sad murmur of the waves when she could bask in summer's golden glory? It must be because the sad murmur also "caresses" this lonely speaker—there is no caress in summer's beauty. The delicious dream, with all of its sensual and sexual implications, was what called to the young woman. Sexual longing is expressed conventionally in images of waves breaking rhythmically on the shore. The "yearning heart," the "delicious dream," the "dip of oars," the "caressing murmur," the "tender music," the "light dying blissfully away" and particularly the verb "crave" suggest sexual fantasy to the modern reader. The poem bears a striking resemblance in both tone and imagery to another passionate poem written perhaps even the same year, Dickinson's "Wild Nights."

> Wild Nights—Wild Nights!
> Were I with thee
> Wild Nights should be
> Our Luxury!
>
> Futile—the Winds—
> To a Heart in port—
> Done with the Compass—
> Done with the Chart!
>
> Rowing in Eden—
> Ah, the Sea!
> Might I but moor-Tonight
> In Thee![8]

Both Thaxter and Dickinson feel the futility of the "Heart in port." Neither compass nor map is needed for the waters into which they desire to row. The poems, with their images of the sea, "owe their persistence, as traditional material of art, to their power of expressing or symbolizing, and so relieving, typical human emotions."[9] Thus it may be assumed that the symbol of the sea might contain roughly similar meanings for Thaxter and Dickinson.

Writing in *After Great Pain: The Inner Life of Emily Dickinson*, psychiatrist John Cody analyzes the multiple meanings of the sea as a symbol in Dickinson's poetry.[10] He speaks of the concept of ego boundaries in which the sane person recognizes clearly the distinction between self and the non-self. Whereas the sea can symbolize the self-immersion that is associated with such negative experiences as loneliness, isolation, or emotional chaos, there is also a positive meaning for the symbol: "merging with a larger security-providing reality in which the self is immersed."[11] Dr. Cody's interpretation of the sea symbol is as follows:

> The common denominator in all these "sea poems" however, regardless of the pleasurability of the feeling, is the poet's experience of a diffusion of herself—of the blurring of her own boundaries until she becomes lost in the infinite or expands into infinity herself.[12]

Cody then goes on to explain what the difference is between the symbol as perceived by the abnormal person and the normal. For the person whose hold on reality is precarious, the symbol involves a threat to the integrity of the personality, but to the normal person whose ego boundaries are clearly recognized, this symbol has a different meaning:

> It should be pointed out that not every experience of a loosening of ego boundaries is indicative of serious mental disorder. Normal persons may have the sensation when thrilled by any of the arts—especially, perhaps, music. The experience may be found in contemplation of nature—a starry night, for example or a startling panoramic view. "Breathtaking" is a word often applied to pleasurable experiences in which the ego undergoes a sudden expansion. A partial loss of ego boundary occurs also at the moment of orgasm.[13]

Cody explains that Dickinson both courted and feared the experience of ego expansion and weakening psychological boundaries. In fact Cody uses the poem "Wild Nights—Wild Nights!" to illustrate Dickinson's potential for strong erotic passion. By analogy, then, it can be argued that Thaxter was probably expressing similar passionate desires in "Land-locked" as well as other poems. Thaxter's immense capacity for enjoyment in both music and sublime landscape are also accounted for in this theory. Psychoanalytic theory, as Cody presents it, rings true for Celia Thaxter, a woman who had clearly defined "ego boundaries," or to put it more plainly, had

no propensity for the psychotic as Dickinson might have
had. Thaxter was no stranger to anxiety or depres-
sion—or grief—but she was always perceived by others
as being sane and hale. Her psychological vulnerability
was revealed only to her confidante, Annie Fields. Given
the gregarious, good-natured, affectionate personality
that so many friends recount in their memories of her,
Celia must have borne the failure of her marriage with
great pain. The monthly and yearly separations so com-
mon to the Thaxters were no inducement to their hap-
piness.

The sexual theme of "Land-locked" is carried fur-
ther in Thaxter's third poem, "Off Shore," *Atlantic*,
September, 1862. The last three stanzas of "Off Shore"
might be read as a continuation of "Land-locked"—or
"Wild Nights."

> Thick falls the dew, soundless on sea and shore:
> It shines on little boat and idle oar,
> Wherever moonbeams touch with tranquil glow.
>
> The waves are full of whispers wild and sweet;
> They call to me,—incessantly they beat
> Along the boat from stern to curved prow.
>
> Comes the careering wind, blows back my hair,
> All damp with dew, to kiss me unaware,
> Murmuring "Thee I Love," and passes on.
>
> Sweet sounds on rocky shores the distant rote;
> Oh could we float forever, little boat,
> Under the blissful sky drifting alone![14]

The sexual theme here is unmistakable. The "careering
wind" as lover passes on leaving the girl in dreamy
detumescence.

The scene of "Off Shore" is a place of privacy and
quiet: "Only the stars behold us where we lie." The set-
ting of the darkness—drifting and dreaming under a
silver moon—suggests a lover's tryst, safe from the
lighthouse beam which is only a slender stream of chang-
ing light. In the final stanzas the light is "tremulous"

and the lighthouse, surely a symbol for Celia's domineering father, stands dark with a fiery crown. Out of his sight, the lovers can float forever, alone.

The visual imagery of the poem is sensual, suggesting a pre-Raphaelite painting or a poem such as Rossetti's "Blessed Damosel." The dream-like quality of the glowing sunset, the silver sparkles, the tremulous crimson, the fiery crown, the damp hair, the murmuring, floating and dreaming—all suggest sexual fantasy.

It is difficult to trace the theme of adult sexuality in Thaxter's poems because after these two early poems with their thinly veiled sexual themes, Celia retreated into privacy about her own intimate life. She avoided the theme of adult sexuality by using the persona of the child (herself) in many poems—or she railed against God rather than against an earthly lover. It would be misleading, however, not to mention some of the biographical information about both Celia and Levi that might clarify the treatment of the sexual themes.

When Celia wrote "Land-locked," and "Off Shore" she was a twenty-six-year-old woman, hopelessly estranged from her husband, yet not free to divorce for the obvious reasons of social convention. More important, Mr. Thaxter was a father substitute for Celia, and she could have left him no more than she could have disowned her own father. Their engagement had taken place when Celia was twelve—if not before—and the marriage to her esteemed tutor, the man who was her father's business partner, was forged by a stronger fire than just youthful passion. It would be impossible to read the motives of a girl the age Celia was when the whole relationship began. It is fair, to assume, however, that her feelings for Levi were inextricably confused with those she held for her father, a man she respected and with whom she identified.

Thomas Laighton must have been a man much like Edward Dickinson, a stern and irascible patriarch, who was willing to put up with a deferring and good-natured wife. Reports are that Thomas Laighton drank too much—most lighthouse keepers did for the practical reason that there was not always fresh water on the tiny islands. He and Levi Thaxter may well have brewed up their scheme for the resort hotel when they were short on work and long on grog. Nevertheless, there was an attraction between the two men, presumably Mr. Laighton admired Thaxter's Harvard polish while Thaxter found Laighton's rough vitality refreshing. Levi was a self-proclaimed invalid, the lame Mr. Laighton was an ambitious entrepreneur. These two men were the only adult males young Celia had ever known, except for old Ben Whaling, her father's assistant, and it would take her years before she could see these men for what they really were.

A further reason Celia could not divorce lay in the fact that she had married "up." Mr. Thaxter was always referred to by the Laighton family as a gentleman, a refining influence on the rough island people.[16] The family was grateful to him for marrying their Celia: it was the sign that they had arrived. Celia, like Browning's "Last Duchess," was supposed to be ever grateful for Thaxter's two hundred year old family name, while Celia's family accepted Levi's eccentricities as a matter of differing social class.

Levi Thaxter's attraction to twelve year old Celia Laighton calls for some explanation. When Levi first saw this child he had come to White Island Lighthouse to recover from a nervous breakdown. It can be shown that his "breakdown" was caused, in part, by his failure to bring under his own command a healthy adult male ego. He had first failed at the bar, perhaps to thwart his aggressive father's desire for him to become a lawyer. He then failed at becoming an actor, in spite of the fact that he apparently had talent, because he was afraid of confronting an audience. As an actor he could try on various masks or roles in hopes of finding a permanent identity—but there was no solid masculine self-concept there when the mask came off. Afraid of failing in all competition with men of his own social class, Levi retreated to a world of poor fishermen and small children where his inadequacies would not be so conspicuous.

In choosing a twelve-year-old girl as his beloved, Levi fortified himself against failure. He was safe in not having to marry her for at least three years—and forces beyond his control could eventually relieve him of his responsibility for the marriage: that is, her father, and the passage of time might intervene. Most important, Levi chose a female who was in no position to reject him. He had already gained her natural affection when he was her tutor; he knew the girl was a genius, and thus his compliments had been sincere. He genuinely wanted to be her parent—and the only way he could do that was outwardly to become her husband. This parent-child relationship seems to be what precluded divorce on the one hand, and the development of a normal sexual relationship on the other.

A final compelling reason for Levi's attraction to Celia was that he was very much drawn to boyishness. Preadolescent Celia had the boyish qualities that Levi was so charmed by—independence, brashness and roughness—all qualities which had been cultivated in her rough island life.

Since Levi Thaxter was never able to endure long without his own boyhood cronies around, finally Celia was simply driven out of the Newtonville house which she referred to as the "Bachelor's Hall." Levi's dearest friend and college roommate, Thomas Wentworth Higginson, shared a disposition similar to Levi's, but Higginson was able to muster a series of careers. Neither Thaxter nor Higginson was able, however, to surmount feelings of inadequacy about his masculinity.[16] Higginson found escape from sexual confrontation in his marriage to an invalid, and thus had an opportunity to live out his feminine instincts in his devoted "mothering" of his wife.[17] Levi, too, took great pleasure in the feminine role of raising his third son, while the two more aggressive boys were left to Celia. In later years Celia wrote that Levi was good at "all womanly things" such as tending the sick and making soup.[18] Levi kept himself surrounded by his gentle friends, John Weiss, William Morris Hunt, Wentworth Higginson, and assorted minor poets and artists, few of whom were ever able to develop any coherent career identity, and all of whom were well rehearsed in the art of the nervous breakdown.

Shortly after Celia wrote "Land-locked" and "Off Shore," two poems which clearly reveal her sexual frustration, she began to find solace and inspiration—poor substitutes—in her friendship with John Greenleaf Whittier. After her father's death in 1866 Celia could begin to build her emotional life around another man, and fortunately Whittier was available. Ironically, Whittier was a man of remarkable similarity to Levi, except on the major issue of having a sense of identity. Tall, bearded, gentle and poetic, Whittier was to become Celia's surrogate husband.

There was yet another man in Celia's life, a man whose temperament and literary taste were akin to Celia's. He was James T. Fields, also a native of Portsmouth, a man safely married to Celia's intimate friend, Annie Fields. Between Fields and Whittier, Celia had the emotional and literary support that was lacking in her relationship with Levi. Fields was not, however, a member of the Cambridge crowd with whom Levi had gone to Harvard. A self-educated country fellow from New Hampshire, Fields had burst upon the Boston literary world just when the Cambridge poets needed his talents as a publishing entrepreneur. Fields was responsible for bringing the fireside poets to an eager audience, and Celia Thaxter was a female type of the poets Fields most admired.

Nonetheless, when James T. Fields asked Celia to revise "Seaward" to fit his idea of what the poem should be, she replied that she could not:

September 23, 1861

Mr. Fields:
I thank you very much for the kind things you

said about my little poem, and am grateful for the trouble you took in looking it over and making suggestions. I am sorry I could not act upon them all. I am not good at making alterations. The only merit of my small productions lies in their straightforward simplicity, and when that bloom is rubbed off by the effort to better them, they lose what little good they originally possessed.

I'm afraid you will not think the unconscious quotation from the "Ancient Mariner" remedied by the mere transposition of words, but I cannot alter it satisfactorily and say what I wish. If the first and fifth verses do not seem to you too objectionable, pray let them pass.

I'm sorry its name is not as felicitous as Land-locked, which Mr. Lowell christened.

Pray pardon me for trespassing on your valuable time, and believe me,

Gratefully yours,
C. Thaxter[19]

Ingratiating as this letter seems on first reading, filled with "pleases" and "pardons" and all manner of self-deprecations, it is a "feminist" document of the first order: a flat-out rejection of patriarchal standards and judgments. Fields, genial soul that he was, probably sighed, when he read the letter, "Ah, poor Celia! What she doesn't know!"

The letter, the first of the extant letters that Thaxter sent to editors, reveals her to be committed in no uncertain terms to the truth about her own experiences. Fields's editorial suggestions went unheeded just as Emily Dickinson quietly ignored Higginson's attempt to alter her form. Here in this brief and seemingly insignificant letter can be seen a twenty-six-year-old woman with no formal education telling the most powerful literary critic and editor in the country that he is wrong about her poem. It is a letter filled with negatives ("I am not good," "I cannot alter," "do not object," "it is not felicitous,"), apologies ("I am grateful," "I am sorry," "I am afraid,"), and most of all *silences!* The letter says, in words that Fields would never understand, "I cannot write any poem *but* this. I cannot lie.'' The language of acquiescense softens her affront to Fields's patriarchal judgment, his implicit request for Thaxter to rewrite her poem in *his* own words.

In order to protect herself from the assaults of patriarchal editors and critics, Thaxter adopted a number of disguises. She needed the distance afforded by the child narrator or the observer/realist. She could never have been a confessional or personal poet—she was too proud to ask for pity—and her grief was all too real. Celia's writing does not reveal her to be introspective; rather, she is a survivor who lives to report the tale. Her self-concept is heroic, as the next poem will begin to reveal, and her psychic survival is based on her wit, her intelligence and her endurance.

"The Spaniards' Graves," (see page 150) appearing in the *Atlantic*, April, 1865, is one of Thaxter's most appealing poems.[20] The speaker is one who "Stands at their bleak graves whose eyes are wet with/Thinking of your woe." The image of the poet who shed tears in behalf of her Spanish sisters is the first in a series of heroic women who pose cosmic questions in Thaxter's poems. Strangely this heroic woman never speaks aloud; both her anguish and her power are repressed. She speaks to herself, and to the imaginary audience of her sisterhood, in dead silence. Her tears never distort reality. Buried in futile dreams, the Spanish sisters endure a living death. In the face of their agony, nature remains unmoved: "Still summer broods o'er that delicious land,/Rich, fragrant, warm with skies of golden glow." There is no consolation, only the sisterhood of grief which spans the oceans and the centuries.

Fresh, specific, dramatic, "The Spaniards' Graves" is a competently written poem which avoids excess sentiment. Indeed there was a shipwreck at the Shoals in 1813, and the sailors' graves can be seen today. The poem takes Celia away from the personal morass of her marriage as seen in the first three poems, and into the boundless subject on which her fame was to rest, the

Isles of Shoals: their history, lore and legend—their cruel
beauty.

In "The Spaniards' Graves" the narrative moves
swiftly. The farewell, the shipwreck, the long wait which
itself takes up four stanzas, the brief moment of
sisterhood in shared grief: the poem is perfectly propor-
tioned. The speaker is not a sentimental grave-stalker,
but rather one who as maiden, wife and mother has
"questioned the distance for the yearning sail." She
speaks as one who has seen the wives of fishermen
paralyzed with fear:

> Weary they watched, till youth and beauty
>   passed,
> And lustrous eyes grew dim and age drew near,
>   And hope was dead at last.

The speaker identifies with the haggard widows of the
sailors, knowing herself a love that is remote, even dead.

With ironic deference, Thaxter wrote to J. T. Fields
that "The Spaniards' Grave" was one of the poems that
"evolved among the pots and kettles."[21]

The heroic woman is only one of Thaxter's literary
disguises. In "Watching" (see page 152), published July
1864, the child narrator seems to have wandered out of
Wordsworth's "Ode" still trailing clouds of glory. By
choosing the child as a speaker, Thaxter could avoid the
inevitable pessimism connected with adult perception
and experience. The Wordsworthian image in the first
two stanzas is charming:

> In childhood's season fair,
> On many a balmy, moonless summer night,
> While wheeled the lighthouse arms of dark
>   and bright
>   Far through the humid air;
>
> How patient have I been,
> Sitting alone, a happy little maid,
> Waiting to see, careless and unafraid,
>   My father's boat come in;[23]

Here again is the familiar scene: waiting, watching, hoping for the sign that never comes. The impatience and the anger are hidden behind the mask of childish faith; clearly there will be "No whisper of thy voice." On first reading, the analogy of the last three stanzas is a perfect statement of faith. On second reading, however, the irony begins to take hold, and the four negatives of the last stanza sound threatening with images of entrapment and impending doom—even claustrophobia. The child is paralyzed with terror: "There was no human sound,/And I was all alone." Voices are heard in the darkness, a rattle of rowlock, then suddenly "loomed the tall sail, smitten suddenly/With the great lighthouse ray!" The child gets one terrifying glimpse of the father:

> I will be patient now,
> Dear Heavenly Father, waiting here for Thee:
> I know the darkness holds Thee. Shall I be
>   Afraid, when it is Thou?

> On thy eternal shore,
> In pauses, when life's tide is at its prime,
> I hear the everlasting rote of Time
>   Beating for evermore.

> Shall I not then rejoice?
> Oh, never lost or sad should child of thine
> Sit waiting, fearing lest there come no sign,
>   No whisper of thy voice!

The unsigned poems, published between 1861 and 1865, constitute the most distinguished group of Thaxter's poems. The poems are fresh, personal, perhaps too revealing of this terribly private woman, but as soon as her signature was added, Celia withdrew the "personal" element from her poems. For the most part, her childhood experiences were relegated to the children's poems which she began to write with increasing frequency. The lonely lover of the early poems was to be incorporated into a heroic personality who transcended sorrow and pain through what Emily Dickinson called "weights of discipline."[24]

The discipline of pain, often the central theme of female poets writing in the late nineteenth century, is most freely revealed in Thaxter's poem, "Sorrow." (see page 159). An odd and unpleasant poem, "Sorrow" is central to the understanding of Thaxter's literary development.[25] Sorrow, personified as God's angel, is taken as the poet's lover.

> I turned and clasped her close with sudden
>   strength,
>   And slowly, sweetly, I became aware
> Within my arms God's Angel stood at length,
>   White-robed and calm and fair.
>
> Upon my lips she laid her touch divine,
>   And merry speech and careless laughter died;
> She fixed her melancholy eyes on mine,
>   And would not be denied.
>
> . . . .
>
> I heard and shrank away from her afraid;
>   But still she held me and would abide;
> Youth's bounding pulses slackened and obeyed,
>   With slowly ebbing tide.

When the poet embraces Sorrow, she is then able to "look beyond the evening star," and know that pain can, with the proper attitude, become an exquisite pleasure.

Unattractive as the logic of this poem may be, the poem is interesting in that it reveals further development of the heroic woman/persona. Celia assumes she is speaking for all women, not just herself. The fact that many of the women in Thaxter's poems are heroic probably owes much to the fact that Celia sought the company of strong, important women while she lived in a family of weak, helpless men—her husband, her sons, her brothers, Levi's friends—all of whose activities she supervised. When she wrote to Annie Fields that she was surrounded by a "howling wilderness of men,"[28] the demands on her had become endless: Karl's constant care, Levi's morbid hypochondria, John's belligerence, Roland's continuing bouts with malaria and depression,

Oscar's continuously broken heart, the insanity and
suicide of William Morris Hunt. In the light of these
tragedies, the beauty of nature was no consolation for
the sorrow that Celia felt. As a poet, Celia did not
cultivate grief for its dramatic effect. A generation
earlier the American poet, Lydia Sigourney, had turned
grief and suffering into a full-time literary occupation,
but whereas Sigourney wailed, Celia Thaxter expressed
sorrow that was rooted in rage. Sorrow seems to have
seduced even Emily Dickinson who wrote of her own
struggle:

> I can wade grief—
> Whole Pools of it—
> I'm used to that—
> But the lest push of Joy
> Breaks up my feet—
> And I tip—drunken—
> Let no Pebble—smile—
> "Twas the New Liquor—
> That was all!

Then Dickinson continues with a metaphor that Celia
Thaxter would have well understood:

> Power is only Pain—
> Stranded, thro'- Discipline,
> Till Weights—will hang—[27]

The discipline of pain was for Celia Thaxter the great
female experience—if not the great human experience of
all time.

Yet another poem, "Rock Weeds" (see page 145),
contains the heroic woman motif, but what dominates
the poem is the erotic imagery, with the storm and the
sea fused to represent the masculine principle. In Thax-
ter's poetry masculinity is associated with storm, rolling
waves, and cold, while *femininity* is suggested by the
island, organic growth, and heat. The masculine is, of
course, active, ominous and almost always destructive,
while the feminine is passive, life giving—the endlessly
waiting victim about to be destroyed. The sexuality in
this poem is violent and ruthless, yet the "iron
shore"—the ego boundary—remains intact. The other

variation on this symbolic rape occurs when the brutal sea destroys a ship such as the *Pocahontus*, itself feminine and life-sustaining, or even the "mad" ghost ship, the *Mystery*, which cruises the high seas as if it were a madwoman racing to and fro in an attic.[28]

By today's standards "Rock Weeds" is not a successful poem, even though it was popular with readers of the *Atlantic* who probably noticed the similarity between the last two stanzas and Lowell's famous lines from "The Vision of Sir Launfal": "And what is so rare as a day in June?"[30] Thaxter herself wanted to avoid moralizing, and in distress she wrote to Annie Fields that her poems were "so didactic and commonplace that I have a kind of loathing for them. Only the stern master necessity would ever encourage me to push them into the light?"[31] The loathing of self, the inevitable fragmentation that comes from self-hatred was not just a humble pose on the poet's part. What Thaxter had written to Annie Fields was a classic statement of the double bind in which female artists find themselves. Gilbert and Gubar speak of the dilemma as:

> The feelings of self-doubt, inadequacy, and inferiority that their education in "femininity" almost seems to have been designed to induce. The necessary converse of the metaphor of literary paternity . . . was a belief that caused literary women like Anne Finch to consider with deep anxiety the possibility that they might be "cyphers," powerless intellectual eunuchs.[32]

It is ironic that there are only two motives that Thaxter and other literary women could admit to: one was that stern master, necessity, and the other was idleness. Elaine Showalter has observed that in the nineteenth century, women writers were forced to be modest, self-deprecating, and subservient, and present their artistic productions as mere trifles designed to distract and divert the reader in moments of idleness.[33] To put the humiliating theory simply: from the writer's idleness came the literature that filled the reader's idleness. The value of both the work of literature and the act of reading it went, supposedly, unrecognized.

A reining in of the power of female literature is nowhere more evident than in a letter Whittier wrote to Mrs. Thaxter upon the popular success of her next poem, "The Wreck of the Pocahontas." (see page 141). After Whittier had read the rave reviews that the poem had brought he sent Thaxter a letter of congratulations—and a warning:

March 29, 1867

> I suspect thee are in the predicament of the
> man who says he "woke up one morning and
> found himself famous." But I hope thee will still
> recognize thy old friends when thee meets them.
> Don't believe the newspapers. "Be not puffed up,"
> says the apostle. Don't go to being blue. Don't set
> up for a strongminded woman. But surely, the
> poem in the Atlantic is liked by everybody, and all
> the more that its author is not a writer by profes-
> sion. It is so pleasant to know that such things
> can be done by a woman who looks to her own
> household, and makes her own fire-side circle hap-
> py, and knows how to render lighter her daily care
> and labors by throwing over them the charm of
> her free idealization. I think men are inclined to
> deprecate the idea of a merely literary woman. But
> when the charm of true womanliness is preserved,
> when the heart's warmth is not absorbed by the
> intellect and the wife and mother remain intact,
> and to this is added the power to move the public
> heart and satisfy the demands of the highest taste
> and culture, what can we do but admire and say
> God-speed! [34]

Whittier's letter, with all of its sincerity and goodwill, is a manifesto: How to be a Female Literary Success. The ten criteria, five negative and five positive, are rein-forced by Biblical authority in the words of the apostle Paul to the Corinthians. Even though a female poet spoke with "the tongues of men and of angels" if she herself were not an embodiment of charity, her *poetry*

was nothing. She is admonished to "seek not her own."
Whittier's charming little letter can be summarized as
ten commandments for the female writer:

1. Do not be "puffed up."
2. Do not allow the warmth of your heart to be ab-
   sorbed by your intellect.
3. Do not set up for a strong-minded woman.
4. Do not neglect your household duties.
5. Do not be a professional writer.
6. Be a wife and mother.
7. Make your own fireside circle happy.
8. Appeal to the public heart, not the public mind.
9. Satisfy the demands of the highest taste and
   culture.
10. Idealize your daily care and labors, or, to use
    Margaret Fuller's angry term, "Dissimulate!"

The cult of true womanhood which Whittier advocated
in his letter, and which he summarized so succintly, drew
its power from the scriptures and its authority from
tradition.

What Whittier sensed in "The Wreck of the
Pocahontas" was a subtle violation of some unspoken
rules that female writers were supposed to follow. The
speaker of the poem only *half forgets* her grief and pain
and returns to her labors unsatisfied that "At last all
shall be clear." Further, the poet has flagrantly violated
three commandments: She has not allowed her heart to
dominate her intellect, she has appealed to the public
mind, not the public heart, and finally, she has not
idealized her labor: "Sighing I climbed the lighthouse
stair,/Half-forgetting my grief and pain." The questions
the poet raises, behind the guise of childlike honesty, are
not simply rhetorical machinations designed to lead the
reader to conciliating answers. Whittier must have
winced when he read the questions and then have been
relieved to find that the "voice eternal" was allowed to
rumble:

"bow thy head and take
Life's rapture and life's ill,

"And wait. At last all shall be clear."

The poet, madwoman though she might be, is clearly dissatisfied with cosmic put-off. Thus Thaxter escapes the patriarchal strictures, which demand that she accept God's will, by pretending to be a willfull and impertinent child. The power emanates from her *will*—the strong sense of determination, almost a sense of self-begottenness—that was Celia Thaxter. She does not, as Theodore Roethke snivels, "stamp her tiny foot against God."[35] The Celia Thaxter that the poem reveals is not a weary housewife complaining to Annie Fields, but rather the heroic woman who sees "the fated brig/Staggering to her grave," and who firmly identifies with the ship.

What was so attractive about this poem—other than the fact that it was written by a woman for whom writing was not a profession? The appeal must have been first of all in the subject of the shipwreck, that classic struggle between man and nature. If ever a poet had license to be didactic, it was on the cosmic subject of the shipwreck. The poet asks:

Oh wherefore? Are we naught to Thee?
    Like senseless weeds that rise and fall
Upon thine awful sea, are we
    No more then, after all?

It is almost as if the Captain's daughter from "The Wreck of the Hesperus" is speaking the lines. Readers on the New England seacoast could never hear too many tales of the shipwreck, ever the emblem of their stern and harsh Providence.

The last major poem to be published before the first collection in 1872 was "Courage" (see page 160), found in the April, 1870 *Atlantic*.[36] One of Celia's most often reprinted poems, "Courage" further develops the persona of the heroic woman who is, in the end, befriended but not loved by the "power of light." She lifts her head "above the mists," while bearing a burden like Christian's pack. Her rebellious tears are held bravely back . . . as she stands alone against the hostile world.

Indeed, by 1870 Celia was a madwoman—her life seems to have been unbearable at this time. Levi's continuing illness, rheumatism of some kind or tuberculosis, forced him to spend the colder months in the South, so their house in Newtonville had to be let out. Roland left with his father, and the marriage had disintegrated. Celia wrote to her friend Elizabeth Hoxie that she had no place to go for the winter: "Then heaven knows where he [Levi] will go or what we shall do, but something will have to be arranged. 'Come home' I say—there won't be any more home, which makes me feel forlorn."[37]

Celia Thaxter was to publish six more poems in the *Atlantic* in 1870 and 1871 before her first edition of *Poems* was issued in 1872. The poems show an ever increasing anger at the God who allows no explanation for his capricious acts. "The Swallow" (see page 149) contains a stanza that sums up all of Thaxter's suffering:

> Before the gates of his mystery
> > Trembling we knock with an eager hand;
> Silent behind them waiteth He;
> > Not yet may we understand.[38]

The silence in Thaxter's poem is ominous: the poems are negatives—pictures of what has not happened, words that are not spoken—and the repressed anger bubbles to the surface of seemingly pleasant and ladylike poems. For Thaxter the process of writing was a means of dissipating or at least making some rationality out of the madness around and within her; however, the anger is never spent.

Thaxter's anger against God is an extension, even an allegory, of her rage against that "howling wilderness of men" whom she was forced to care for in private, and then defer to in public. These men she served loyally in both body and spirit. They were male household gods to whom she was ever faithful, and who were, in turn, treacherous to her, driving her into private madness. In one letter to Annie Fields, Thaxter expresses her anger toward Levi for deserting her and leaving her penniless. She tries to complete a manuscript as "unfinished." Celia then laments: "Oh Annie, if it were only possible to go back and pick up the thread of one's life anew—I could be 10 years old again—I would climb to my lighthouse top and set at defiance anything in the shape of man. How inexorably sadness grips us."[38] Celia was just ten when Levi came in view of the lighthouse; little did she know that he would bring a premature ending to not only her childhood, but also her happiness.

She couldn't laugh about Levi, but she could laugh about the remote God that was supposed to be such a refuge in time of trouble. In another letter to Annie, Celia wrote with abandon:

November 13, 1875

> I must tell you! I came home like a raving lion
> and tore my new bonnet limb from limb, cut off
> half a yard of that heaven-aspiring coronet, and in
> the twinkling of an eye turned the whole structure
> into one of grace and elegance. (Ahem!) But really,
> you would imagine me to be at least ten years
> younger, and that *the peace which somebody said
> the consolations of religion failed to bring*, is
> mine—that of being fitly bonneted![39]

The lighthearted mood of that letter was not to last long, for Celia was to spend the next two years caring for her invalid mother, even during the long winters on the islands. Almost two years to the day, Celia was to write another letter about her religious beliefs, but the mood was to be somber:

November 14, 1877

> Dearest Annie,
>   This morning, at half past seven, the sweetest
> mother in the world went, God alone knows where,
> away from us! There is no comfort for us any-
> where except by the gradual hand of time. The

"consolations of religion" I cannot bear. I can
bear my anguish better than their emptiness,
though I am crushed breathless by my sorrow. It
seems as if I could never fill my lungs with air
again, as if I never wished to look upon the light
of day.[40]

Thaxter thought the submission of her will to any God
was humiliating; she quested endlessly for nontradi-
tional religious experience: spiritualism, Buddhism,
Christian Science, psychic experience. In the end she
was most comfortable with a gentle pantheism sup-
ported by stoic patience. She would be true only to
herself.

Celia Thaxter, *circa* 1873. PPL.

3

Drifting
1872–1884

Parting is all we know of heaven,
And all we need of hell.[1]
Emily Dickinson

The truth about Celia Thaxter's most productive decade remains elusive. The first story to be told is that of a genuinely talented writer meeting the demands and the deadlines of numerous editors, and then being paid for her efforts in both public affection and in cash. It is the story of a successful writer who kept James R. Osgood and Company (later Houghton Mifflin) from going bankrupt after the disastrous fire in the publishing district of Boston in 1872. Outwardly Thaxter was, by any standard, one of the most successful women in America, but inwardly there was the turmoil and the agony that Margaret Fuller had predicted would be the price of success.

For all practical purposes, the Thaxter marriage ended when Celia's first volume, *Poems*, was issued in 1872. Levi had financed the first five hundred volume edition and had chosen the arrangement of the twenty-nine poems. Eager readers paid one dollar for the volume, which sold out immediately, but Celia paid for her success in a different currency. The price she paid is found in the "second-story," the story of her personal life, the full account of which has never been assembled. Marital and domestic troubles continued to drain away

73

the energies Thaxter wanted to spend on her writing. Poetry was her lifeline, as she revealed in a letter to James T. Fields ten years earlier:

> Verses can grow when prose can't, ... The rhymes
> in my head are all that keep me alive, I do believe,
> lifting me in a half unconscious condition over the
> ashes heap, so that I don't half realize how dry
> and dusty it is! ... I wish you'd tell A. [Annie]
> that I have had infinite satisfaction and refresh-
> ment out of her tickets to the Emerson lectures
> already, and forgot all weariness and perplexity on
> the crest of a breaker of earthly bliss while Emer-
> son discourses.[2]

Ten more dreary years of housekeeping and invalid tending had ensued between this letter and the publication of *Poems*. The poet's skill, versatility and vision had continued to grow in spite of adversity, but Celia was not confident that her poems were good. Her talent had expanded to include children's poetry and the prose of the Shoals papers. Celia's response to all this acclaim was to make plans to give up her career—the price had been too high in terms of her family relationships. She had written to her brother, Cedric, about plans to give up, but he retorted only with some teasing: "You say you are going to stop writing. Whatever you do, never do that, unless you wish to consign us to an early grave. But perhaps you do want to kill us, in your puss-proud grandeur."[3] Always the joker, Cedric was really belittling Celia in this letter, teasing her about her increasingly demanding audience.

Only a few days after Celia had received Cedric's belittling letter, Whittier wrote to tell Celia of Horace Greeley's enthusiasm for her work:

> I must tell thee that many people spoke of thy
> "Shoals" papers in strong terms of admiration.
> Poor Alice Cary—who is very ill,—and her
> sister—among others. One day when I sat by her
> bed-side Horace Greeley came in. He spoke of
> Boston writers and magazines and then said in his

slow Yankee drawl: "Well—the best prose writing
I have seen for a long time is Mrs. Thaxter's Isles
of Shoals in the Atlantic. Her pen-pictures are
wonderfully well done." Now that I call praise
worth having.[4]

Celia had indeed become one of the brightest stars in
literary Boston. As her friend Elizabeth Stuart Phelps
wrote, "Celia was the best of good company, the most
fearless, the most independent of beings."[5] Howells
wrote his impression of Celia about this time: "She was
in presence what her work was, fine, frank, and
finished."[6]

But Celia herself was filled with self-doubts; her hus-
band and sons virtually ignored her career, and she was
forced to turn outside her home ever increasingly for en-
couragement and for advice. A series of letters written to
Annie Fields in 1872 and 1873 reveal more dramatically
than an analysis could the despondency that Celia faced.
She was a prisoner held captive in her own kitchen, over-
whelmed with exhaustion and even physical illness, try-
ing desperately to retain her sanity. Her story is a
perfect example of what Sandra Gilbert and Susan
Gubar call "the common, female impulse to struggle free
from social and literary confinement through strategic
redefinitions of self, art, and society."[7]

Celia's efforts to redefine herself, art, and society
consumed the decade of the 1870's, the most difficult of
the redefinitions being that of self. As her role as wife
and mother disintegrated, she was forced to build a new
indentity based on her literary success and, most unex-
pectedly, on her relationship with her own mother. This
second experience, on the outside, looks like a dreary
resignation to invalid nursing, but in reality, it was
much more. During the five years preceding her
mother's death in 1877, Celia began to articulate to
herself, and finally in her poems, an awareness of the
silent bond of what Gilbert and Gubar call the "female
subculture."[8] Upon this awareness is built, slowly but
securely, her literary identity, her definition of her art. A

more extensive discussion of this redefinition will be found in Chapter Four of this study, but suffice it to say at this point that Thaxter's literal return to her mother brought forth all that is the best, all that is enduring in her art.

Poems, 1872, marks the end of what may be called the first stage of Thaxter's literary life, centered, as it was, around Levi and the Cambridge literary establishment. *Poems*, 1874, marks the beginning of the second stage with its growing commitment to female experience, and thus to the female literary imagination. While *Poems*, 1872, contained only five new poems in addition to those published in the *Atlantic* for the preceding ten years, *Poems*, 1874, burst forth with twenty-eight new poems, all fresh from the sources of Thaxter's new-found literary power—her own *female* experience. Gone were her imitations of Lowell and Longfellow, gone were the lines of iambic pentameter through which she had conformed to partriarchal poetics.

The five new poems in 1872 included "The Sandpiper" (see page 147) on which her fame was to rest. In this lovely poem, the speaker is the same child the readers had met in "Watching," and "The Wreck of the Pocahontas." The faith this child of nature exhibits in God's providence perhaps refreshed weary believers, while for those readers who could not accept the consolations of faith, "The Sandpiper" was a charming picture of childhood innocence. Simple enough to be enjoyed by children, "The Sandpiper" has been anthologized at least thirty times and is the one poem of Thaxter's that receives attention today.

*   *   *   *   *

Out of the bonfires of a broken home and heart came Celia's best poetry. Gone were the lines with lush and dreamy summer evenings, comforting flowers, and murmuring sea. The new poems had a new voice, sharpened

imagery, and less melody; narrative dominated, whether
the poem was a simple ballad or a dramatic monologue.
For the first time money was coming in from *Scribners*,
from *Atlantic*, from *Young Folks*, and from *Harpers*, and
Celia was able to save enough to buy a set of Browning's
poems.[9]

By the mid-1870's Celia's sons were grown, and all
but Karl were away from home. Levi had for twenty
years refused to sail to the islands, and he had sunk into
sardonic isolation. Young Roland by this time had begun
to take his anger out on his mother, presumably for
deserting their Newtonville home. Roland felt his
primary loyalty was to his father, not his mother; unfor-
tunately he had had to choose between them.

When Celia retreated to her childhood home and the
care of her mother, it seemed that all the attention and
affection she had withheld from Levi and the children
she now lavished on Eliza Laighton. Poor Karl was also
in her care, his only alternative being a state mental
institution.

The four years that Thaxter spent writing *Among
the Isles of Shoals*, 1869–1873, had led her back to a rich
vein of material: tales of man and the sea. Immersed in
the history of the islands, Thaxter became recognized as
an early folklorist.[10] Well she knew the daily struggles
against the sea—and loneliness, hunger and heartbreak.
She had witnessed the shipwrecks, and she had consoled
the wives of fishermen who had failed to return. She was
not a romantic folklorist, seeking out the quaint and the
picturesque in everyday life; rather, she was a realist
whose methods of reporting had become widely
respected.[11]

Separated from her husband, Celia began to write
poems about unfaithful lovers. A dramatic monologue
entitled "At the Breaker's Edge" (see page 169) reveals
the poet at a spiritual nadir as she waits, like the Indian
maiden in "Heartbreak Hill" with a heart of stone. She
addresses an impersonal God who is the epitome of all
unfaithful lovers:

Thou art the cold, the swift fire that consumes;
   Thy vast, unerring forces never fail;
And thou art in the frailest flower that blooms,
   As is the breath of this tremendous gale.

Yet, though thy laws are clear as light, and prove
   Thee changeless, ever human weakness craves
Some deeper knowledge for our human love
   That looks with sad eyes o'er its wastes of
      graves,

And hungers for the dear hands softly drawn,
   One after one, from out our longing grasp.
Dost Thou reach out for them? In the sweet dawn
   Of some new world thrill they within thy
      clasp?

Ah! what am I, thine atom, standing here
   In presence of thy pitiless elements,
Daring to question thy great silence drear,
   No voice may break to lighten our suspense!

Thou only, infinite Patience, that endures
   Forever! Blind and dumb I cling to Thee.
Slow glides the bitter night, and silent pours
   Thine awful moonlight on the winter sea.[12]

"Blind and dumb" stands the victim, contemplating the breaker's edge and the "awful moonlight" which no longer "sends its silver sparkles down," as it had in a poem a decade earlier.

The faithless lover turns into a demon-lover in Thaxter's next poem, "A Tryst" (see page 162). Once again the subject is a shipwreck, but not a specific one as Thomas Hardy had in mind when he wrote "The Convergence of the Twain" in 1912. The image of the ship and iceberg as ill-fated lovers whose meeting is decreed by Fate is the kind of cosmic theme Thaxter found most attractive. Hardy may well have been familiar with Thaxter's poem when he wrote about the Titanic. The image of Death, riding the iceberg, recalls other faithless or destructive lovers which have populated Thaxter's poems. Death is proud, disdainful and silent, his eyes riveted on his victim:

Ever Death rode upon its solemn heights,
    Ever his watch he kept;
Cold as its heart through changing days and
  nights
    Its changeless purpose slept.

Death is merciless, not even allowing time for prayer:

O helmsman, turn thy wheel! Will no surmise
    Cleave through the midnight drear?
No warning of the horrible surprise
    Reach thine unconscious ear?

She rushed upon her ruin. Not a flash
    Broke up the waiting dark;
Dully through wind and sea one awful crash
    Sounded, with none to mark.

Scarcely her crew had time to clutch despair,
    So swift the work was done:
Ere their pale lips could frame a speechless
  prayer,
    They perished, every one!

And thus the poem ends with no comment, no explanation. "The Wreck of the Pocahontas," ten years earlier, was told by a child who was able to rekindle her faith and to light the lamps of the lighthouse again. In "A Tryst" the tragedy is neither seen nor heard by a soul; at least the ill-fated *Pocahontas* knew her destroyer, and her crew had time to prepare for death.

In 1884 the explorer Adolphus W. Greely returned from an Arctic expedition, when for some time all thought that there would be no rescue. Greely took pains to seek out Celia Thaxter and tell her that in those grim days of despair he had read aloud to his men from her book of poems, many of which had an appeal for the rough sailors; moreover, they had especially found comfort and hope in her poem, "A Tryst."[13] Only six out of the original crew of twenty-five survived the expedition. What hope they found there has escaped this reader's imagination!

The human tragedy of "The Watch of Boon Island"

The Appledore Hotel photographed from the porch of
Celia Thaxter's cottage. UNH.

(see page 172) and "A Tryst" is portrayed in cosmic
terms, but a more gentle and personal portrait of human
suffering is found in the 1874 *Poems* in what might be
called Thaxter's best poem, "In Kittery Churchyard"
(see page 167). The subtitle of the poem refers to the
gravestone which the speaker in the poem reads with
tender sympathy: "Mary, wife of Charles Chauncey, died
April 23, 1758, in the 24th year of her age." The dramatic
monologue begins with the speaker/poet in the church-
yard. This lovely poem avoids moralizing the senten-
tiousness. The speaker in "In Kittery Churchyard" does
not "embrace sorrow;" rather, she speaks of a controlled
and tender sympathy, the mood of which contrasts with
the sparkling summer day. As the speaker kneels at the
grave of sweet Mary Chauncey, she feels a moment of
shared sisterhood much as she did at the graves of the
Spanish sailors. The speaker is clearly in sympathy with
Mary, a Victorian "Angel-woman" who has un-
questionably gone to "that happy shore." But, the
speaker of the poem will not admit to the commonplace

consolation that death rescues Mary from the trials of life on earth: Mary is simply cheated out of a life. The "happy shore" to which she has supposedly gone does not offer reparation.

"In Kittery Churchyard" is the only poem of Thaxter's that allows the male consciousness to be revealed. The characterization of Charles Chauncey is balanced, yet tender. There is really none of the unfaithful lover theme here; it is time that "deals firmly yet kindly" with Charles. There is a chill of irony in the line, "Doubtless he found another mate," although Charles is clearly not in the same league with the faithless lovers of "A Tryst" and "Heartbreak Hill" (see page 165). Charles' grief, however, is obviously for *himself*: "What joy for *me*, what joy on earth is left?" The value of Mary's life lies clearly in what joy she could have brought to Charles, selfless as she supposedly is. Time, which has been "firm and kind" to Charles, has been treacherous to his bride, Mary, a woman whose gentle and beautiful face was only one source of her husband's happiness. The grief of Charles Chauncey "appeals" to the speaker not in a morbid sense, but in an artistic sense: the poet tries to balance out the joy and sorrow of life, an effort which leaves her in "foolish" tears.

Most of the poems in the 1874 volume shared with "In Kittery Churchyard" a heightened intensity of visual imagery. The 1872 poems had been written more for the ear, but by 1874 Thaxter was beginning a second career as a painter and the poems benefit from her growing concern with the visual. Thaxter replaced words like "pain" with metaphors such as the one that occurs in the last stanza of "Guendolen":

> We go our separate ways on earth, and pain,
> God's shaping chisel, waits us as the rest.[14]

"God's shaping chisel" is a grim metaphor; but it is an effective one that makes the reader wince.

In conclusion, it might be said that the 1874 poems were richer in imagery and freer from didacticism than the early poems. The poet's sense of irony deepens and the cosmic questions become implied rather than stated. Thaxter moves away from the child/persona toward an objective speaker who is more reporter than commentator. Nature's beauty is still immense, but it no longer consoles the heartsick and weary. Nor does the splendid beauty of nature compensate man for his suffering. Ultimately, death is the only faithful lover, and joy is defined in the negative: "relief from pain."

*   *   *   *   *

As seaweed lives out of the cold, dark bottom of the sea, and as land weeds grow out of barren soil, so *Driftweed* grew out of Celia Thaxter's darkest and most barren hours. The years between *Poems*, 1874, and *Driftweed*, 1878, were a time of experiment in Thaxter's poetry and in her life. Her attention began to turn from poetry to painting, and her family concerns turned completely from Newtonville back to the islands. Success, recognition, both fame and fortune were now hers, thanks to the two editions of *Poems* and *Among the Isles of Shoals*, 1873. A Boston publisher begged her to write a story about the ghastly murder that occurred on Smuttynose Island in 1873, and in the interest of justice, she said, she wrote *A Memorable Murder*, 1875[15] (see page 217). Her career was at its crest.

In 1873, the wave of self-confidence Thaxter must have felt with her hard-won recognition perhaps gave her the courage to make the difficult decision of leaving her husband and two younger sons and the Newtonville home. (Karl would always be with her.) She put the best possible face on the situation when she wrote to her confidante Annie Fields:

> My mother has been so poorly I could not leave
> her, and she would not leave my brothers, so I
> must leave my family to take care of themselves
> and stay with her, for our family is so destitute of
> women it is really forlorn! No sister, daughters,

Eliza Laighton. UNH.

> aunts, cousins, nothing but a howling wilderness
> of men! So it all comes on my shoulders. I would
> fain unite the duties of existence and have my
> mother at home with me, but alas fate has ar-
> ranged it otherwise.[16]

Celia did not explain why she could not unite the duties
of existence; she may well have been looking for an ex-
cuse to leave the Newtonville house, a place she had
always detested. Except for Karl, her sons were no
longer dependent on her, and Levi Thaxter had begun
his series of ornithological expeditions to Florida and to
the West Indies. The morose invalid hiked and camped
throughout the southern states for months at a time,

often taking Roland with him. Then he would return to Newtonville, to the "Bachelor's Hall," and sulk out the summer season while his wife enjoyed the social and cultural life of the Appledore Hotel.

Although Celia Thaxter saw her husband and sons occasionally during the five years she cared for her mother, the separation of the Thaxter family did not solve any problems. Celia lived in mortal terror of Karl's being sent off to an insane asylum when his attempts to hold a job failed. Levi ignored his son's pathetic situation and went off on his trips, hunting rare birds and mushrooms, while Celia was left with the daily burden of Karl's care. As early as 1870, Eliza Laighton's strength began to fail, and by 1872 she demanded Celia's presence at her bedside, an exhausting vigil which would not end until 1877. Shortly after Mrs. Laighton's death, Celia had to face another dilemma:

> Oh Annie, burn up this note straightway & do not breathe the madness to anybody, but do you know Mr. Thaxter refuses to have any servant at Newtonville, no not if I pay her wages & board besides, & if I go home into the turmoil of that kitchen eternally, I shall go under & I am in despair.
>
> I had all my family here last week & I did beg so hard to be allowed to have one person to help do the work, but this poor man said no—and Annie, I don't want to go home. If he only would let me pay her & pay him for allowing me to have her! I would rejoice to do it. It is all madness, . . .
>
> I enclosed a line to James T. Fields for I have yielded to everybody, at last, about printing a new volume of poems, and I want to ask him about it.
>
> Ah, the world is good to me—But my place is in that drear despairing Newtonville where I am not wanted—where they would like to keep me away. What shall I do? I can earn enough to pay a servant and live decently![17]

Annie Fields did not burn up the letter as her friend requested, and Celia Thaxter much against her will did return to the housekeeping drudgery of Newtonville. She wanted to devote her energies to painting and poetry, but Levi won the battle of wills and no servant was hired. At this point Thaxter's financial prospects and literary reputation were well established, so what power did Levi have to consign her to the kitchen? Was Karl the pawn? Did Levi's eccentric lifestyle depend on complete privacy? Celia hated her life in Newtonville and took every opportunity to escape to the homes of friends. She described to Annie Fields how busy her days were:

March 7, 1878

> ... First I made a pudding and did other cooking, then went for a scamper on horseback for two hours in the country. Home again, I wrote a sonnet to Modjeska whose singing I enjoyed with you. Then I painted a small cup for an order; and felt the day went better than usual, so before going to bed I made brown bread and buns.[18]

And thus it was in a period of five years that Celia Thaxter plunged from the heights of her career into physical, spiritual, and artistic exhaustion. Her life had become frantic and fragmented, and so had her poetry.

The *Driftweed* poems reflect Thaxter's frustration and loneliness in the face of her disintegrating family life. Certainly there were some sunny days when *Poems* was reissued to meet popular demand in 1876, and when friends such as the Fieldses and Whittier joined her for holidays, and when summer vacationers at the Appledore Hotel shared their spirited hours with her. Overwhelmed by her mother's death, Celia must have mourned for the fading of all of her childhood dreams as much as for the loss of her parent. The obvious failure of her marriage and family life was excruciating to one whose own childhood had been unusually happy.

Celia remained strangely silent on the subject of her arranged marriage with Levi Thaxter, and when she came to that point in the autobiography she had begun about 1874, she could write no further. Did her father

betray her just to get money to finance the hotel scheme
back in 1847? Did she marry Levi by choice? One conclu-
sion seems inescapable: the marriage denied Celia con-
trol over her own life, and her internal rage would not be
stilled until Levi's death in 1884. During the decade of
the 1870's, she was truly a madwoman in the attic.

Living up to her own reputation must have been an
additional burden for Thaxter, to whom, Wentworth
Higginson said, fame came too quickly.[19] As soon as she
had begun signing the poems in the *Atlantic*, she ex-
perienced some of the stings of success. She had written
Lizzie Whittier:

> I almost grow to dislike the aspect of the "human
> shape divine" in a perfectly whole-sale manner. If
> people would only let an unoffending Christian
> alone! But when an unknown creature in pet-
> ticoats comes up to me and inquires if I am the
> "Rose of the Isles," a decided loathing of my kind
> possesses my soul. Dear friend, forgive my in-
> tolerance and uncharitableness—if you had passed
> through so much of that sort of thing as I have,
> even you, I think would lose patience.[20]

Whittier enjoyed teasing Celia about her popularity,
while at the same time he prided himself in having
recognized her talent. He wrote a note in 1874:

> I wonder what the Islands would be without
> thee—a mere pile of rocks, I imagine, dead as the
> moon's old volcanic mountains. Thee have given
> them an atmosphere. Does thee know that Parton
> in his lecture on "Fashion" introduces thee as the
> best-dressed lady he ever saw? Such is the penalty
> of writing and making books!"[21]

Whittier's continual delight in Thaxter's growing
reputation was expressed in a letter he wrote the next
year:

March, 1875

> . . . and is it so strange to thee that the good
> people of Portsmouth should be glad and proud of

one who has made her name a household word in
thy land, and has made their river and harbor and
outlying islands immortal in song? How glad I am
that I can say to thee, "I told thee so years
ago!"[22]

Even the humble Quaker could not resist saying, "I told
you so," and the success which at first had seemed so
gratifying began to be a burden for Thaxter. Despite the
fact that *Poems*, 1874, was reissued in 1876, there was
still a demand for a new volume: hence, *Driftweed*, 1878.
When Thaxter wrote to Annie Fields that she had
yielded to everybody, at last, about printing a new
volume, she sought James T. Fields's advice.[23] She must
have felt some hesitation about bringing out a new
volume, perhaps because there had been little time since
1874 to refresh her spirits as well as her poetry. With the
demand for a new volume coming every two years, when
was there the time for experimenting, time to grow and
mature as a poet?

Driftweed contained fifty-eight poems, half of which
had appeared in magazines the previous two years. The
twenty-nine new poems, most of which were written in
that two year period, had the sound of the already
familiar Thaxter poems, but not the music. The little
volume opened with a representative Thaxter poem,
"Contrast" (see page 178). It contained all the elements
her readers hoped to find: The grandeur of sky and sea,
the music of wind and wave, and the narrative which
ends in peaceful resolution.

"A Faded Glove" (see page 179), the second poem in
Driftweed, departs from Thaxter's familiar topic of
nature. The poet sent this experimental poem to
Harpers, which published it the same month that the
Atlantic published "Contrast." Thaxter evidently felt
unsure about "The Faded Glove," and so she wrote to
her dear friend Whittier for his advice:

Have you happened to see a poem called "A Fad-
ed Glove," in this month's *Harpers* Magazine? I
wonder if you think it too highly colored, I would

like to know. It is rather new to me, writing in
that sort of style, and I have my doubts about it.
But people say, "Put more human interest into
your poems!" That must be my excuse.[24]

What Thaxter didn't see was that "Contrast" did have
human interest in the theme of man's powerlessness in
the face of nature. The "human interest" in "A Faded
Glove" was artificial in its sentimentality. But Whittier
would never criticize Thaxter, and so he wrote:

Thy poem in "Harper's" is very sweet and tender
in sentiment and feeling. It is in a rather new vein,
but the vigor of the language betrays its author-
ship. Whether thee speak of the sea or not, the
strength of the wind and waters is in thy verse.[25]

What did Whittier mean when he referred to the vigor of
the language, the "strength of the wind and the water,"
in her verse? The poem is filled with cliches about
romance such as "I would have been content that night
to die." Whittier must have been referring to the nar-
rative strength of the poem, the rush of psychological
turmoil behind the static scene. The contrast between
the girl's whirling emotions and her decorous behavior
gives high drama to the story: the young girl, standing
alone and fastening her glove looks up only to catch the
gaze of a man who breaks the static scene by bending to
kiss her hand. The rest of the poem describes the girl's
rapturous thoughts as she stands apart from the festive
merrymakers, lost in a dream of perfect love, while "not
a word the mystic silence broke." Fifty years later, the
grandmother tells her little granddaughter that:

The glove is faded, but immortal joy
    Lives in the kiss; its memory cannot fade;
And when Death's clasp this pale hand shall
    destroy,
    The sacred glove shall in my grave be laid.[26]

Presumably this is the first time the grandmother has
even translated her memory of the glorious moment into
language, and the portrait of idealized love is offered as a

gift to the child, "my lily yet unsought." In "A Faded
Glove," outwardly there is little happening, except for
the gallant kiss. The young girl says nothing, but rather
has an instantaneous understanding of the power of
love.

The grandmother in "A Faded Glove" is one of the
few heroic women found in the *Driftweed* poems. This
woman describes herself as one set apart from her
sisters, one who has extraordinary powers of insight and
understanding. She makes the sweep from un-
consciousness to consciousness in an instant, and is fifty
years later still capable of feeling immortal joy even as
death's hand reaches out to clasp hers. At the touch of
Death's hand, the grandmother bequeaths to her grand-
daughter the female legacy of silence, the tradition of the
unspoken word which binds successive generations of
female art. Glorious was that moment when the majestic
lover said, "I am your slave." Glorious was the power
she felt at her command: it is the one instant in her life
where she tastes of the forbidden fruit implicitly denied
all women, that intoxicating *power* which Thaxter
euphemistically calls "love."

The life led by the other females in the poem, the
sisters, is depicted as being meaningless:

> Down the echoing stair
> Swept voices, laughter, wafts of melody,—
> My sisters three, in draperies light as air;

They are not ready for the epiphany for which she,
dressed in bridal white, is prepared. They participate in
an "empty show," a "Phantasmagoria of light and
flowers," brilliant hours of music, beauty. They remain
ignorant, like the little granddaughter, of the most ex-
quisite of pleasures—*power*.

Admittedly this is a radical interpretation of a seem-
ingly simple poem. The point is, however, that Thaxter
articulated in this poem—perhaps even uncon-
sciously—a philosophy of female experience that unites
her with her "matrilineal heritage of literary strength."[27]

Once she has tasted of this power, she will forever
hunger after it. Its nourishment will sustain her life.

"A Faded Glove" was written the same year that
Thaxter began writing the autobiography that Whittier
insisted she must write. There are some remarkable
similarities between "A Faded Glove" and the two court-
ship scenes in the autobiography. In both the poem and
the autobiography the young girl thrills to the attention
of a majestic male, and yet she remains inarticulate. In
the autobiography Thaxter refers to herself as
"Hjelma," a young orphan girl who is distinguished
from the coarse fishermen who raise her not only by her
beauty but by her moral and aesthetic superiority. Their
petty concerns of everyday life seem crass to Hjelma
who goes about her work dreaming of the smell of
flowers and the colors of the sunset. When Laban, the
noble and fair-haired son of a fisherman asks why she
can't love him, Hjelma is speechless—words can't con-
vey her reasons. Somehow her natural nobility forbids
her from ever being one of the ordinary folk. Inarticulate
as Hjelma is, the young fisherman still gets the message
and takes to the open sea with his wounded heart.
Hjelma seems to relish her power over him. The final
passage from the autobiographical fragment reveals
their last encounter:

> Presently Hjelma turned to look at Laban, he
> was gazing at her, with such an expression in his
> face that all Hjelma's soul began to flutter like a
> frightened bird, across his eyes lay a dreamy mist,
> intense, like the mirage she had seen afar brooding
> on the horizon in summer weather. Her impulse
> was to rise and flee but as if drawn by a power too
> strong for him Laban came nearer, and would
> have taken her hand in his but she drew herself
> gently and simply away.
> "Hjelma," he cried and she could hardly
> recognize Laban's familiar voice in those tones
> made harsh with emotion. "Hjelma, don't go,
> don't hate me, Hjelma! I want you to love me.
> Hjelma, for as long as I live I shall never love
> anyone but you."

> Poor Hjelma! What has happened to her!
> Yesterday she was a beautiful child, laughing
> under the clear sky at the edge of the foam, today,
> a cloud was hanging over her life whose power of
> ill she could not measure.[28]

Power is the theme of this particular excerpt; in response to Laban's pressuring of Hjelma to love him, the young girl remains silent. She knows that silence, non-compliance, is her ultimate weapon of self-defense. She, like a frightened bird, wishes to flee, but since she cannot escape him physically, she simply denies his presence by not answering him. Yesterday, when she was a child, she could laugh, but today—facing the dreary prospect of a traditional female role as Laban's wife—she retreats into herself and remains mute.

In an earlier scene of the autobiography, Hjelma has tried to flee the dark cottage where she is consigned to meaningless labor and surrounded by women whose bitterness, misery and even stupidity demoralize her. She can flee, however, only through her imagination. Nature is her true mother, and beauty is her refuge. When Laban asks why she doesn't love him, she flees from his boat. The spatial imagery of enclosure and escape, so common in the writing of nineteenth-century women, dominates the autobiographical fragment.

> The room she entered was dingy and dark, smell-
> ing of tobacco and the cooking stove, a few rough
> tables and chairs its only furniture except the
> stove whose cozy black funnel reached the ceiling.
> Some shelves on one side held plates, cups and
> tins, an ugly square clock with a clattering tick oc-
> cupied the center of the opposite wall, a yellow
> Farmer's Almanac hung on a nail beneath. The
> place was anything but agreeable . . . Near the
> stove in a corner sat a deaf old woman, gray and
> bent and toothless, some knitting held in her shak-
> ing hands. She looked up with her bleared eyes as
> she recognized the sounds of discontent.[29]

The autobiographical fragment also contains some interesting descriptions of women who are trapped in the

patriarchal notions of female beauty as well as patriar-
chal "houses." A description of the peevish Aunt
Clarissa reveals all that young Hjelma does *not* want to
become:

> a tall, spare woman, dressed in a faded calico of no
> particular color, rushed out of the door, scattering
> in confusion the hens that were peacefully burrow-
> ing in the warm dry earth under the windows. Her
> face was red with worry and hurry, her thin grey
> hair twisted tightly into one hard, round, defiant
> button in the middle of the back of her head. Her
> lean bare arms were steaming with suds, the
> Saturday's scrubbing and cooking were in full
> blast.[30]

Clarissa is a comic version of the gaunt and faded women
that lived out their empty lives in Sarah Orne Jewett's
fiction. This characterization, along with the one that
follows, are Thaxter's only bits of comic writing. Some
arrogance lies behind these negative portraits of women
who serve, in the autobiography, only as foils for
Hjelma's natural loveliness:

> She sat still with her elbows on her knees and
> her firm little beautiful chin resting in the palms
> of her hands, while her eyes wandered off again
> over the blue sparkling plain of the sea.
> Her companion observed her intently. Her
> Norwegian father had given her the blond hair and
> fair skin of his race and from her Yankee mother,
> from the blood of heaven knows which of all the
> races of the earth inherited eyes of midnight
> darkness, and her yellow hair had caught a redder,
> richer hue. The shorter locks struggled out of the
> heavy tawny braid that lay over her young
> shoulders, and curled about her ears, and over her
> forehead it arched in a mist of sunny rings. Her
> mouth was large, with grave and noble curves, she
> had the Norse composure of expression, but her
> brilliant eyes contradicted her otherwise quiet
> aspect, they seemed to see everything, they went
> everywhere.
> She was fourteen, but rather small for her age,
> her slender figure was clad in a gown of coarse

brown gingham of primitive make and innocent of
any attempt at ornament; in the front of the waist
she had pinned a little bunch of purple hepaticas,
not to adorn herself, but to keep the flowers from
the warmth of her hand till she could put them in
water at home. The big braid down her back was
tied with a ribbon of dark purple, dull and worn,
but still keeping its royal color and making a love-
ly harmony with the golden head and rough brown
gown.[31]

Hjelma in the plain brown gown with no furbelows
and no attempt at ornament; the shapely and
gracious lines of her young figure, her bright hair
touched with gold over her dark eyes. She was a
picture. A charming air of modesty and integrity
pervaded her whole aspect. She drew your eyes to
her again and again with a sense of pleasure and
refreshment.[32]

In contrast to the delicate beauty of Hjelma is the
daughter of the family, the comic "Lowizy Immogeen"
(with the accent on the last syllable):

a type of being often seen among her class. Her
face was trivial, dull, infinished, ineffectual, her
hay colored hair was curled elaborately in coarse,
frizzy ringlets, her eyes and complexion were of
the same tone as her hair, colorless, pasty, with a
freckle or two, her figure was not so bad, only she
had arrayed herself in so many hoops and
flounces, and her gown of bright green alpaca was
so fearfully and wonderfully made that the eye
turned away in despair from the picture. She had
a brick red ribbon round her neck and another in
her hair, a Brummagen locket and chain, long ear-
rings glittered in her ears and her not overclean
hands were covered with rings. Her hat, who dares
essay a description of that amazing structure hav-
ing no more relation to her head than a wheelbar-
row or a watering pot, tied on at hap-hazard, if
such a thing could be. . . . Lowizy Immogeen
laughed like a horse jockey and tho her mother
seemed to have lost the power of laughter, she did
not look displeased at the prowess of her infant.[33]

These are the models of femininity young Hjelma rejected, their distorted faces matching their distorted lives. These women serve their "Lords of creation" for no reward whatsoever—except stinking fish. Even though Thaxter stopped the autobiography at this point, it is obvious that she thought she was escaping this arduous life by her marriage to her esteemed tutor.

The three examples of young women inarticulate about their responses to men were evidently written within the same year, all three occurring in experimental forms of writing. James T. Fields had urged Thaxter to put more human interest into her writing, and Whittier had encouraged her to try autobiography. Celia wrote to Whittier of her frustration in trying to write the autobiographical novel:

> "My Novel?" My dear friend, it is nowhere. Twice I essayed to begin, wrote a chapter and flung it to the four winds, in wrath and scorn. Nay, good friend, I'll think I'll even "stick to my last," the Muse. I am not to be the author of *the* Novel par excellence, of America, that is certain. But I do think that if I could have had some critical and sympathising friend at hand, to whom I could have turned for advice, with whom I could have talked about it I might have had some measure of success.[34]

Thaxter's talent might have expanded to include the novel if she had had the uninterrupted time to concentrate on the longer form, but she never really had time to try new forms and themes, as financial necessity kept fueling her creativity.

In general, the experiments failed, but they are useful for the biographer who is looking for clues to the mysteries of Thaxter's romantic life—if indeed she ever had one. "A Faded Glove" is one of only a dozen or so poems on romance, all of which have the theme of the gallant and majestic lover hovering around an inarticulate and bewildered girl. Celia seemed never to have had a romantic attachment to a man: Levi she married out of youthful ignorance and family duty, and Whittier

she worshipped from a distance. To what degree she suf-
fered is clear in her early poems and autobiographical
fragment.

A letter to James T. Fields reveals Thaxter's
thoughts about the title of the *Driftweed* volume:

November 12, 1878

Dear Friend:
Let me keep the title *Driftweed*. Don't you see
it is more than a name and signifies something,
namely—as the water is God to the seaweeds,
making them to live out of the cold and dark bot-
tom of the sea, and as the sun is God to the land
weeds making them grow out of barren, "bare-
blown rock," so is our God, to our barren lives.
And as these little verses are weeds that sprang
out of the rock and never knew cultivation. Don't
you know I never went to school? I can fancy you
smiling and saying to your self that there is little
need of telling you that.[35]

Thaxter's uncultivated "weeds" sold very well, thanks
to the three earlier editions of *Poems* and *Among the
Isles of Shoals*. Successful sales had been particularly
important for Thaxter who since 1872 had received little
or no monetary support from her husband. In order to
meet her own financial needs, she took orders for special
copies of *Driftweed* in which she painted watercolors ap-
propriate to the poems. She received as much as twenty-
five dollars a volume, volumes which today sell for
around five hundred dollars apiece as collector's items.

Thaxter's financial straits must have been
humiliating, for she had to sell poems to pay for the
small necessities of life. She wrote to Annie Fields in
January of 1877: "O that I were something besides the
ignoramus that I am! Am I writing? Nothing—hardly
have done enough to provide shoes and gloves for the
winter—I haven't got an idea in my stupid head."[36] A
year later she wrote her friend that the dressmaker was
making new dresses out of old ones. Thaxter had com-
plained of being penniless as early as April of 1873 when

she wrote to Annie that she was busily "stockpiling"
poems for future use, should she remain without funds,
as she did. It is embarrassing to find that in even as late
as 1888 she says: "I write a 'poem' for my kitchen stove,
& another for my parlor carpet, & another for the parlor
stove & another for my sheets & pillowcases & so on."[37]
In 1892, just two years before her death:

> I am too "poor" to afford even so small a journey
> just now, unless it were some dire necessity.
> Every summer before these last two I have been
> able to do something to keep my winter expenses,
> making a hundred dollars or so by reading at the
> Shoals or with my painting or something—but I
> couldn't do it this year & so I must print this
> article I have been saving for a rainy day.[38]

This rehearsal of her financial worries serves to for-
tify a central point in Thaxter's literary history: after
the 1874 edition of *Poems*, Thaxter became more of what
is called today a freelance writer than a poet. The distinc-
tion is crucial because the professional writer and the
poet bring different goals to their work. The professional
writer usually contracts with a publisher or editor to pro-
duce a specific piece of material for a specific audience at
a specific time. The professional writer has a competence
of expression, a precise mastery of his material, and he
does not necessarily cultivate a unique personal voice in
the writing. The poet, on the other hand, is more con-
cerned with his personal vision, and ideally, with the
"meter making argument" of which Emerson spoke. In
the case of poets like Celia Thaxter and J.G. Whittier,
the poet has a moral obligation to his fellow man.

During the mid 1870's, Celia Thaxter made a painful
but necessary transition from being a poet of genuine
talent to being a professional writer or a journalist—also
of genuine talent. Unfortunately, she did not seem to ar-
ticulate this distinction clearly to herself, and hence the
agonizing letters of those years with self-deprecating
references to her lack of poetic inspiration and produc-
tion. Virtually all of her good (or best) poems were writ-

ten before 1875; most of those that followed were pale
imitations of the early poems. The *Driftweed* poems
could, of course, please the Thaxter readers who wanted
more of the same, but they could not please the reader
who demanded a growth of vision and widening of ex-
perience and perception.

The success of Thaxter's *Poems* and *Among the
Isles of Shoals* proved to be a burden because the
publishers and editors demanded more . . . and fast. Dur-
ing the first six months of 1873, book trade had been
slow in Boston, but by June, Osgood's publicity releases
showed that sales were up, the three best sellers being
Mrs. Whitney's *The Other Girls*, which sold over ten
thousand copies, Howells' *A Chance Acquaintance*, and
Thaxter's *Among the Isles of Shoals*. By 1875, Hurd and
Houghton chose Thaxter's *Poems* as one of only eight
books to be promoted in *Publishers Weekly* during the
Book Fair and the Trade Sales.[39] Because Thaxter was a
proven money-maker, Osgood begged her for more
autobiographical material similar to *Among the Isles of
Shoals*, and Hurd and Houghton reprinted the 1874
Poems in 1876 with no revisions, just a fancier binding.
The poems of 1878, *Driftweed*, were as eagerly awaited
by her publisher as by her public. Gone was Thaxter's
freedom to try something new; the insistent cry (that she
chose to hear) was for more of the same, and that meant
the money she so desperately needed. She felt helpless:

May 1, 1877

> . . . It makes me rage against my woman's fate
> of helplessness,—or if only I had money that
> would be power to have at least weekly com-
> munication with the land—But why rage against
> stupid fate! I can't help anything but must sub-
> mit—submit—submit—Nobody cares whether we
> hear or not—only I fret and suffer & strive for
> patience.[40]

Celia Thaxter's failure to achieve economic security
or self-sufficiency seems to be an obvious deterrent to

her artistic growth. With all of her talent and even genius, she was forced by necessity to become at times a hack writer, spinning out verses for Christmas cards and art prints.

Celia Thaxter, *circa* 1880. PPL.

4

On Quiet Waters
1884–1894

The Leaves like Women interchange
Exclusive Confidence—
Somewhat of nods and somewhat
Portentous inference.[1]

Emily Dickinson

After Levi Thaxter's death in 1884, Celia was set free from the prison of her marriage. The last ten years of her life were reasonably calm; she was no longer forced into madness. Her reading public lavished their praises upon everything she wrote, while Houghton Mifflin rejected Higginson's first edition of Emily Dickinson's poems because they already had a "female" poet. Thaxter's poems were in their sixteenth edition.[2] Celia's creative powers were reborn when her husband died, and thus she was able to write some of her finest poems in the last decade of her life. In addition to her writing, she continued to paint seascapes and botanical subjects. In fact, her paintings became more profitable than her poetry. Even her hobbies had to become means of earning a living. She could seldom afford to play.

Artists make conscious choices about the forms they use. Immortal fame might be won by the composer of symphonies, the sculptor of stone, or the epic poet, but artists who choose gardening or china painting or hymns and songs have committed themselves to minor forms of artistic expression in their culture. Those artists, know-

101

ing their work may be enjoyed by people on a daily basis, do not expect their art to outlive them.

Celia Thaxter chose to pursue minor art forms, and no one in her day was any more proficient than she was. Her skill in gardening led to a fine book, *An Island Garden*. The china she painted brings hundreds of dollars on the antique market even today in New England. The hymns and songs she wrote are still sung, and her lyric sea poems hold special attraction for vacationers along the Atlantic coast of New England. A used book dealer on Cape Cod reports that there are several requests every summer for Thaxter's poems.[3]

Being a popular artist has its own rewards, several of which Celia Thaxter was able to enjoy in her lifetime. Although she never achieved great financial success, she did have the satisfaction of earning an income from her art. Her greatest reward, however, was the recognition she received from the very beginning to the very end of her career, the recognition coming from all of the people whose praises would mean the most: Emerson, Hawthorne, Howells, Whittier, Dickens, James and Annie Fields, Jewett, Larcom, Phelps—the list seems endless. When one looks at the life and work of someone like Thaxter, who without the advantages of education or social class became such an accomplished artist in several fields, there is always the wish that the artist might have tried a more complex, demanding, permanent, or prestigious art form.

Wistful thinking of what might have been leads to the interesting question of what forms of artistic expression are open to given members of any culture. Celia Thaxter was limited in what art forms were open to her. She had to choose among the forms that called for the minimum of formal training. Her apprenticeship as a poet was brief, and she attained her early reputation somewhat by the good fortune of being married to a man whose literary connections were firmly established. The five years of publishing her unsigned poems in the *Atlantic*, the gentle criticism and warm encouragement by

J.T. Fields were about all she had of training before she was presented to the *Atlantic* readers as a poet of some status. Levi Thaxter's continued interest in the literary issues of the day was another source of her education as were his many Harvard friends.

A second limitation on Thaxter's choice of art forms was the matter of financial need. Thaxter had to choose art forms that sold immediately—china milk jugs, juvenile poems and stories, magazine verse. All three forms she could turn out rather quickly, so facile were her varied talents. She had a solid sense of pride in her work, fortunately, so nothing she ever sold was shoddy, but she was limited in her range of growth and interest by pressing monetary matters.

During the 1880's Celia Thaxter's career as a freelance writer continued to flourish. A few months of respite came in the winter of 1881 when she accompanied her brother Oscar Laighton on a whirlwind tour of Europe. Travel essays had been much in vogue in the *Atlantic* since the early days of Howells and Twain, but the trip abroad did not lead Thaxter to any new material for her writing. A few poems and letters written from Europe reveal the same interest in nature and local color that were found in Thaxter's descriptions of her own islands. One of the few literary moments of the trip came in her brief visit with Robert Browning who knew of Levi Thaxter's reading of his poetry in America.

When Thaxter returned from Europe, her family sold their Newtonville house and bought the Champernowne Farm at Kittery Point, Maine, where the sons from then on worked and lived. The change of scene must have perked up Levi Thaxter's spirits, for in 1881 and 1882 he gave a number of successful Browning readings in Boston. Meanwhile, Celia took an apartment near her husband's in Boston where she could hide away with Karl when his fits of temper, as they called them, made it impossible for him to live on the farm. Illness cut short Levi's late blooming career, and his wife was able to visit his bedside before he died on May 31, 1884.

Celia Thaxter's famed parlor on Appledore Island. PPL.

During the next few years Celia Thaxter traveled back and forth between the Boston apartment, the Kittery Point farm, and the summer hotel on Appledore. These were times of weariness when nothing she could do was enough to satisfy her sons who must have harbored some resentment of the fact that their mother had not filled the traditional maternal role in their lives. Letters between Celia and her son John during these years reveal the painful failure of Thaxter family life. A letter from Celia to her son John reveals the tension within the family:

June 22, 1885

> I think your letter is very unkind indeed, & cross & horrid & I think you are cross to me continually, & you have no reason to be, & ought to have more consideration than to "jaw" at me the way you do. You don't know how it sounds & how it hurts me. You have no friend like your mother & you might be good to her while you have her . . .

> I think your attitude toward Lony [Roland] is
> unkind & unpleasant, if he is inclined to throw
> cold water it is because you are inclined to spend
> too freely. He knew how papa strove to save & get
> along & he feels from papa's point of view that
> you spend unnecessarily sometimes. A half dollar
> for oranges, or a little sum here or there, *so hard
> to earn*, so easy to spend, for things *not necessary*.
> I don't say anything when it is something to
> forward earning your living, which I know how
> hard you are trying to do. But Lony's instincts
> are toward saving a penny where yours are to
> spend it.
>
> Do try to be good to him & pleasant to him,
> don't get into a way of looking at him as anything
> but the most friendly of brothers. It makes me
> ache to think of it all. Do be nice at meals—if you
> only knew how dreadful it was for people who
> listen, you would never do it.
>
> There—all this is in return for your scolding at
> me. There is no use in making life any more
> unpleasant than it is by fretting and fuming. I
> know how "demnition" hard a grind existence is &
> I respect all your efforts & sympathize keenly in
> all your ups and downs, my dear & all your trials.
> But I don't deserve that you should fling out at
> me & "jaw" at me like this, & I shan't bear it.[4]

The raw emotion revealed in this and other letters be-
tween Celia and John centers on John's inability to keep
peace with his brothers, and on Celia's precarious finan-
cial position.

Despite the family problems—most of which can be
traced directly to Thaxter's choice of being a poet in ad-
dition to her traditional feminine role as a wife and
mother—the years of the 1880's were as productive as
the preceding decade had been. Thaxter's *Stories and
Poems for Children* in 1883 contained ten stories and
seventy-one poems, many of which had been published
earlier in *St. Nicholas*, the leading juvenile magazine of
the day. Thaxter's talent as a writer of children's
literature was early recognized by such eminent editors
as Lucy Larcom and Mary Mapes Dodge. Larcom wrote
of her admiration for Celia Thaxter as early as 1867
when the two women first met:

> For you are an enchantress. It is a gift to attract
> and to *hold* as you can, and rare even among
> women. To some it is a snare, but I do not believe
> it ever can be to you, because the large generosity
> of the sea was born into you. How can you help it,
> if your waves overblow with music, and all sorts
> of mysterious wealth upon others of us humans?[5]

The gift of enchantment, commonly known as the skill of a good storyteller, had been lavished on Thaxter. Storytelling must have filled many long and lonely hours at the White Island Lighthouse, with sea captains and stranded sailors, warmed by the generous hearth and a winter's supply of grog. The drama of life at sea had played endlessly in those early days, and young Celia Laighton had learned to create her own world by imposing narrative upon the random events of the life about her. Every bird and every flower came to life in her consciousness, and as an adult she had only to reach back to that rich storehouse for the materials of her children's literature. The stories she told had been written in her own memory years earlier; now she merely transcribed them.

The characters in her little narratives, either poems or stories, were the familiar island birds—the burgomaster gull, the great white owl, the shag and the kittiwake. Thaxter's fondness for little girls is revealed in several poems and letters, all of which are conspicuous for their lack of equally charming little boys. When boys do appear in the stories and poems, they are most often destructive—killers of birds—while the little girls are always preservers of life.

Children have always seemed to enjoy the kind of poetry Celia Thaxter was more proficient at writing. Strong regular rhythms, close rhymes, alliteration and onomatopoeia conspire to make the lively, musical poems that the island poet wrote so easily. One historian of children's literature places Thaxter in the same class with Robert Louis Stevenson, William Blake, Christina Rossetti, Edward Lear, Lewis Carroll and Eugene Field.[6]

This historian of children's literature is impressed with Thaxter's lack of sentimentality and moralizing, two flaws which pervade much juvenile literature. In discussing "The Sandpiper," Thaxter's most famous poem, he says: "Perhaps 'The Sandpiper' does represent, as John Burroughs has said, the woman's point of view, as Bryant's 'To a Waterfowl' represents a man's. But there is no trace of sentimentality in 'The Sandpiper,' not in anything Celia Thaxter ever wrote."[7] Then this critic makes a telling point about Thaxter's juvenile literature which applies as well to the rest of her writing: "She is, above all, hale and sane." His remarks are concluded by a discussion of Thaxter's "good sense" which may account for the lack of humor in her verse. Thaxter is never silly or condescending.

Celia Thaxter was able to treat her topics with a realism that was unusual in children's literature of that time. The death of the burgomaster gull, cited earlier in chapter 2, is told in grim detail as is the death of a canary in "The Butcher-Bird"[8] (see page 209). In these poems nature is as ruthless as it is lovely. An early poem, "Jack Frost" (see page 211), illustrates Thaxter's realism:

> Rustily creak the crickets: Jack Frost came down
>   last night,
> He slid to the earth on a starbeam, keen and
>   sparkling bright;
> He sought in the grass for the crickets with
>   icy spear,
> So sharp and fine and fatal, and he stabbed them
>   far and near.
> Only a few stout fellows, thawed by the morning
>   sun,
> Chirrup a mournful echo of by-gone frolic and fun.[9]

Writing for children was not the specialized business in the nineteenth century that it is today with controlled vocabularies and schoolboard censorship. Many of the poets and novelists of the late nineteenth century wrote for and about children as a matter of course. In America, Twain, Whittier, Longfellow and Aldrich joined Thaxter in addressing the children, while in England, Dickens,

Carroll, Lear, Christina Rossetti and Walter de la Mare
chose the child as the audience as well as the subject for
some of their work.

The sane and hale good sense so evident in Thaxter's
children's poetry is really more representative of the
poet's basic stance than are some of those despairing
poems of *Driftweed*. Thaxter was, in many ways, a poet
of reason. Her endless questioning of "why?" for all of
human experience was her attempt to impose order on
her increasingly chaotic life. The balancing of good and
evil, calm and storm in her writing came from her own
rage for order. Celia Thaxter was not trained in the
language of philosophical discourse nor was she sup-
ported by an absolute religious creed. She sought control
of her life to a degree uncommon for women of her time,
and in seeking that control she had to risk emotional, in-
tellectual and financial insecurity. When, for example in
the early 1880's Thaxter became interested in psychic
experience, she pursued the subject with vigor. Poets are
always found at the frontiers of psychological ex-
perience, and like Whitman's interest in phrenology,
Thaxter's interest in the psychic experience was a
necessary step in her personal development as a poet.
One literary historian, Perry Westbrook, finds Thaxter's
interest in the psychic phenomena embarrassing—she
should have known better![10] But, it can also be argued
that Thaxter was quick to reject the power of a seance
once she submitted her experience to scientific investi-
gation. Her temperament demanded that she recognize
what was reasonable and positive in all human experi-
ence, and her curiosity about the human mind was one of
the true signs of her poetic genius.

Religion was always to pose a difficulty for Celia
Thaxter, who had not been raised with a traditional
Christian faith. Her expansive mind demanded that she
combine the best of theology, Buddhism and Christiani-
ty, into a strong and practical belief. She had little
tolerance for the narrowness of conventional New
England piety, and even toward the end of her life when

she finally confessed to a Christian faith, she would not associate herself with a church or a denomination. Several of her more traditionally Christian friends such as Elizabeth Stuart Phelps and Annie Fields tried to bring Celia to a more orthodox position, but she managed to resist their efforts. Her religious belief could best be described as being anchored somewhere between Whittier's Quakerism and the pantheism of a sea nymph.

Celia Thaxter included in her last major collection of poems in 1886 a long poem called "Questions." The poem reflects Thaxter's reluctance to accept simplistic answers to cosmic questions; the poem also reflects her awareness of modern science and the problems that it raised in the face of traditional Christian belief. Speaking of our "steadfast planet" spinning through space, the poet says:

> We only know it keeps it place,
>   An atom in the universe,
> As through the awful realms of space
>   The mighty hosts of stars disperse.
>
> We know the hand that holds in check
>   The whirling worlds, each in its course,
> And saves the universe from wreck
>   And peril, this tremendous Force
>
> Holds likewise all our little lives;
>   The suns and stars do all obey
> His bidding, never planet strives
>   To swerve from its appointed way.[11]

Thaxter's poems on religious subjects never have the shrill tone that is found in the religious poems of Lucy Larcom or Elizabeth Stuart Phelps. Instead there is a steady and reasoned confidence in the order of the universe, and unlike the other two poets, she finds comfort in her belief that God is *not* personally involved in her daily life except through the ongoing laws of nature.

Thaxter had long been interested in the religious, the philosophical and the psychic. In the *American*

Annie Fields. UNH.

Notebooks, 1852, Hawthorne mentions that he saw a tract on spiritual mediums on the Thaxter's table when he visited them on the islands.[12] The death of her mother, the disintegration of her family life, and her self-concept as a failed poet left Thaxter at times groping for answers to the meaning of human suffering. Her talent, however, did not lie in dealing with the abstract; it lay in her ability to deal with the real world which came to her through her senses. What she could see, what she could hear, what she could smell, taste and touch were the basis of her art. Thaxter shares with Melville the power of rendering into language the awful moods of the ocean. Her reader experiences an almost kinesthetic response to her poetry in which the rhythm of the sea is found.

Celia Thaxter was a woman of great common sense, vigorous physical energy, magnificent intelligence. Her best moments came in the world of action, not in the world of reflection. In the 1880's she gave numerous poetry readings, not the least of which were given at the Women's State Reformatory at Sherborn, Massachusetts.[13] She loved social interaction and she gloried in friendship and conviviality. She had experienced enough loneliness at the lighthouse to last a lifetime, as she told a friend. Never did she seek enduring fame—she much preferred to please her friends and her audience immediately.

Thaxter's status as a popular poet won her a commission from the Lothrop Company of Boston to write verses to accompany art prints which were then bound into Christmas and gift volumes, a profitable new idea in the publishing world. Thaxter found the task formidable, and wrote to Whittier of her frustration.

June 24, 1888

I am writing poems (?) by the yard to fit 26 Wide Awake art prints to be made into a Xmas book, an edition deluxe. You may believe it is no small job! I have twelve done and 14 more to do. Bismillah! but some of them are posers! It takes a heap of

human ingenuity to get the better of them. But I
trust I shall come off victorious, tho' sometimes it
really does look hopeless. I have been getting
ready a new vol. to be printed in the autumn. And
when I have done such a thing I always think
what an idiot I am to imagine there is anything I
could say worth preserving in a book, and regret
my temerity.[14]

In this letter can be seen Mrs. Thaxter's dilemma—her
self-concept as a poet in conflict with her commitments
as a freelance writer. Two years earlier, her *Idyls and
Pastoral: A Home Gallery of Poetry and Art* had been a
success for Lothrop, and even earlier she had won
several contests for Christmas card verse sponsored by
the Prang Company. In 1882 she was paid one thousand
dollars for the first prize verse, "Thine own wish I wish
thee." Another contest sponsored by Prang paid Thax-
ter two thousand dollars for the first prize verse entitled
"Drifting on Rosy Vapors." These are high prices even
by today's standards, and they testify to Thaxter's suc-
cess as a popular artist.

*   *   *   *   *

Although it was freelance writing that kept Thaxter
constantly busy the last decade of her life, in 1886 she
brought out her last major book of poetry. Some poems
are obvious potboilers, but there are enough good lyrics
and narratives to reclaim for Thaxter the title of poet.

"The Cruise of the Mystery" (see page 188) is not
the work of a freelance writer; the poem reveals the
talent of a poet. Thaxter's poetic voice is clear and cer-
tain when she builds on her skill at rendering narrative.
Poems like "The Cruise of the Mystery" could be en-
joyed by schoolchildren—or anyone—and deserve a
place in the history of American poetry along with
Longfellow's "Wreck of the Hesperus," and "Skeleton in
Armour," and Holmes's "The Chambered Nautilus."
"The Cruise of the Mystery" is clearly the strongest nar-
rative poem in Thaxter's last major collection.

In the 1886 collection there is an odd group of poems written to her mother who died in 1877. Presumably these poems were written early in the 1880's when Thaxter was participating in seances to make contact with the spirit of her mother. Typical of the tone in these poems is the first stanza of "Impatience" (see page 194).

Only to follow you, dearest, only to find you!
    Only to feel for one instant the touch of your
        hands;
Only to tell you once of the love you left behind
    you,—
    To say the world without you is like a desert
        sand;[16]

The poem continues with impassioned pleading which seems more appropriate to a lover's complaint:

I did not dream it was you who kindled the
    morning
    And folded the evening purple in peace so
    sweet;
But you took the whole world's rapture without a
    warning,
    And left me naught save the print of your
    patient feet.

I count the days and the hours that hold us
    asunder;
    I long for Earth's friendly hand which shall
    rend in twain
With the glorious lightning flash and the golden
    thunder,
    These clouds of the earth, and give me my
own again!

The love poems addressed to her mother are an odd lot; they follow no familiar tradition in western literature. The elegaic tradition includes such types of grief as one lover for another, one noble friend for another, or a parent mourning for a lost child, but the poem of grief written by a daughter for her mother is difficult to find until the twentieth century. The language

of the poems leaves the modern reader somewhat uncom-
fortable for it is too close to the language of lovers. The
poem, "A Song of Hope" will serve as an example:

> Beloved, beloved! Is there no morning breeze
>   To clear our sky and chase our mists away,
> Like this great air that sweeps the freshing seas,
>   And wakes the old sad world to glad new day?
>
> Sweeter than morning, stronger than the gale,
>   Deeper than ocean, warmer than the sun,
> My love shall climb, shall claim thee, shall prevail
>   Against eternal darkness, dearest one![16]

How painful to read these lines, how sad to recognize
that nineteenth-century American culture had no elegaic
tradition to express what so many daughters must have
felt. Thaxter's awkward attempts to deal with this
agonizing experience of a daughter's grief over the loss
of her mother are perhaps a sad commentary on the
cultural values of the day. In Thaxter's day, a mother's
care for her daughter extended far beyond childhood—it
was often a young woman's mother who took care of her
during childbirth, tended the sick babies, helped with
the seasonal burdens of food preparation. It was the
mother who served as doctor, lawyer, minister and
marriage counselor to her daughter, and it was often the
mother who lightened the heavy load of domestic
responsibility.

It is ironic that women who have nursed the sick and
the dying have seldom been writers or even the subjects
of elegies. The grand elegies of Milton, Shelley and
Tennyson were written by poets who did not, of course,
attend the dying friends whose memories they have so
artfully preserved. Granted, the "high" elegies such as
"Lycidas," "Adonais," and "In Memorium" are philo-
sophical poems which go beyond the simple fact of the
death of a friend, but elegies for women in nineteenth-
century America are few, and elegies written by women
of that century are even fewer.

The poems Celia Thaxter wrote on her mother's

death are not elegies in the formal sense of the tradi-
tion—but what else are they? They have a lyrical quality,
certainly, but they are more than lyrics because they are
addressed to a specific person, and they treat a specific
subject. They do not fit comfortably in the twentieth-
century confessional mode, nor are they songs. The im-
agery in the death poems derives from the many seances
Celia attended in order to make contact with the spirit of
her departed mother. Years earlier Whittier had en-
couraged Celia to develop her psychic powers, never an-
ticipating the psychological turmoil that would engulf
her when her mother died.[17]

Celia Thaxter's groping for a tradition or a form for
the mourning poems might be compared to the
uneasiness Theodore Roethke describes at the end of his
"Elegy for Jane":

> If only I could nudge you from this sleep,
> My maimed darling, my skittery pigeon.
> Over this damp grave I speak the words of my
>   love:
> I, with no rights in this matter,
> Neither father nor lover.[18]

Neither father nor lover, Celia Thaxter seized the right
to speak of her grief for her mother and in so doing,
broke some new ground for women's claim to poetic
territory.

The old territory of the romantic love poem was less
fertile ground for Thaxter's imagination. In *The Cruise
of the Mystery and Other Poems* Thaxter included some
poems on the subject of love that she had been asked to
write for a new women's magazine. She wrote to Annie
Fields that she had "tried to bring out a love poem for a
new illustrated journal although in far from a romantic
mood."[19] The romantic poems are narratives with the
same old pattern of the inarticulate woman averting her
eyes from the lurid gaze of her heroic lover. In a word,
the love poems are awkward, perhaps a painful reflection
on Thaxter's own romantic experience. A few examples
will illustrate sufficiently the limitations of Thaxter's

Celia Thaxter's cottage and garden, Appledore Island.
UNH.

romantic verse. Obviously, development of character
was not Thaxter's forte, as the last stanzas of "Two"
demonstrate:

> O sweet and awful Love! O power supreme,
>   Mighty and sacred, terrible art thou!
> Beside thee Life and Death are but a dream;
>   Before thee all must bow.
>
> When in the west the sunset's crimson flame
>   Burned low and wasted, and the cool winds
>   blew,
> Watching the steadfast sky she heard her name
>   Breathed in the voice she knew.
>
> Joy shook her heart, nor would its pulse be stilled;
>   Her fair cheek borrowed swift and sunset's
>   bloom.
> A presence beautiful and stately filled
>   The silence of the room.

> "Hast thou no word of welcome?" for indeed
>> Like some mute marble goddess proud stood
>> she;
> She turned. "O king of men!" she cried, "what
>> need
> That I should welcome thee?"
>
> Her eyes divine beneath her solemn brows
>> Met his clear gaze and measured strength for
>> strength.
> She dropped, as to the sun the lily bows,
>> Into his arms at length.
>
> Wide swung heaven's gates for them; no more
>> they knew.
> The silent stars looked in, they saw them not.
> The slow winds wandered soft through dusk and
>> dew,
> But earth was all forgot.[20]

The interesting point of this poem occurs when their gazes meet "strength for strength," the phrase revealing Thaxter's full recognition of female sexuality.

The discussion of Thaxter's love poems would not be complete without reference to her sonnet "O were I loved as I desire to be!"—a poem which the poet chose not to publish. Perhaps the sonnet was too painfully close to her own experience—there is no way of knowing anything about the composition of the sonnet which was published in *The Heavenly Guest*. It should be remembered that Thaxter had written Annie Fields that she put her heart and soul into the sonnets.

> O were I loved as I desire to be!
>> What is there in the great sphere of the earth
> Or range of evil between death and birth
>> That I should fear, if I were loved by thee?
> All the inner, all the outer world of pain
>> Clear love would pierce and cleave, if thou
>> wast mine;
> As I have heard that somewhere in the main
>> Fresh water springs come up through bitter
>> brine,
> 'Twere joy, not fear, clasped hand in hand with
>> thee

> To wait for death,—mute, careless of all ills
>   Apart upon a mountain, tho's the surge
>   Of some new deluge from a thousand hills
> Flung leagues of roaring foam into the gorge
>   Below us, as far as eye could see![21]

Celia Thaxter's biography could be written around this sonnet and her mastery of poetic technique is nowhere more evident. There is one other sonnet in *Cruise of the Mystery* which might serve as a companion poem to "O were I loved as I desire to be." It speaks of the fulfillment of love with memorable imagery and may have been written to Whittier:

> As happy dwellers by the seaside hear
>   In every pause the sea's mysterious sound,
>   The infinite murmur, solemn and profound,
> Incessant, filling all the atmosphere,
>   Even so I hear you, for you do surround
> My newly-waking life, and break for aye
>   About the viewless shores, till they resound
> With echoes of God's greatness night and day.
> Refreshed and glad I feel the full flood-tide
>   Fill every inlet of my waiting soul;
>   Long-striving, eager hope, beyond control,
> For help and strength at last is satisfied;
>   And you exalt me, like the sounding sea,
>   With ceaseless whispers of eternity.[22]

Celia Thaxter's best sonnets are as strong as any written in American literature; in fact, they compare favorably with those of Elizabeth Barrett Browning. Thaxter's love for the sonnet form was based in her yearning for reason, order and structure. In the sonnet she was able to meld the cosmic with the intimate without sounding shrill. Finally, the sonnet form gave Thaxter the opportunity to move away from the concrete realities of narrative into the realm of reason where she longed to dwell.

The last volume of verse that Celia Thaxter herself published was entitled simply *Verses*, 1891, and on the title page was an advertisement "with twenty-five full-page illustrations by famous artists." Evidently a gift volume, the publisher was D. Lathrop of Boston, the firm for which Thaxter had worked most steadily during the preceding decade. There had been time for reading and writing after 1887 when Thaxter had evidently suffered a heart attack which she endured with stoicism: "Neuralgic swords playing across the region of my heart and cutting through, tearing across the spine are not very pleasant companions to deal with!"[23] These symptoms of heart disease were to plague Thaxter until her death, but they did not halt her amazing literary productivity. She continued to publish her poems and the autobiographical account, *An Island Garden*. Upon her death were found over one hundred unpublished poems, later to be collected into *The Heavenly Guest*.

Celia Thaxter's late poems reveal a mind and an artistic sensibility still growing, still responding vigorously to the world around her. *Verses*, 1891, contains Thaxter's poetry at its worst—and at its best, the unevenness due, perhaps, to the fact that she no longer sought critical opinion and approval. Thaxter's inability to come to terms with her mother's death is revealed in the poem "Lost" where she opens with the pleading line:

> Low burns the sunset and the dark is near:
> O where is home! O where my mother's face![24]

"Lost" is the only one of twenty-five poems in *Verses* that is despairing. The others are light and even joyous as the opening stanza from "The Dream Peddler" will illustrate:

> Lo, I come from dreamland dim,
> Down the drowsy air I swim,
> Ringing soft a pleasant tune,
> Through the sharp horns of the moon;
> All that fancy fine can paint
> Of fair or sweet or wild or quaint,
> Though your brain I'll set adrift,
> When my slender wand I lift.[25]

The Poems in *Verses* are clearly written for family reading, but they are not distinctly juvenile poetry. The poem "On the Beach" reveals quite another of Thaxter's well-known themes:

The slow, cool emerald breaker curving clear
   Along the sparkling edge of level sand,
Shatters its crystal arch, and far and near
   In broken splendor spills upon the land.
With rush and whisper siren-sweet and soft
   Gently salutes the children of the earth,
And catching every sunbeam from aloft
   Flashes it back in summer mood of mirth;
And with a flood of strong refreshment pours
   Health and delight among the sounding
      shores.

Amid its frolic foam and scattered spray
   Tossed lightly, like some dreaming lion's
      mane,
The tired dwellers of the city play.
   Forgetful for awhile of care and pain,
While peace broods over all, nor does it seem
   As if the sleeping lion could awake;
And yet, when passed is this sweet summer dream
   What roar of thunder on the coast will break
When winter's tempests rage in sullen wrath—
   Death and disaster in their cruel path—
And hurl against the sandy margin gray
   Devouring fury, tumult and dismay![26]

The method of this poem harks back to "Land-locked"
and "Contrast."

A final poem from *Verses*, "On Quiet Waters," has
the same pre-Raphaelite imagery and the same sexual
implications found in Thaxter's early poem, "Rock Little
Boat." The poem has the musical quality of the early
poem and ends with the same image of "Rowing in
Eden" that Emily Dickinson had used in "Wild
Nights—Wild Nights" also published in 1891.

O lightly moored the lilies lie,
And look up to the golden sky.
Softly they breathe into the air
Their holy fragrance everywhere:
Delicate, dewy-fresh and sweet,
It steals our charmed sense to greet.
In each pure chalice, dazzling white,
Sits thronged a spirit of delight.

Our grateful souls with joy to fill,
A pleasure sacred, deep and still,
O lightly moored the lilies lie
Afloat beneath the glowing sky!
From shadow cool to sunshine clear
Safe past the changing shores we steer,
And watch the swallow dip his wing,
And hear the hidden thrushes sing
Each to his mate within the wood,
Safe in their happy solitude.
O perfect morn! O peaceful time!
O life that blossoms at its prime!
We dream in Eden, thou and I,
Afloat beneath the golden sky.[27]

When in 1935 on Celia Thaxter's centenary her brother Oscar Laighton published *The Heavenly Guest*, another chapter had to be written on the subject of Thaxter as a poet. Among the papers found after her death were some fine poems that Annie Fields, Rose Lamb and Sarah Orne Jewett chose not to include in the Appledore Edition of Thaxter's poems in 1896.

Celia Thaxter in her garden, *circa* 1890. UNH.

5

Farewells Fond and Brief

The summer's songs are hushed. Up the lone shore
The weary waves wash sadly, and a grief
Sounds in the wind, like farewells fond and brief.
The cricket's chirp but makes the silence more.[1]

from "Twilight"

Down Time's quaint stream
Without an oar
We are enforced to sail
Our port a secret
What Skipper would
Incur the Risk
What Buccaneer would ride
Without a surety from the Wind
Or schedule of the Tide—[2]

Emily Dickinson

Sunset and evening star,
    And one clear call for me!
And may there be no moaning of the bar
    When I put out to sea,
But such a tide as moving seems asleep,
    Too full for sound and foam,
When that which drew from out the boundless deep
    Turns again home.[3]

Tennyson

In 1894, the summer season at the Appledore Hotel
had been especially glorious. Each evening Celia Thaxter
had read her well loved poetry to an admiring and en-
thusiastic audience. In fact, she had even written some
new poems which she intended to bring out in a volume
later that year. Thaxter and her two friends, Annie
Fields and Sarah Orne Jewett, had spent sunny days re-
exploring the Isles of Shoals, the scene of all that was
beautiful in the poet's life. Death came unexpectedly
that August at a time when Celia Thaxter had com-
pletely reawakened in her heart the joy and peace she
had known as a child at the White Island Lighthouse.

The story of Thaxter's simple burial in a flower filled
grave on Appledore Island was carried by the same
newspapers and magazines which had published her
poems. Obituaries praised not only her poetry but also
her life. To separate the praise of the art from the praise
of the artist is a large task in the case of Thaxter because
always her art is discussed in the light of her dramatic
and admirable personality. A typical obituary, unsigned,
glowed with praise for the beloved poet:

> The late Celia Thaxter held a unique place, if not
> in American literature, where other women poets
> have sung with equal sweetness, yet certainly in
> the hearts of many hundred admirers, of whom
> some loved her poems, some her personality,
> some—and they were not few—her wondrous
> garden, and the radiance of bloom and color which
> seem to emanate from her unpretentious little
> vine-hung cottage to glorify the whole rocky isle of
> Appledore.[4]

Yet another obituary expresses no reservation about her
important role in American literature: "When 'Land-
locked' [sic] was first published, there could be no ques-
tion as to what standing its author was in the future to
occupy among poets." Mr. Alfred R. Hussey, literary
editor of the *Boston Christian Register*, wrote: "Nothing
remains to indicate her method of work or of what in-
fluences affected her. She seemed to have no trial flights

of song, rather she burst forth full-throated with "Landlocked. [sic].'" That she "burst forth full-throated" was indeed a sign to the popular audience that Celia Thaxter was a true poet. Mr. Hussey predicted that the basis of Thaxter's fame would lie in her eminence in poetry as well as in prose.

Shortly before the publication of the Appledore Edition of the *Poems*, 1896, came an edition of the *Letters*, 1895, edited by Annie Fields and Rose Lamb. Reviewers realized that the editors had selected those parts of the letters which reinforced the public image of Celia Thaxter *they* thought people wanted to retain.

The *Boston Beacon* calls Celia Thaxter "one of the most genuine of American poets," and says that her letters are a "noteworthy example of unpremeditated art." This particular review stressed how Celia Thaxter fit the romantic notion of the untutored poet, filled with natural song and wisdom, à la Robert Burns. The *Boston Herald* extravagantly compared Thaxter's letters to those of Mde. Sevigne or Charles Lamb.

A minor chord, however, sounded in some other reviews. One anonymous reviewer stated, "Her letters lack that piercing modern note, we must solace ourselves with its pleasantness." That same reviewer perceived that "the editors suppressed too much." Yet another review of the *Letters* pointed out that Celia Thaxter, as revealed in those letters, lacks the introspection found in such a poet as Emily Dickinson. The *Philadelphia Ledger* published a harsh commentary: "The letters unfold the daily life of a busy woman, who seems to have passed the great part of her existence in general housework, invalid-nursing and flower tending, and to whose career the vocation of a poet was merely accidental."

This review sums up the first premise of patriarchal criticism: female experience is an inferior variation on the human experience. It is this premise that haunts all of female literary history.

Glowing praise for Celia Thaxter was rekindled in 1896 when the "Appledore Edition" of *Poems* was

Celia Thaxter with grandson Charles Eliot Thaxter. UNH.

brought out. The edition was hurriedly assembled by Annie Fields, Rose Lamb, Sarah Orne Jewett and Roland Thaxter, all of whom must have had some fear that Celia would be forgotten unless this supposedly complete edition were published quickly. Unfortunately the edition is incomplete, although most of the major poems are there. In the preface to the Appledore Edition, Miss Jewett wrote with remarkable perceptiveness about the poems:

> They seem to make something like a journal of her daily life and thought, and to mark the constantly increasing power of observation which was so marked a trait in her character. In the earliest of her poems there is much to be found of that strange insight and anticipation of experience which comes with such gifts of writing as hers, but as life went on it seemed as if sorrow were visible to her eyes, a shrouded figure walking in the daylight.[5]

Even Miss Jewett separates the "gifts of nature," and the "gifts of writing." She concludes the preface with the observation that "there was something bright in her spirit that will forever shine."[6]

On the whole, the reviews of both the *Letters* and the *Poems* were positive, even laudatory. A reviewer in the *Portland Morning Advertizer* meant to praise the poet when he wrote, "her poems are womanly but not intellectual, reflective of feeling rather than thought." In other words, Thaxter's poetry is the writing of a *true* woman. Another anonymous reviewer compliments Thaxter by comparing her to Rudyard Kipling—a man's poet—and goes on to say that she is "a person of rare and gifted nature, limited in both temperament and experience, and beset by the double disadvantage of repression and flattery." No wonder there were madwomen in the attics!

A final review takes Thaxter's prose and poetry into account, and represents best what she meant to her readers: "The five volumes now hold place in many libraries and scores of the poems of Celia Thaxter are

cherished in memories of men and women who have felt
their ethical as well as their lyric quality, their heart-beat
of human experience, and their courage that faith gives
the soul." The courage that faith gives the soul is il-
lustrated in the little poem, "Courage," published in the
Atlantic, in April, 1870:

> Because I hold it sinful to despond,
>   And will not let the bitterness of life
> Blind me with burning tears, but look beyond
>   Its tumult and its strife;
>
> Because I lift my head above the mist,
>   Where the sun shines and the broad breezes
>   blow,
> By every ray and every raindrop kissed
>   That God's love doth bestow;
>
> Think you I find no bitterness at all?
>   No burden to be borne, like Christian's pack?
> Think you there are no ready tears to fall
>   Because I keep them back?[7]

She assures her readers that in every rebellious tear "He
makes a rainbow shine," and that "One golden day
redeems a dreary year." To rebell against the bitterness
and pain of life is as futile as flailing against a hurricane.
Thaxter's duty as a popular poet was to remind her au-
dience of what they already hoped was true. Her poetry
dignified and elevated their daily efforts to wrest a living
from the barren New England landscape.

The quantity and range of material that Thaxter
published indicates to some degree how popular a writer
she was. Her name in the table of contents meant more
sales and increased readerships for struggling maga-
zines of New England. Elizabeth Stuart Phelps described
Celia as "one of the brightest figures in literary Boston
for many years," and then went on with an interview
which revealed Thaxter's grace, beauty and unaffected
manner:

> Celia was always sure of a welcome, and was the
> best of company—everyone wanted her. Hearty,

wholesome, she rose through a decorous drawing
room like a breeze from her own island waves. She
was never afraid to be herself. Her vigorous phy-
sique had much to do with this, for she had had
her share of the sorrows of life.[8]

A history of Atlantic coast resorts and hotels in 1878
refers to "the ballads founded on the romantic scenes
that have occurred on the Isles of Shoals...
and...given Mrs. Thaxter a well known position as a
writer of picturesque verse."[9]

At the turn of the century, William D. Howells
fondly recalled Celia Thaxter in *Literary Friends and
Acquaintances*:

When I saw Celia Thaxter she was just beginning
to make her effect with those poems and sketches
which the sea signs and flashes around the Isles of
Shoals. There her girlhood had been passed in the
freedom as wild as a curlew's. She was a most
beautiful creature still very young, with a slender
figure; she was in presence what her work was:
fine, frank, and finished. I do not know whether
other witnesses of our literary history feel that the
public has failed to keep her fully in mind as her
work merited; but I do not think there can be any
doubt but that our literature would be sensibly
the poorer without her work. Something strangely
full and bright came to her verse from that
mystical environment of the ocean. Her gift, in-
deed, could not satisfy itself with the terms of one
art alone,[10]

and thus Howells goes on to say that she remains in his
mind a vivid and distinct personality. Howells's ap-
preciation for Celia Thaxter is of a balanced kind, based
on his recognition of her honesty and her profession-
alism. That she was "fine, frank and finished" suggests
that Howells saw in Thaxter the commendable personal
qualities respected in any age.

A more charged enthusiasm for all that was Celia
Thaxter can be seen in the many poems her death in-
spired. The following sonnet was found in the Ports-
mouth, New Hampshire, Public Library, written in a

decidedly nineteenth-century handwriting by poet Benjamin Collins Woodbury.

A Face:

On Viewing a Portrait of Celia Thaxter
in the Portsmouth Public Library

The glory of that face—I wonder who
Thou art! Such only can immortal be—
A face like those whose shining glories see
So sad and tender, beautiful and true.

The face of one who joy and pain once knew
But looked from bondage of the flesh and free
Hath flown in transport up to Heaven and Thee

An angel face of God's Immortal few.
Still on the breezes rising homeward float
Thy songs that from the crags of Appledore

Reverberate in airy fluted note;
Thy music flying to that farther shore
As if upon the ear from angel throat
Resounds in echoes dying nevermore.[11]

That Celia Thaxter and her poetry were loved by an enthusiastic audience can be attested to by not only this sonnet but by other poems on her life published in *The Heavenly Guest: A Collection of Unpublished Writing By and About Celia Thaxter* in 1935 on the centenary of her birth.[12] These poems were a fond public's tribute to a poet who spoke sometimes to them, but most often, for them.

Who was this audience that responded so deeply to what Nina Baym calls the "literature of consolation?"[13] They were people who had some education, some skill in reading. People who had the leisure to read to their families around the fires and stoves of rural New England. They were people for whom duty, discipline, self-control and sacrifice were not sentimental abstractions, but rather methods of getting through a hard world. They read Thaxter along with Whittier, Dickens,

Twain, and Longfellow. They were people whose ears were tuned to the old Protestant hymns and the King James Version of the Bible. Some may have memorized the Psalms and even a passage or two from Shakespeare. Browning would have been too mysterious, and Emily Dickinson, if they had read her, would have been dismissed as an incompetent. But most important, Thaxter's audience—and it still exists today—was not aesthetically critical of a poem which expressed clearly its ethical and moral beliefs. Poetry delighted because it edified, and Thaxter's verse did both. The phrase, "How True!" summed up an aesthetic for the audience.

Earlier in the century, Edgar Allan Poe had delineated what would be the qualities of an American poet in his discussion of Mrs. Lydia Sigourney. His characterization fits Thaxter remarkably well:

> Among those high qualities which give her beyond
> doubt, a title to the sacred name of poet are an
> acute sensibility to natural loveliness—a quick and
> perfectly just conception of the moral and physical
> sublime—a calm and unostentatious vigor of
> thought—mingled delicacy and strength of expres-
> sion—and above all, a mind nobly and exquisitely
> attuned to the gentle charities and lofty pieties of
> life.[14]

Poe's genuine concern for the development of a truly American literature allowed him to find merit in a poet such as Lydia Sigourney who, it might be imagined, affronted his personal literary tastes. Even though Poe did scribble in the margins a deprecating reference to women poets—"speak if you can commend—be silent, if not"— he saw that Sigourney played a necessary part in developing the role of the poet, as well as the poetry, of America.

It might be too extreme to say that Sigourney prepared the way for Celia Thaxter, but it can be stated that they shared a female literary tradition. Other than Elizabeth Barret Browning, who could have been Thaxter's literary mothers? She speaks of only three:

Charlotte and Elizabeth Brontë and Elizabeth Barrett
Browning. Thaxter reproached her friend Elizabeth Hox-
ie for even daring to ask if she cared about Charlotte
Brontë:

> To think of your asking a question as "Do I care
> about Charlotte Brontë!" As if I did not care
> everything I am capable of caring for anything!
> As if Levi and I hadn't read her books with rap-
> ture, and hadn't looked forward to the publishing
> of Mrs. Gaskell's book about her as one of the
> most interesting things that could happen; as if
> we didn't lament her loss to the world every year
> of our lives! Oh, Lizzie! I'm ashamed that you
> know so little of your friends.[15]

To the same Mrs. Hoxie, Celia Thaxter raved about Bar-
rett Browning:

> We draw the table up to the roaring fire, and I
> take my work, and Levi reads to me; first he read
> "Aurora Leigh" (and you're an abominable woman
> for not thinking it the beautifullest book that was
> ever written.)[16]

Thaxter's tone in this letter is not comic scolding, it is
genuine anger at the fact that Elizabeth Curzon Hoxie
with her fine education does not appreciate her literary
matrilineage. Recall that in her autobiographical frag-
ment, Thaxter patterns her story after "Aurora Leigh,"
the story of the abandoned female artist.

Who else could Thaxter have turned to? Surely Celia
was aware of the legendary Margaret Fuller Ossoli
whose teachings reached her indirectly through Levi
Thaxter and Wentworth Higginson. Celia Thaxter,
writing alone in the kitchen or alone on the islands, was
one of the creators of an American tradition for female
writers. Her friendships with Harriet Beecher Stowe,
Helen Hunt Jackson, Elizabeth Stuart Phelps, Lucy
Larcom, Harriet Spofford, Rose Terry, Elizabeth Whit-
tier, Sarah Orne Jewett and, of course, Annie Fields
make up one of the first, if not one of the strongest, net-
works of female literary support, inspiration, and power.
Thaxter was a favorite of all these women who were bent

on turning their own experience into literature. Although this coterie met either at the Shoals or in Annie Fields's salon in Boston, clearly it was Thaxter who was perceived by the others as the most original talent in the group. If Thaxter's matrilineage were only dimly recognized, her literary sisterhood was probably the single greatest source of joy in her life.

From a twentieth-century perspective, it is difficult to evaluate the role of a poet like Celia Thaxter. The final, and perhaps central, fact about Thaxter's poetry is that is was written for oral performance, and therein should lie the ultimate test for its effectiveness. Even though the poem that is read or recited can be printed, the text of that poem includes not only the words but also the tone, gesture, expression, mode, the overall performance context of the poem.[17]

Performance interested Celia Thaxter. Her letters and the letters and reminiscences of her many friends abound with references to Thaxter reading her own poems not only at the Appledore Hotel, but also at dinners, parties, and on quiet evenings with family and with friends. One of the most amusing stories of Celia's readings is told by Mr. A.M. DeWolfe Howe in *Memories of a Hostess*. Among the guests at a dinner party where Celia read her poem, "The Tryst," were James and Annie Fields, William Morris Hunt, Longfellow, Holmes, and Emerson. Impressed with the poem, Emerson asked if he could try reading it aloud. Celia was not satisfied with the sage of Concord's performance of her poem, and there, in front of that distinguished audience, Celia coached Emerson into a better reading by insisting he stress the lines that "carried over." Mr. Howe reports that Emerson took her criticism graciously and was finally able to read the poem to Thaxter's satisfaction.[18]

In Thaxter's salon at Appledore, the highlight of every evening, after the Beethoven sonatas and the Bach trios, was Celia Thaxter's reading. Annie Fields reports that Celia "read with an exceptionally beautiful voice which completely satisfied any ear."[19] Celia's poetry comes to life in that atmosphere of island beauty—the music, the brilliant flowers, the golden sunset, and the murmur of the sea.

In evaluating oral poetry, the personality and reputation of the poet must be taken into account as part of the text.[20] Most of the obituaries and reviews mentioned earlier in the chapter do not make the distinction between the poet and the poems and therein lies further evidence for Celia Thaxter as an oral poet: Celia's personality was as well known as her poetry was. Although she occasionally lamented the lack of privacy her status brought, she was always gracious when visitors to Appledore Island and the hotel would barge into her cottage just to gawk at the most famous "Rose of the Island." Celia was a gregarious person and would visit for hours with pilgrims to her cottage. Judging by her endless rounds of social engagements, she must have been the most delightful, and pleasant of conversationalists, and she endured the occasional winters she spent on the island with great pain: "I am too much alone," she wrote Annie Fields after a winter on the island. "I wish the sea would stop its roar!"[21]

As the poet-performer, Celia was most impressive, not only because of her reading skill, but also because of her beauty. That she was a beautiful young woman was attested to by Hawthorne and Howells, but with age, Celia's attractiveness did not fade. Pictures of her in later years reveal her to be a statuesque woman with wavy, white hair and a suntanned, rosy complexion. The subject of many paintings and photographs, Thaxter always took great pride in her appearance. Avoiding all jewelry and ornamentation, except for an occasional fresh rose, she never changed her style, and always dressed in black, white or gray. Her presence was dramatic indeed.

One interviewer in a Boston newspaper described her as a "western woman—open, untutored, strong, cheerful, not subtle or sophisticated." That she was unsophisticated is simply unimaginable, given the social circles of Boston into which she was welcomed. What this interviewer must be trying to report is that Celia always seemed to be natural and unaffected, judging by her quick smile and her hearty laugh. Certainly she was not above playing the role of the rustic—much to her own amusement—because this is often a valuable role for the poet-performer: the audience enjoys feeling that he or she is one of them. Nonetheless her friendships ranged from some of the most brilliant writers and artists of her time to the simple fishermen of the islands who spoke little English. She was truly the "first lady" of the Isles of Shoals, always ready to tend a sick child or feed a starving sailor.

Recognized, then, as one who understood the common lot of human suffering, Celia was well qualified to sing songs of courage and hope to her audience. She could speak of duty, discipline, self-control and sacrifice without sounding a false note. To her audience and to her friends, Celia Thaxter was that heroic woman who had passed all of the tests of character life could bring her, and thus she was qualified to speak as a poet.

In the final analysis the obituaries and subsequent literary history written shortly after Thaxter's death were all based on the assumption that she would not be remembered as an important poet—first because she was a woman, and second because she was so popular: since her personality was an integral part of the text of each poem, that the poetry would die along with the ephemeral personality of the poet. The fact is, however, that personality need not be ephemeral if enough of it can be captured in biography; but, biography can be accomplished only when a culture learns to value the life and work of a poet—such as Celia Thaxter—and thus preserve for future generations not only the poetry and prose of that writer, but also the letters, pictures, stories and reminiscences of that writer's life.

Thanks to the social revolution which has called for the total re-evaluation of female experience, one dimension of which is literary expression, the labor and pleasures of telling the first and second stories of Celia

Thaxter's life can proceed. Margaret Fuller spoke often of her desire to redeem—revalue—American woman-hood. Fuller's dream is still alive today in the scholar-ship, the teaching, and the ideals of people who re-evaluate the lost or forgotten work of those who have attempted to record the richness of human experience in literature.

> Glory is that bright tragic thing
> That for an instant
> Means Dominion—
> Warms some poor name
> That never felt the Sun,
> Gently replacing
> In oblivion—[22]

Emily Dickinson

Poems

LAND-LOCKED

Black lie the hills; swiftly doth daylight flee;
  And, catching gleams of sunset's dying smile,
  Through the dusk land for many a changing mile
The river runneth softly to the sea.

O happy river, could I follow thee!
  O yearning heart, that never can be still!
  O wistful eyes, that watch the steadfast hill,
Longing for level line of solemn sea!

Have patience; here are flowers and songs of birds,
  Beauty and fragrance, wealth of sound and sight,
  All summer's glory thine from morn till night,
And life too full of joy for uttered words.

Neither am I ungrateful; but I dream
  Deliciously how twilight falls to-night
  Over the glimmering water, how the light
Dies blissfully away, until I seem

To feel the wind, sea-scented, on my cheek,
  To catch the sound of dusky flapping sand
  And dip of oars, and voices on the gale
Afar off, calling low,—my name they speak!

O Earth! thy summer song of joy may soar
  Ringing to heaven in triumph. I but crave
  The sad, caressing murmur of the wave
That breaks in tender music on the shore.

OFF SHORE

Rock, little boat, beneath the quiet sky;
Only the stars behold us where we lie,—
Only the stars and yonder brightening moon.

On the wide sea to-night alone are we;
The sweet, bright summer day dies silently,
Its glowing sunset will have faded soon.

Rock softly, little boat, the while I mark
The far off gliding sails, distinct and dark,
Across the west pass steadily and slow.

But on the eastern waters sad, they change
And vanish, dream-like, gray, and cold, and strange,
And no one knoweth whither they may go.

We care not, we, drifting with wind and tide,
While glad waves darken upon either side,
Save where the moon sends silver sparkles down,

And yonder slender stream of changing light,
Now white, now crimson, tremulously bright,
Where dark the lighthouse stands, with fiery crown.

Thick falls the dew, soundless on sea and shore:
It shines on little boat and idle oar,
Wherever moonbeams touch with tranquil glow.

The waves are full of whispers wild and sweet;
They call to me,—incessantly they beat
Along the boat from stern to curvèd prow.

Comes the careering wind, blows back my hair,
All damp with dew, to kiss me unaware,
Murmuring "Thee I love," and passes on.

Sweet sounds on rocky shores the distant rote;
Oh could we float forever, little boat,
Under the blissful sky drifting alone!

EXPECTATION

Throughout the lonely house the whole day long
    The wind-harp's fitful music sinks and swells,—
A cry of pain, sometimes, or sad and strong,
    Or faint, like broken peals of silver bells.

Across the little garden comes the breeze,
    Bows all its cups of flame, and brings to me
Its breath of mignonette and bright sweet-peas,
    With drowsy murmurs from the encircling sea.

In at the open door a crimson drift
    Of fluttering, fading woodbine leaves is blown,
And through the clambering vine the sunbeams sift,
    And trembling shadows on the floor are thrown.

I climb the stair, and from the window lean
    Seeking thy sail, O love, that still delays;
Longing to catch its glimmer, searching keen
    The jealous distance veiled in tender haze.

What care I if the pansies purple be,
    Or sweet the wind-harp wails through the slow
        hours;
Or that the lulling music of the sea
    Comes woven with the perfume of the flowers?

Thou comest not! I ponder o'er the leaves,
    The crimson drift behind the open door:
Soon shall we listen to a wind that grieves,
    Mourning this glad year, dead forevermore.

And, O my love, shall we on some sad day
  Find joys and hopes low fallen like the leaves,
Blown by life's chilly autumn wind away
  In withered heaps God's eye alone perceives?

Come thou, and save me from my dreary thought!
  Who dares to question Time, what it may bring?
Yet round us lies the radiant summer, fraught
  With beauty: must we dream of suffering?

Yea, even so. Through this enchanted land,
  This morning-red of life, we go to meet
The tempest in the desert, hand in hand,
  Along God's paths of pain, that seek his feet.

But this one golden moment,—hold it fast!
  The light grows long: low in the west the sun,
Clear red and glorious, slowly sinks at last,
  And while I muse, the tranquil day is done.

The land breeze freshens in thy gleaming sail!
  Across the singing waves the shadows creep:
Under the new moon's thread of silver pale,
  With the first star, thou comest o'er the deep.

THE WRECK OF THE POCAHONTAS

I lit the lamps in the lighthouse tower,
  For the sun dropped down and the day was dead.
They shone like a glorious clustered flower,—
  Ten golden and five red.

Looking across, where the line of coast
  Stretched darkly, shrinking away from the sea,
The lights sprang out at its edge,—almost
  They seemed to answer me!

O warning lights! burn bright and clear,
    Hither the storm comes! Leagues away
It moans and thunders low and drear,—
    Burn till the break of day!

Good-night! I called to the gulls that sailed
    Slow past me through the evening sky;
And my comrades, answering shrilly, hailed
    Me back with boding cry.

A mournful breeze began to blow;
    Weird music it drew through the iron bars;
The sullen billows boiled below,
    And dimly peered the stars;

The sails that flecked the ocean floor
    From east to west leaned low and fled;
They knew what came in the distant roar
    That filled the air with dread!

Flung by a fitful gust, there beat
    Against the window a dash of rain:
Steady as tramp of marching feet
    Strode on the hurricane.

It smote the waves for a moment still,
    Level and deadly white for fear;
The bare rock shuddered,—an awful thrill
    Shook even my tower of cheer.

Like all the demons loosed at last,
    Whistling and shrieking, wild and wide,
The mad wind raged, while strong and fast
    Rolled in the rising tide.

And soon in ponderous showers, the spray
    Struck from the granite, reared and sprung
And clutched at tower and cottage gray,
    Where overwhelmed they clung

Half drowning to the naked rock;
    But still burned on the faithful light,
Nor faltered at the tempest's shock,
    Through all the fearful night.

Was it in vain? That knew not we.
    We seemed, in that confusion vast
Of rushing wind and roaring sea,
    One point whereon was cast

The whole Atlantic's weight of brine.
    Heaven help the ship should drift our way!
No matter how the light might shine
    Far on into the day.

When morning dawned, above the din
    Of gale and breaker boomed a gun!
Another! We who sat within
    Answered with cries each one.

Into each other's eyes with fear
    We looked through helpless tears, as still,
One after one, near and more near,
    The signals pealed, until

The thick storm seemed to break apart
    To show us, staggering to her grave,
The fated brig. We had no heart
    To look, for naught could save.

One glimpse of black hull heaving slow,
    Then closed the mists o'er canvas torn
And tangled ropes swept to and fro
    From masts that raked forlorn.

Weeks after, yet ringed round with spray
    Our island lay, and none might land;
Though blue the waters of the bay
    Stretched calm on either hand.

And when at last from the distant shore
    A little boat stole out, to reach
Our loneliness, and bring once more
    Fresh human thought and speech,

We told our tale, and the boatmen cried:
    " 'Twas the Pocahontas,—all were lost!
For miles along the coast the tide
    Her shattered timbers tossed."

Then I looked the whole horizon round,—
    So beautiful the ocean spread
About us, o'er those sailors drowned!
    "Father in heaven," I said,—

A child's grief struggling in my breast,—
    "Do purposeless thy children meet
Such bitter death? How was it best
    These hearts should cease to beat?

"Oh wherefore? Are we naught to Thee?
    Like senseless weeds that rise and fall
Upon thine awful sea, are we
    No more then, after all?"

And I shut the beauty from my sight,
    For I thought of the dead that lay below;
From the bright air faded the warmth and light,
    There came a chill like snow.

Then I heard the far-off rote resound,
    Where the breakers slow and slumberous rolled,
And a subtile sense of Thought profound
    Touched me with power untold.

And like a voice eternal spake
    That wondrous rhythm, and, "Peace, be still!"
It murmured, "bow thy head and take
    Life's rapture and life's ill,

"And wait. At last all shall be clear."
    The long, low, mellow music rose
And fell, and soothed my dreaming ear
    With infinite repose.

Sighing I climbed the lighthouse stair,
    Half forgetting my grief and pain;
And while the day died, sweet and fair,
    I lit the lamps again.

ROCK WEEDS

So bleak these shores, wind-swept and all the year
    Washed by the wild Atlantic's restless tide,
You would not dream that flowers the woods hold dear
    Amid such desolation dare abide.

Yet when the bitter winter breaks, some day,
    With soft winds fluttering her garments' hem,
Up from the sweet South comes the lingering May,
    Sets the first wind-flower trembling on its stem;

Scatters her violets with lavish hands,
    White, blue and amber; calls the columbine,
Till like clear flame in lonely nooks, gay bands
    Swinging their scarlet bells, obey the sign;

Makes buttercups and dandelions blaze,
    And throws in glimmering patches here and there,
The little eyebright's pearls, and gently lays
    The impress of her beauty everywhere.

Later, June bids the sweet wild rose to blow;
    Wakes from its dream the drowsy pimpernel;
Unfolds the bindweed's ivory buds, that glow
    As delicately blushing as a shell.

Then purple Iris smiles, and hour by hour,
    The fair procession multiplies; and soon,
In clusters creamy white, the elder-flower
    Waves its broad disk against the rising moon.

O'er quiet beaches shelving to the sea
    Tall mulleins sway, and thistles; all day long
Flows in the wooing water dreamily,
    With subtile music in its slumberous song.

Herb-robert hears, and princess'-feather bright,
    And goldthread clasps the little skull-cap blue;
And troops of swallows, gathering for their flight,
    O'er goldenrod and asters hold review.

The barren island dreams in flowers, while blow
    The south winds, drawing haze o'er sea and land;
Yet the great heart of ocean, throbbing slow,
    Makes the frail blossoms vibrate where they stand;

And hints of heavier pulses soon to shake
    Its mighty breast when summer is no more,
And devastating waves sweep on and break,
    And clasp with girdle white the iron shore.

Close folded, safe within the sheltering seed,
    Blossom and bell and leafy beauty hide;
Nor icy blast, nor bitter spray they heed,
    But patiently their wondrous change abide.

The heart of God through his creation stirs,
    We thrill to feel it, trembling as the flowers
That die to live again,—his messengers,
    To keep faith firm in these sad souls of ours.

The waves of Time may devastate our lives,
    The frosts of age may check our failing breath,
They shall not touch the spirit that survives
    Triumphant over doubt and pain and death.

THE SANDPIPER

Across the narrow beach we flit,
    One little sandpiper and I,
And fast I gather, bit by bit,
    The scattered driftwood bleached and dry.
The wild waves reach their hands for it,
    The wild wind raves, the tide runs high,
As up and down the beach we flit,—
    One little sandpiper and I.

Above our heads the sullen clouds
    Scud black and swift across the sky;
Like silent ghosts in misty shrouds
    Stand out the white lighthouses high.
Almost as far as eye can reach
    I see the close-reefed vessels fly,
As fast we flit along the beach,—
    One little sandpiper and I.

I watch him as he skims along,
    Uttering his sweet and mournful cry.
He starts not at my fitful song,
    Or flash of fluttering drapery.
He has no thought of any wrong;
    He scans me with a fearless eye,
Stanch friends are we, well tried and strong,
    The little sandpiper and I.

Comrade, where wilt thou be to-night
    When the loosed storm breaks furiously?
My driftwood fire will burn so bright!
    To what warm shelter canst thou fly?
I do not fear for thee, though wroth
    The tempest rushes through the sky:
For are we not God's children both,
    Thou, little sandpiper and I?

TWILIGHT

September's slender crescent grows again
    Distinct in yonder peaceful evening red,
    Clearer the stars are sparkling overhead,
And all the sky is pure, without a stain.

Cool blows the evening wind from out the West
    And bows the flowers, the last sweet flowers that
        bloom,—
    Pale asters, many a heavy-waving plume
Of goldenrod that bends as if opprest.

The summer's songs are hushed. Up the lone shore
    The weary waves wash sadly, and a grief
    Sounds in the wind, like farewells fond and brief.
The cricket's chirp but makes the silence more.

Life's autumn comes; the leaves begin to fail;
    The moods of spring and summer pass away;
    The glory and the rapture, day by day,
Depart, and soon the quiet grave folds all.

O thoughtful sky, how many eyes in vain
    Are lifted to your beauty, full of tears!
    How many hearts go back through all the years,
Heavy with loss, eager with questioning pain,

To read the dim Hereafter, to obtain
    One glimpse beyond the earthly curtain, where
    Their dearest dwell, where they may be or e'er
September's slender crescent shines again!

THE SWALLOW

The swallow twitters about the eaves;
    Blithely she sings, and sweet and clear;
Around her climb the woodbine leaves
    In a golden atmosphere.

The summer wind sways leaf and spray,
    That catch and cling to the cool gray wall;
The bright sea stretches miles away,
    And the noon sun shines o'er all.

In the chamber's shadow, quietly,
    I stand and worship the sky and the leaves,
The golden air and the brilliant sea,
    The swallow at the eaves.

Like a living jewel she sits and sings;
    Fain would I read her riddle aright,
Fain would I know whence her rapture springs,
    So strong in a thing so slight!

The fine, clear fire of joy that steals
    Through all my spirit at what I see
In the glimpse my window's space reveals,—
    That seems no mystery!

But scarce for her joy can she utter her song;
    Yet she knows not the beauty of skies or seas.
Is it bliss of living, so sweet and strong?
    Is it love, which is more than these?

O happy creature! what stirs thee so?
    A spark of the gladness of God thou art.
Why should we seek to find and to know
    The secret of thy heart?

Before the gates of his mystery
    Trembling we knock with an eager hand;
Silent behind them waiteth He;
    Not yet may we understand.

But thrilling throughout the universe
    Throbs the pulse of his mighty will,
Till we gain the knowledge of joy or curse
    In the choice of good or ill.

He looks from the eyes of the little child,
    And searches souls with their gaze so clear;
To the heart some agony makes wild
    He whispers, "I am here."

He smiles in the face of every flower;
    In the swallow's twitter of sweet content
He speaks, and we follow through every hour
    The way his deep thought went.

Here should be courage and hope and faith;
    Naught has escaped the trace of his hand;
And a voice in the heart of his silence saith,
    One day we shall understand.

THE SPANIARDS' GRAVES

AT THE ISLES OF SHOALS

O sailors, did sweet eyes look after you
    The day you sailed away from sunny Spain?
Bright eyes that followed fading ship and crew,
    Melting in tender rain?

Did no one dream of that drear night to be,
    Wild with the wind, fierce with the stinging snow,

When on yon granite point that frets the sea,
    The ship met her death-blow?

Fifty long years ago these sailors died:
    (None know how many sleep beneath the waves:)
Fourteen gray headstones, rising side by side,
    Point out their nameless graves,—

Lonely, unknown, deserted, but for me,
    And the wild birds that flit with mournful cry,
And sadder winds, and voices of the sea
    That moans perpetually.

Wives, mothers, maidens, wistfully, in vain
    Questioned the distance for the yearning sail,
That, leaning landward, should have stretched again
    White arms wide on the gale,

To bring back their beloved. Year by year,
    Weary they watched, till youth and beauty
        passed,
And lustrous eyes grew dim and age drew near,
    And hope was dead at last.

Still summer broods o'er that delicious land,
    Rich, fragrant, warm with skies of golden glow:
Live any yet of that forsaken band
    Who loved so long ago?

O Spanish women, over the far seas,
    Could I but show you where your dead repose!
Could I send tidings on this northern breeze
    That strong and steady blows!

Dear dark-eyed sisters, you remember yet
    These you have lost, but you can never know
One stands at their bleak graves whose eyes are wet
    With thinking of your woe!

WATCHING

In childhood's season fair,
On many a balmy, moonless summer night,
While wheeled the lighthouse arms of dark and bright
    Far through the humid air;

How patient have I been,
Sitting alone, a happy little maid,
Waiting to see, careless and unafraid,
    My father's boat come in;

Close to the water's edge
Holding a tiny spark, that he might steer
(So dangerous the landing, far and near)
    Safe past the ragged ledge.

I had no fears,—not one;
The wild, wide waste of water leagues around
Washed ceaselessly; there was no human sound,
    And I was all alone.

But Nature was so kind!
Like a dear friend I loved the loneliness;
My heart rose glad, as at some sweet caress,
    When passed the wandering wind.

Yet it was joy to hear,
From out the darkness, sounds grow clear at last,
Of rattling rowlock, and of creaking mast,
    And voices drawing near!

"Is 't thou, dear father? Say!"
What well-known shout resounded in reply,
As loomed the tall sail, smitten suddenly
    With the great lighthouse ray!

I will be patient now,
Dear Heavenly Father, waiting here for Thee:
I know the darkness holds Thee. Shall I be
    Afraid, when it is Thou?

  On thy eternal shore,
In pauses, when life's tide is at its prime,
I hear the everlasting rote of Time
    Beating for evermore.

    Shall I not then rejoice?
Oh, never lost or sad should child of thine
Sit waiting, fearing lest there come no sign,
    No whisper of thy voice!

IN MAY

That was a curlew calling overhead,
    That fine, clear whistle shaken from the clouds:
See! hovering o'er the swamp with wings outspread,
    He sinks where at its edge in shining crowds
The yellow violets dance as they unfold,
In the blithe spring wind, all their green and gold.

Blithe south-wind, spreading bloom upon the sea,
    Drawing about the world this band of haze
So softly delicate, and bringing me
    A touch of balm that like a blessing stays;
Though beauty like a dream bathes sea and land,
For the first time Death holds me by the hand.

Yet none the less the swallows weave above
    Through the bright air a web of light and song,
And calling clear and sweet from cove to cove,
    The sandpiper, the lonely rocks among,
Makes wistful music, and the singing sea
Sends its strong chorus upward solemnly.

O Mother Nature, infinitely dear!
   Vainly I search the beauty of thy face,
Vainly thy myriad voices charm my ear;
   I cannot gather from thee any trace
Of God's intent. Help me to understand
Why, this sweet morn, Death holds me by the hand.

I watch the waves, shoulder to shoulder set,
   That strive and vanish and are seen no more.
The earth is sown with graves that we forget,
   And races of mankind the wide world o'er
Rise, strive, and vanish, leaving naught behind,
Like changing waves swept by the changing wind.

"Hard-hearted, cold, and blind," she answers me,
   "Vexing thy soul with riddles hard to guess!
No waste of any atom canst thou see,
   Nor make I any gesture purposeless.
Lift thy dim eyes up to the conscious sky!
God *meant* that rapture in the curlew's cry.

"He holds his whirling worlds in check; not one
   May from its awful orbit swerve aside;
Yet breathes He in this south-wind, bids the sun
   Wake the fair flowers He fashioned, far and wide,
And this strong pain thou canst not understand
Is but his grasp on thy reluctant hand."

A SUMMER DAY

At daybreak in the fresh light, joyfully
   The fishermen drew in their laden net;
The shore shone rosy purple, and the sea
   Was streaked with violet;

And pink with sunrise, many a shadowy sail
    Lay southward, lighting up the sleeping bay;
And in the west the white moon, still and pale,
    Faded before the day.

Silence was everywhere. The rising tide
    Slowly filled every cove and inlet small;
A musical low whisper, multiplied,
    You heard, and that was all.

No clouds at dawn, but as the sun climbed higher,
    White columns, thunderous, splendid, up the sky
Floated and stood, heaped in his steady fire,
    A stately company.

Stealing along the coast from cape to cape
    The weird mirage crept tremulously on,
In many a magic change and wondrous shape,
    Throbbing beneath the sun.

At noon the wind rose, swept the glassy sea
    To sudden ripple, thrust against the clouds
A strenuous shoulder, gathering steadily,
    Drove them before in crowds;

Till all the west was dark, and inky black
    The level-ruffled water underneath,
And up the wind cloud tossed,—a ghostly rack,
    In many a ragged wreath.

Then sudden roared the thunder, a great peal
    Magnificent, that broke and rolled away;
And down the wind plunged, like a furious keel,
    Cleaving the sea to spray;

And brought the rain sweeping o'er land and sea.
    And then was tumult! Lightning sharp and
        keen,
Thunder, wind, rain,—a mighty jubilee
    The heaven and earth between!

Loud the roused ocean sang, a chorus grand;
   A solemn music rolled in undertone
Of waves that broke about, on either hand,
   The little island lone;

Where, joyful in his tempest as his calm,
   Held in the hollow of that hand of his,
I joined with heart and soul in God's great psalm,
   Thrilled with a nameless bliss.

Soon lulled the wind, the summer storm soon died;
   The shattered clouds went eastward, drifting slow;
From the low sun the rain-fringe swept aside,
   Bright in his rosy glow,

And wide a splendor streamed through all the sky;
   O'er sea and land one soft, delicious blush,
That touched the gray rocks lightly, tenderly;
   A transitory flush.

Warm, odorous gusts blew off the distant land,
   With spice of pine-woods, breath of hay new
      mown,
O'er miles of waves and sea scents cool and bland,
   Full in our faces blown.

Slow faded the sweet light, and peacefully
   The quiet stars came out, one after one:
The holy twilight fell upon the sea,
   The summer day was done.

Such unalloyed delight its hours had given,
   Musing, this thought rose in my grateful mind,
That God, who watches all things, up in heaven,
   With patient eyes and kind,

Saw and was pleased, perhaps, one child of his
   Dared to be happy like the little birds,

Because He gave his children days like this,
    Rejoicing beyond words;

Dared, lifting up to Him untroubled eyes
    In gratitude that worship is, and prayer,
Sing and be glad with ever new surprise,
    He made his world so fair!

BEFORE SUNRISE

This grassy gorge, as daylight failed last night,
    I traversed toward the west, where, thin and
        young,
Bent like Diana's bow and silver bright,
    Half lost in rosy haze, a crescent hung.

I paused upon the beach's upper edge:
    The violet east all shadowy lay behind;
Southward the lighthouse glittered o'er the ledge,
    And lightly, softly blew the western wind.

And at my feet, between the turf and stone,
    Wild roses, bayberry, purple thistles tall,
And pink herb-robert grew, where shells were strown
    And morning-glory vines climbed over all.

I stooped the closely folded buds to note,
    That gleamed in the dim light mysteriously,
While, full of whispers of the far-off rote,
    Summer's enchanted dusk crept o'er the sea.

And sights and sounds and sea-scents delicate,
    So wrought upon my soul with sense of bliss,
Happy I sat as if at heaven's gate,
    Asking on earth no greater joy than this.

And now, at dawn, upon the beach again,
    Kneeling I wait the coming of the sun,

Watching the looser-folded buds, and fain
    To see the marvel of their day begun.

All the world lies so dewy-fresh and still!
    Whispers so gently all the water wide,
Hardly it breaks the silence: from the hill
    Come clear bird-voices mingling with the tide.

Sunset or dawn: which is the lovelier? Lo!
    My darlings, sung to all the balmy night
By summer waves and softest winds that blow,
    Begin to feel the thrilling of the light!

Red lips of roses, waiting to be kissed
    By early sunshine, soon in smiles will break.
But oh, ye morning-glories, that keep tryst
    With the first ray of daybreak, ye awake!

O bells of triumph, ringing noiseless peals
    Of unimagined music to the day!
Almost I could believe each blossom feels
    The same delight that sweeps my soul away.

O bells of triumph! delicate trumpets, thrown
    Heavenward and earthward, turned east, west,
        north, south,
In lavish beauty, who through you has blown
    This sweet cheer of the morning with calm mouth?

'T is God who breathes the triumph; He who
        wrought
    The tender curves, and laid the tints divine
Along the lovely lines; the Eternal Thought
    That troubles all our lives with wise design.

Yea, out of pain and death his beauty springs,
    And out of doubt a deathless confidence:
Though we are shod with leaden cares, our wings
    Shall lift us yet out of our deep suspense!

Thou great Creator! Pardon us who reach
    For other heaven beyond this world of thine,
This matchless world, where thy least touch doth
       teach
    Thy solemn lessons clearly, line on line.

And help us to be grateful, we who live
    Such sordid, fretful lives of discontent,
Nor see the sunshine nor the flower, nor strive
    To find the love thy bitter chastening meant.

SORROW

Upon my lips she laid her touch divine,
    And merry speech and careless laughter died;
She fixed her melancholy eyes on mine,
    And would not be denied.

I saw the west wind loose his cloudlets white
    In flocks, careering through the April sky;
I could not sing though joy was at its height,
    For she stood silent by.

I watched the lovely evening fade away;
    A mist was lightly drawn across the stars;
She broke my quiet dream, I heard her say,
    "Behold your prison bars!

"Earth's gladness shall not satisfy your soul,
    This beauty of the world in which you live;
The crowning grace that sanctifies the whole,
    That, I alone can give."

I heard and shrank away from her afraid;
    But still she held me and would still abide;
Youth's bounding pulses slackened and obeyed,
    With slowly ebbing tide.

"Look thou beyond the evening star," she said,
   "Beyond the changing splendors of the day;
Accept the pain, the weariness, the dread,
   Accept and bid me stay!"

I turned and clasped her close with sudden strength,
   And slowly, sweetly, I became aware
Within my arms God's angel stood at length,
   White-robed and calm and fair.

And now I look beyond the evening star,
   Beyond the changing splendors of the day,
Knowing the pain He sends more precious far,
   More beautiful, than they.

COURAGE

Because I hold it sinful to despond,
   And will not let the bitterness of life
Blind me with burning tears, but look beyond
   Its tumult and its strife;

Because I lift my head above the mist,
   Where the sun shines and the broad breezes blow,
By every ray and every raindrop kissed
   That God's love doth bestow;

Think you I find no bitterness at all?
   No burden to be borne, like Christian's pack?
Think you there are no ready tears to fall
   Because I keep them back?

Why should I hug life's ills with cold reserve,
   To curse myself and all who love me? Nay!
A thousand times more good than I deserve
   God gives me every day.

And in each one of these rebellious tears,
    Kept bravely back, He makes a rainbow shine;
Grateful I take his slightest gift, no fears
    Nor any doubts are mine.

Dark skies must clear, and when the clouds are past,
    One golden day redeems a weary year;
Patient I listen, sure that sweet at last
    Will sound his voice of cheer.

Then vex me not with chiding. Let me be.
    I must be glad and grateful to the end.
I grudge you not your cold and darkness,—me
    The powers of light befriend.

REMEMBRANCE

Fragrant and soft the summer wind doth blow.
    Weary I lie, with heavy, half-shut eyes,
    And watch, while wistful thoughts within me
        rise,
The curtain idly swaying to and fro.

There comes a sound of household toil from far,
    A woven murmur: voices shrill and sweet,
    Clapping of doors, and restless moving feet,
And tokens faint of fret, and noise, and jar.

Without, the broad earth shimmers in the glare,
    Through the clear noon high rides the blazing
        sun,
    The birds are hushed; the cricket's chirp alone
With tremulous music cleaves the drowsy air.

I think,—"Past the gray rocks the wavelets run;
    The gold-brown seaweed drapes the ragged ledge;
    And brooding, silent, at the water's edge
The white gull sitteth, shining in the sun."

A TRYST

From out the desolation of the North
    An iceberg took it away,
From its detaining comrades breaking forth,
    And traveling night and day.

At whose command? Who bade it sail the deep
    With that resistless force?
Who made the dread appointment it must keep?
    Who traced its awful course?

To the warm airs that stir in the sweet South,
    A good ship spread her sails;
Stately she passed beyond the harbor's mouth,
    Chased by the favoring gales;

And on her ample decks a happy crowd
    Bade the fair land good-by;
Clear shone the day, with not a single cloud
    In all the peaceful sky.

Brave men, sweet women, little children bright
    For all these she made room,
And with her freight of beauty and delight
    She went to meet her doom.

Storms buffeted the iceberg, spray was swept
    Across its loftiest height;
Guided alike by storm and calm, it kept
    Its fatal path aright.

Then warmer waves gnawed at its crumbling base,
    As if in piteous plea;
The ardent sun sent slow tears down its face,
    Soft flowing to the sea.

Dawn kissed it with her tender rose tints, Eve
    Bathed it in violet,

The wistful color o'er it seemed to grieve
    With a divine regret.

Whether Day clad its clefts in rainbows dim
    And shadowy as a dream,
Or Night through lonely spaces saw it swim
    White in the moonlight's gleam,

Ever Death rode upon its solemn heights,
    Ever his watch he kept;
Cold at its heart through changing days and nights
    Its changeless purpose slept.

And where afar a smiling coast it passed,
    Straightway the air grew chill;
Dwellers thereon perceived a bitter blast,
    A vague report of ill.

Like some imperial creature, moving slow,
    Meanwhile, with matchless grace,
The stately ship, unconscious of her foe,
    Drew near the trysting place.

For still the prosperous breezes followed her,
    And half the voyage was o'er;
In many a breast glad thoughts began to stir
    Of lands that lay before.

And human hearts with longing love were dumb,
    That soon should cease to beat,
Thrilled with the hope of meetings soon to come,
    And lost in memories sweet.

Was not the weltering waste of water wide
    Enough for both to sail?
What drew the two together o'er the tide,
    Fair ship and iceberg pale?

There came a night with neither moon nor star,
    Clouds draped the sky in black;

With fluttering canvas reefed at every spar,
    And weird fire in her track,

The ship swept on; a wild wind gathering fast
    Drove her at utmost speed.
Bravely she bent before the fitful blast
    That shook her like a reed.

O helmsman, turn thy wheel! Will no surmise
    Cleave through the midnight drear?
No warning of the horrible surprise
    Reach thine unconscious ear?

She rushed upon her ruin. Not a flash
    Broke up the waiting dark;
Dully through wind and sea one awful crash
    Sounded, with none to mark.

Scarcely her crew had time to clutch despair,
    So swift the work was done:
Ere their pale lips could frame a speechless prayer,
    They perished, every one!

IMPRISONED

Lightly she lifts the large, pure, luminous shell,
    Poises it in her strong and shapely hand.
"Listen," she says, "it has a tale to tell,
    Spoken in language you may understand."

Smiling, she holds it at my dreaming ear:
    The old, delicious murmur of the sea
Steals like enchantment through me, and I hear
    Voices like echoes of eternity.

She stirs it softly. Lo, another speech!
    In one of its dim chambers, shut from sight,

Is sealed the water that has kissed the beach
  Where the far Indian Ocean leaps in light.

Those laughing ripples, hidden evermore
  In utter darkness, plaintively repeat
Their lapsing on the glowing tropic shore,
  In melancholy whispers low and sweet.

O prisoned wave that may not see the sun!
  O voice that never may be comforted!
You cannot break the web that Fate has spun;
  Out of your world are light and gladness fled.

The red dawn nevermore shall tremble far
  Across the leagues of radiant brine to you;
You shall not sing to greet the evening star,
  Nor dance exulting under heaven's clear blue.

Inexorably woven is the weft
  That shrouds from you all joy but memory;
Only this tender, low lament is left
  Of all the sumptuous splendor of the sea.

HEARTBREAK HILL

In Ipswich town, not far from the sea,
  Rises a hill which the people call
Heartbreak Hill, and its history
  Is an old, old legend, known to all.

The selfsame dreary, worn-out tale
  Told by all peoples in every clime,
Still to be told till the ages fail,
  And there comes a pause in the march of Time.

It was a sailor who won the heart
  Of an Indian maiden, lithe and young;

And she saw him over the sea depart,
    While sweet in her ear his promise rung;

For he cried, as he kissed her wet eyes dry,
    "I'll come back, sweetheart; keep your faith!"
She said, "I will watch while the moons go by:"
    Her love was stronger than life or death.

So this poor dusk Ariadne kept
    Her watch from the hilltop rugged and steep;
Slowly the empty moments crept
    While she studied the changing face of the deep,

Fastening her eyes upon every speck
    That crossed the ocean within her ken;
Might not her lover be walking the deck,
    Surely and swiftly returning again?

The Isles of Shoals loomed, lonely and dim,
    In the northeast distance far and gray,
And on the horizon's uttermost rim
    The low rock heap of Boon Island lay.

And north and south and west and east
    Stretched sea and land in the blinding light,
Till evening fell, and her vigil ceased,
    And many a hearth-glow lit the night,

To mock those set and glittering eyes
    Fast growing wild as her hope went out.
Hateful seemed earth, and the hollow skies,
    Like her own heart, empty of aught but doubt.

Oh, but the weary, merciless days,
    With the sun above, with the sea afar,—
No change in her fixed and wistful gaze
    From the morning-red to the evening star!

Oh, the winds that blew, and the birds that sang,
    The calms that smiled, and the storms that rolled,

The bells from the town beneath, that rang
    Through the summer's heat and the winter's cold!

The flash of the plunging surges white,
    The soaring gull's wild, boding cry,—
She was weary of all; there was no delight
    In heaven or earth, and she longed to die.

What was it to her though the Dawn should paint
    With delicate beauty skies and seas?
But the sweet, sad sunset splendors faint
    Made her soul sick with memories:

Drowning in sorrowful purple a sail
    In the distant east, where shadows grew,
Till the twilight shrouded it, cold and pale,
    And the tide of her anguish rose anew.

Like a slender statue carved of stone
    She sat, with hardly motion or breath.
She wept no tears and she made no moan,
    But her love was stronger than life or death.

He never came back! Yet faithful still,
    She watched from the hilltop her life away.
And the townsfolk christened it Heartbreak Hill,
    And it bears the name to this very day.

IN KITTERY CHURCHYARD

"Mary, wife of Charles Chauncy, died April 23, 1758,
in the 24th year of her age."

Crushing the scarlet strawberries in the grass,
I kneel to read the slanting stone. Alas!
How sharp a sorrow speaks! A hundred years
And more have vanished, with their smiles and tears,
Since here was laid, upon an April day,
Sweet Mary Chauncy in the grave away,—

A hundred years since here her lover stood
Beside her grave in such despairing mood,
And yet from out the vanished past I hear
His cry of anguish sounding deep and clear,
And all my heart with pity melts, as though
To-day's bright sun were looking on his woe.
"Of such a wife, O righteous Heaven! bereft,
What joy for me, what joy on earth is left?
Still from my inmost soul the groans arise,
Still flow the sorrows ceaseless from mine eyes."
Alas, poor tortured soul! I look away
From the dark stone,—how brilliant shines the day!
A low wall, over which the roses shed
Their perfumed petals, shuts the quiet dead
Apart a little, and the tiny square
Stands in the broad and laughing field so fair,
And gay green vines climb o'er the rough stone wall,
And all about the wild birds flit and call,
And but a stone's throw southward, the blue sea
Rolls sparkling in and sings incessantly.
Lovely as any dream the peaceful place,
And scarcely changed since on her gentle face
For the last time on that sad April day
He gazed, and felt, for him, all beauty lay
Buried with her forever. Dull to him
Looked the bright world through eyes with tears so dim!
"I soon shall follow the same dreary way
That leads and opens to the coasts of day."
His only hope! But when slow time had dealt
Firmly with him and kindly, and he felt
The storm and stress of strong and piercing pain
Yielding at last, and he grew calm again,
Doubtless he found another mate before
He followed Mary to the happy shore!
But none the less his grief appeals to me
Who sit and listen to the singing sea
This matchless summer day, beside the stone
He made to echo with his bitter moan,
And in my eyes I feel the foolish tears
For buried sorrow, dead a hundred years!

AT THE BREAKERS' EDGE

Through the wide sky thy north wind's thunder
    roars
  Restless, till no cloud is left to flee,
And down the clear, cold heaven unhindered pours
    Thine awful moonlight on the winter sea.

The vast, black, raging spaces, torn and wild,
    With an insensate fury answer back
To the gale's challenge; hurrying breakers, piled
    Each over each, roll through the glittering track.

I shudder in the terror of thy cold,
    As buffeted by the fierce blast I stand,
Watching that shining path of bronzèd gold,
    With solemn, shadowy rocks on either hand;

While at their feet, ghastly and white as death,
    The cruel, foaming billows plunge and rave.
O Father! where art Thou? My feeble breath
    Cries to Thee through the storm of wind and wave.

The cry of all thy children since the first
    That walked thy planets' myriad paths among;
The cry of all mankind whom doubt has cursed,
    In every clime, in every age and tongue.

Thou art the cold, the swift fire that consumes;
    Thy vast, unerring forces never fail;
And Thou art in the frailest flower that blooms,
    As in the breath of this tremendous gale.

Yet, though thy laws are clear as light, and prove
    Thee changeless, ever human weakness craves
Some deeper knowledge for our human love
    That looks with sad eyes o'er its wastes of graves,

And hungers for the dear hands softly drawn,
    One after one, from out our longing grasp.
Dost Thou reach out for them? In the sweet dawn
    Of some new world thrill they within thy clasp?

Ah! what am I, thine atom, standing here
    In presence of thy pitiless elements,
Daring to question thy great silence drear,
    No voice may break to lighten our suspense!

Thou only, infinite Patience, that endures
    Forever! Blind and dumb I cling to Thee.
Slow glides the bitter night, and silent pours
    Thine awful moonlight on the winter sea.

WHEREFORE

Black sea, black sky! A ponderous steamship driving
    Between them, laboring westward on her way,
And in her path a trap of Death's contriving
    Waiting remorseless for its easy prey.

Hundreds of souls within her frame lie dreaming,
    Hoping and fearing, longing for the light:
With human life and thought and feeling teeming,
    She struggles onward through the starless night.

Upon her furnace fires fresh fuel flinging,
    The swarthy firemen grumble at the dust
Mixed with the coal—when suddenly upspringing,
    Swift through the smoke-stack like a signal thrust,

Flares a red flame, a dread illumination!
    A cry,—a tumult! Slowly to her helm

The vessel yields, 'mid shouts of acclamation,
  And joy and terror all her crew o'erwhelm;

For looming from the blackness drear before them
  Discovered is the iceberg—hardly seen,
Its ghastly precipices hanging o'er them,
  Its reddened peaks, with dreadful chasms between,

Ere darkness swallows it again! and veering
  Out of its track the brave ship onward steers,
Just grazing ruin. Trembling still, and fearing,
  Her grateful people melt in prayers and tears.

Is it a mockery, their profound thanksgiving?
  Another ship goes shuddering to her doom
Unwarned, that very night, with hopes as living
  With freight as precious, lost amid the gloom,

With not a ray to show the apparition
  Waiting to slay her, none to cry "Beware!"
Rushing straight onward headlong to perdition,
  And for her crew no time vouchsafed for prayer.

Could they have stormed Heaven's gate with anguished
      praying,
  It would not have availed a feather's weight
Against their doom. Yet were they disobeying
  No law of God, to beckon such a fate.

And do not tell me the Almighty Master
  Would work a miracle to save the one,
And yield the other up to dire disaster,
  By merely human justice thus outdone!

Vainly we weep and wrestle with our sorrow—
  We cannot see his roads, they lie so broad:
But his eternal day knows no to-morrow,
  And life and death are all the same with God.

THE WATCH OF BOON ISLAND

They crossed the lonely and lamenting sea;
  Its moaning seemed but singing. "Wilt thou dare,"
He asked her, "brave the loneliness with me?"
  "What loneliness," she said, "if thou art there?"

Afar and cold on the horizon's rim
  Loomed the tall lighthouse, like a ghostly sign;
They sighed not as the shore behind grew dim,
  A rose of joy they bore across the brine.

They gained the barren rock, and made their home
  Among the wild waves and the sea-birds wild;
The wintry winds blew fierce across the foam,
  But in each other's eyes they looked and smiled.

Aloft the lighthouse sent its warnings wide,
  Fed by their faithful hands, and ships in sight
With joy beheld it, and on land men cried,
  "Look, clear and steady burns Boon Island light!"

And, while they trimmed the lamp with busy hands
  "Shine far and through the dark, sweet light!"
    they cried;
"Bring safely back the sailors from all lands
  To waiting love,—wife, mother, sister, bride!"

No tempest shook their calm, though many a storm
  Tore the vexed ocean into furious spray;
No chill could find them in their Eden warm,
  And gently Time lapsed onward day by day.

Said I no chill could find them? There is one
  Whose awful footfalls everywhere are known,
With echoing sobs, who chills the summer sun,
  And turns the happy heart of youth to stone;

Inexorable Death, a silent guest
    At every hearth, before whose footsteps flee
All joys, who rules the earth, and, without rest,
    Roams the vast shuddering spaces of the sea.

Death found them; turned his face and passed her by,
    But laid a finger on her lover's lips,
And there was silence. Then the storm ran high,
    And tossed and troubled sore the distant ships.

Nay, who shall speak the terrors of the night,
    The speechless sorrow, the supreme despair?
Still like a ghost she trimmed the waning light,
    Dragging her slow weight up the winding stair.

With more than oil the saving lamp she fed,
    While lashed to madness the wild sea she heard.
She kept her awful vigil with the dead,
    And God's sweet pity still she ministered.

O sailors, hailing loud the cheerful beam,
    Piercing so far the tumult of the dark,
A radiant star of hope, you could not dream
    What misery there sat cherishing that spark!

Three times the night, too terrible to bear,
    Descended, shrouded in the storm. At last
The sun rose clear and still on her despair,
    And all her striving to the winds she cast,

And bowed her head and let the light die out,
    For the wide sea lay calm as her dead love.
When evening fell, from the far land, in doubt,
    Vainly to find that faithful star men strove.

Sailors and landsmen look, and women's eyes,
    For pity ready, search in vain the night,

And wondering neighbor unto neighbor cries,
  "Now what, think you, can ail Boon Island light?"

Out from the coast toward her high tower they sailed;
  They found her watching, silent, by her dead,
A shadowy woman, who nor wept, nor wailed,
  But answered what they spake, till all was said.

They bore the dead and living both away.
  With anguish time seemed powerless to destroy
She turned, and backward gazed across the bay,—
  Lost in the sad sea lay her rose of joy.

BEETHOVEN

I

O sovereign Master! stern and splendid power,
  That calmly dost both Time and Death defy;
Lofty and lone as mountain peaks that tower,
  Leading our thoughts up to the eternal sky:
Keeper of some divine, mysterious key,
  Raising us far above all human care,
Unlocking awful gates of harmony
  To let heaven's light in on the world's despair;
Smiter of solemn chords that still command
  Echoes in souls that suffer and aspire,
In the great moment while we hold thy hand,
  Baptized with pain and rapture, tears and fire,
God lifts our saddened foreheads from the dust,
The everlasting God, in whom we trust!

II

O stateliest! who shall speak thy praise, who find
    A fitting word to utter before thee?
Thou lonely splendor, thou consummate mind,
    Who marshalest thy hosts in majesty;
Thy shadowy armies of resistless thought,
    Thy subtile forces drawn from Nature's heart,
Thy solemn breathing, mighty music, wrought
    Of life and death—a miracle thou art!
The restless tides of human life that swing
    In stormy currents, thou dost touch and sway;
Deep tones within us answer, shuddering,
    At thy resounding voice—we cast away
All our unworthiness, made strong by thee,
Thou great uplifter of humanity!

III

And was it thus the master looked, think you?
    Is this the painter's fancy? Who can tell!
These strong and noble outlines should be true:
    On the broad brow such majesty should dwell.
Yea, and these deep, indomitable eyes
    Are surely his. Lo, the imperial will
In every feature! Mighty purpose lies
    About the shut mouth, resolute and still.
Observe the head's pathetic attitude,
    Bent forward, listening,—he that might not hear!
Ah, could the world's adoring gratitude,
    So late to come, have made his life less drear!
Hearest thou, now, great soul beyond our ken,
Men's reverent voices answering thee, "Amen"?

THE WHITE ROVER

They called the little schooner the White Rover,
    When they lightly launched her on the brimming
        tide;
Stanch and trim she was to sail the broad seas over,
    And with cheers they spread her snowy canvas wide;

And a thing of beauty, forth she fared to wrestle
    With the wild, uncertain ocean, far and near,
And no evil thing befell the graceful vessel,
    And she sailed in storm and sunshine many a year.

But at last a rumor grew that she was haunted;
    That up her slender masts her sails had flown
Unhelped by human hands, as if enchanted,
    As she rocked upon her moorings all alone.

Howe'er that be, one day in winter weather,
    When the bitter north was raging at its worst,
And wind and cold vexed the roused sea together,
    Till Dante's frozen hell seemed less accurst,

Two fishermen, to draw their trawls essaying,
    Seized by the hurricane that ploughed the bay,
Were swept across the waste; and hardly weighing
    Death's chance, the Rover reefed and bore away

To save them—reached them, shuddering where they
        waited
    Their quick destruction, tossing white and dumb,
And caught them from perdition; then, belated,
    Strove to return the rough way she had come.

But there was no returning! Fierce as lightning
    The eager cold grew keener, more intense.
Across her homeward track the billows, whitening,
    In crested mountains rolling, drove her thence;

Till her brave crew, benumbed, gave up the battle,
    Clad in a mail of ice that weighed like lead;
They heard the crusted blocks and rigging rattle,
    They saw the sails like sheets of iron spread.

And powerless before the gale they drifted,
    Till swiftly dropped the black and hopeless night.
The wild tornado never lulled nor shifted,
    But drove them toward the coast upon their right,

And flung the frozen schooner, all sail standing,
    Stiff as an iceberg on the icy shore;
And half alive, her torpid people, landing,
    Crept to the lighthouse, and were safe once more.

Then what befell the vessel, standing solemn
    Through that tremendous night of cold and storm,
Upon the frost-locked land, a frigid column,
    Beneath the stars, a silent, glittering form?

None ever saw her more! The tide upbore her,
    Released her fastened keel, and ere the day,
Without a guide, and all the world before her,
    The sad, forsaken Rover sailed away.

But sometimes, when in summer twilight blending
    Sunset and moonrise mingle their rich light,
Or when on noonday mists the sun is spending
    His glory, till they glimmer thin and white,

Upon the dim horizon melting, gleaming,
    Slender, ethereal, like a lovely ghost
Soft looming, in the hazy distance dreaming,
    Or gliding like a film along the coast,

I seem to see her yet: and skippers hoary,
    Sailors and fishermen, will still relate
Among their sea-worn mates the simple story
    Of how the wandering Rover met her fate;

And shake their heads: "Perhaps the tempest wrecked
    her,
  But snug and trim and tidy, fore and aft,
I've seen the vessel since, or else her spectre,
    Sailing as never yet sailed earthly craft,

Straight in the wind's teeth; and with steady motion
    Cleaving a calm as if it blew a gale!"
And they are sure her wraith still haunts the ocean,
    Mocking the sight with semblance of a sail.

CONTRAST

The day is bitter. Through the hollow sky
    Rolls the clear sun, inexorably bright,
Glares on the shrinking earth, a lidless eye,
    Shedding no warmth, but floods of blinding light.

The hurricane roars loud. The facile sea
    With passionate resentment writhes and raves
Beneath its maddening whip, and furiously
    Responds with all the thunder of its waves.

The iron rock, ice-locked, snow-sheathed, lies still,
    The centre of this devastated world,
Beaten and lashed by wind and sea at will,
    Buried in spray by the fierce breakers hurled.

Cold, raging desolation! Out of it,
    Swift-footed, eager, noiseless as the light,
Glides my adventurous thought, and lo, I sit
    With Memnon and the desert in my sight.

Silence and breathless heat! A torrid land,
    Unbroken to the vast horizon's verge,
Save once, where from the waste of level sand
    All motionless the clustered palms emerge.

Hot the wide earth and hot the blazing sky,
    And still as death, unchanged since time began.
Far in the shimmering distance silently
    Creeps like a snake the lessening caravan.

And on the great lips of the statue old
    Broods silence, and no zephyr stirs the palm.
Nature forgets her tempests and her cold.
    And breathes in peace. "There is no joy but
        calm."

A FADED GLOVE

My little granddaughter, who fain would know
    Why, folded close in scented satin fine,
I keep a relic faded long ago,
    This pearl-gray, dainty, withered glove of mine,

Listen: I'll tell you. It is fifty years
    Since the fair day I laid my treasure here.
But yesterday to me the time appears;
    Ages ago to you, I know, my dear.

Upon this palm, now withered as my cheek,
    Love laid his first kiss, doubting and afraid:
Oh, swift and strong across me while I speak
    Comes memory of Love's might, my little maid!

I yet was so unconscious! 'Twas a night—
    Some festal night; my sisters were above,
Not ready quite; but I, cloaked all in white,
    Waited below, and, fastening my glove,

Looked up with smiling speech to him who stood
    Observing me, so still and so intent,

I wondered somewhat at his quiet mood,
    Till it flashed on me what the silence meant.

What sudden fire of dawn my sky o'erspread!
    What low melodious thunder broke my calm!
Could I be dreaming that this glorious head
    Was bending low above my girlish palm?

His majesty of mien proclaimed him king;
    His lowly gesture said, "I am your slave;"
Beneath my feet the firm earth seemed to swing,
    Unstable as storm-driven wind and wave.

Ah, beautiful and terrible and sweet
    The matchless moment! Was it life or death,
Or day or night? For my heart ceased to beat,
    And heaven and earth changed in a single breath.

And, like a harp some hand of power doth smite
    To sudden harmony, my soul awoke,
And, answering, rose to match his spirit's height
    While not a word the mystic silence broke.

'Twas but an instant. Down the echoing stair
    Swept voices, laughter, wafts of melody,—
My sisters three, in draperies light as air;
    But like a dream the whole world seemed to me,

As, steadying my whirling thoughts, I strove
    To grasp a truth so wondrous, so divine.
I shut this hand, this little tinted glove,
    To keep its secret mine, and only mine.

And like an empty show the brilliant hours
    Passed by, with beauty, music, pleasure thronged,
Phantasmagoria of light and flowers;
    But only one delight to me belonged,

One thought, one wish, one hope, one joy, one fear,
  One dizzy rapture, one star in the sky,—
The solemn sky that bent to bring God near:
  I would have been content that night to die.

Only a touch upon this little glove,
  And, lo, the lofty marvel which it wrought!
You wonder; for as yet you know not love,
  Oh, sweet my child, my lily yet unsought!

The glove is faded, but immortal joy
  Lives in the kiss; its memory cannot fade;
And when Death's clasp this pale hand shall destroy,
  The sacred glove shall in my grave be laid.

TWO SONNETS

Not so! You stand as long ago a king
  Stood on the seashore, bidding back the tide
That onward rolled resistless still, to fling
  Its awful volume landward, wild and wide.
And just as impotent is your command
  To stem the tide that rises in my soul.
It ebbs not at the lifting of your hand,
  It owns no curb, it yields to no control;
Mighty it is, and of the elements,—
  Brother of winds and lightning, cold and fire,
Subtle as light, as steadfast and intense;
  Sweet as the music of Apollo's lyre.
You think to rule the ocean's ebb and flow
With that soft woman's hand? Nay, love, not so.

And like the lighthouse on the rock you stand,
    And pierce the distance with your searching eyes;
Nor do you heed the waves that storm the land
    And endlessly about you fall and rise,
But seek the ships that wander night and day
    Within the dim horizon's shadowy ring;
And some with flashing glance you warn away,
    And some you beckon with sweet welcoming.
So steadfast still you keep your lofty place,
    Safe from the tumult of the restless tide,
Firm as the rock in your resisting grace,
    And strong through humble duty, not through
        pride.
While I—I cast my life before your feet,
And only live that I may love you, sweet!

LARS

"Tell us a story of these isles," they said,
    The daughters of the West, whose eyes had seen
For the first time the circling sea, instead
    Of the blown prairie's waves of grassy green:

"Tell us of wreck and peril, storm and cold,
    Wild as the wildest." Under summer stars,
With the slow moonrise at our back, I told
    The story of the young Norwegian, Lars.

That youth with the black eyebrows sharply drawn
    In strong curves, like some sea-bird's wings
        outspread
O'er his dark eyes, is Lars, and this fair dawn
    Of womanhood, the maiden he will wed.

She loves him for the dangers he has past.
    Her rosy beauty glowed before his stern

And vigilant regard, until at last
    Her sweetness vanquished Lars the taciturn.

For he is ever quiet, strong, and wise;
    Wastes nothing, not a gesture nor a breath;
Forgets not, gazing in the maiden's eyes,
    A year ago it was not love, but death,

That clasped him, and can hardly learn as yet
    How to be merry, haunted by that pain
And terror, and remembering with regret
    The comrade he can never see again.

Out from the harbor on that winter day
    Sailed the two men to set their trawl together.
Down swept the sudden snow-squall o'er the bay,
    And hurled their slight boat onward like a feather.

They tossed they knew not whither, till at last
    Under the lighthouse cliff they found a lee,
And out the road-lines of the trawl they cast
    To moor her, if so happy they might be.

But quick the slender road-lines snapt in twain
    In the wild breakers, and once more they tossed
Adrift; and, watching from his misty pane,
    The lighthouse keeper muttered, "They are lost!"

Lifted the snow: night fell; swift cleared the sky;
    The air grew sharp as death with polar cold;
Raged the insensate gale, and flashing high
    In starlight keen the hissing billows rolled.

Driven before the wind's incessant scourge
    All night they fled,—one dead ere morning lay.
Lars saw his strange, drawn countenance emerge
    In the fierce sunrise light of that drear day,

And thought, "A little space and I shall be
    Even as he," and, gazing in despair

O'er the wide, weltering waste, no sign could see
    Of hope, or help, or comfort, anywhere.

Two hundred miles before the hurricane
    The dead and living drove across the sea.
The third day dawned. His dim eyes saw again
    The vast green plain, breaking eternally

In ghastly waves. But in the early light,
    On the horizon glittering like a star,
Fast growing, looming tall, with canvas white,
    Sailed his salvation southward from afar!

Down she bore, rushing o'er the hills of brine,
    Straight for his feeble signal. As she past,
Out from the schooner's deck they flung a line,
    And o'er his head the open noose was cast.

Clutching with both hands the bowline knot
        Caught at his throat, swift drawn through fire he
        seemed,
Whelmed in the icy sea, and he forgot
        Life, death, and all things,—yet he thought he
        dreamed

A dread voice cried, "We've lost him!" and a sting
    Of anguish pierced his clouded senses through;
A moment more, and like a lifeless thing
    He lay among the eager, pitying crew.

Long time he swooned, while o'er the ocean vast
    The dead man tossed alone, they knew not where;
But youth and health triumphant were at last,
    And here is Lars, you see, and here the fair

Young snow-and-rose-bloom maiden he will wed.
    His face is kindly, though it seems so stern.
Death passed him by, and life begins instead,
    For Thora sweet and Lars the taciturn.

BEETHOVEN

If God speaks anywhere, in any voice,
    To us, his creatures, surely here and now
    We hear Him, while the great chords seem to bow
Our heads, and all the symphony's breathless noise
    Breaks over us with challenge to our souls!
Beethoven's music! From the mountain peaks
    The strong, divine, compelling thunder rolls,
And, "Come up higher, come!" the words it speaks,
    "Out of your darkened valleys of despair,
Behold, I lift you upon mighty wings
    Into Hope's living, reconciling air!
Breathe, and forget your life's perpetual stings;
    Dream,—folded on the breast of Patience sweet,
    Some pulse of pitying love for you may beat!"

THE SUNRISE NEVER FAILED
US YET

Upon the sadness of the sea
The sunset broods regretfully;
From the far lonely spaces, slow
Withdraws the wistful afterglow.

So out of life the splendor dies;
So darken all the happy skies;
So gathers twilight, cold and stern;
But overhead the planets burn;

And up the east another day
Shall chase the bitter dark away;

What though our eyes with tears be wet?
The sunrise never failed us yet.

The blush of dawn may yet restore
Our light and hope and joy once more.
Sad soul, take comfort, nor forget
That sunrise never failed us yet!

SONNET

As happy dwellers by the seaside hear
    In every pause the sea's mysterious sound,
    The infinite murmur, solemn and profound,
Incessant, filling all the atmosphere,
    Even so I hear you, for you do surround
My newly-waking life, and break for aye
    About the viewless shores, till they resound
With echoes of God's greatness night and day.
Refreshed and glad I feel the full flood-tide
    Fill every inlet of my waiting soul;
    Long-striving, eager hope, beyond control,
For help and strength at last is satisfied;
    And you exalt me, like the sounding sea,
    With ceaseless whispers of eternity.

MUTATION

About your window's happy height
    The roses wove their airy screen:
More radiant than the blossoms bright
    Looked your fair face between.

The glowing summer sunshine laid
    Its touch on field and flower and tree;

But 't was your golden smile that made
    The warmth that gladdened me.

The summer withered from the land,
    The vision from the window passed:
Blank Sorrow looked at me; her hand
    Sought mine and clasped it fast.

The bitter wind blows keen and drear,
    Stinging with winter's flouts and scorns,
And where the roses breathed I hear
    The rattling of the thorns.

LOVE SHALL SAVE US ALL

O Pilgrim, comes the night so fast?
    Let not the dark thy heart appall,
Though loom the shadows vague and vast,
    For Love shall save us all.

There is no hope but this to see
    Through tears that gather fast and fall;
Too great to perish Love must be,
    And Love shall save us all.

Have patience with our loss and pain,
    Our troubled space of days so small;
We shall not reach our arms in vain,
    For Love shall save us all.

O Pilgrim, but a moment wait,
    And we shall hear our darlings call
Beyond death's mute and awful gate,
    And Love shall save us all!

THE CRUISE OF THE MYSTERY

The children wandered up and down,
    Seeking for driftwood o'er the sand;
The elder tugged at granny's gown,
    And pointed with his little hand.

"Look! look!" he cried, "at yonder ship
    That sails so fast and looms so tall!"
She turned, and let her basket slip,
    And all her gathered treasure fall.

"Nay, granny, why are you so pale?
    Where *is* the ship we saw but now?"
"Oh, child, it was no mortal sail!
    It came and went, I know not how.

"But ill winds fill that canvas white
    That blow no good to you and me.
Oh, woe for us who saw the sight
    That evil bodes to all who see!"

They pressed about her, all afraid:
    "Oh, tell us, granny, what was she?"
"A ship's unhappy ghost," she said,
    "The awful ship, the Mystery."

"But tell us, tell us!" "Quiet be!"
    She said. "Sit close and listen well,
For what befell the Mystery
    It is a fearful thing to tell!"

———

She was a slave-ship long ago.
    Year after year across the sea
She made a trade of human woe,
    And carried freights of misery.

One voyage, when from the tropic coast
    Laden with dusky forms she came,—
A wretched and despairing host,—
    Beneath the fierce sun's breathless flame

Sprang, like a wild beast from its lair,
    The fury of the hurricane,
And sent the great ship reeling bare
    Across the roaring ocean plain.

Then terror seized the piteous crowd:
    With many an oath and cruel blow
The captain drove them, shrieking loud,
    Into the pitch-black hold below.

Shouting, "Make fast the hatchways tight!"
    He cursed them: "Let them live or die,
They'll trouble us no more to-night!"
    The crew obeyed him sullenly.

Has hell such torment as they knew?
    Like herded cattle packed they lay,
Till morning showed a streak of blue
    Breaking the sky's thick pall of gray.

"Off with the hatchways, men!" No sound!
    What sound should rise from out a grave?
The silence shook with dread profound
    The heart of every seaman brave.

"Quick! Drag them up," the captain said,
    "And pitch the dead into the sea!"
The sea was peopled with the dead,
    With wide eyes staring fearfully.

From weltering wave to wave they tossed,
    Two hundred corpses, stiff and stark,
At last were in the distance lost,
    A banquet for the wandering shark.

Oh, sweetly the relenting day
   Changed, till the storm had left no trace,
And the whole awful ocean lay
  As tranquil as an infant's face.

Abaft the wind hauled fair and fine,
   Lightly the ship sped on her way;
Her sharp bows crushed the yielding brine
   Into a diamond dust of spray.

But up and down the decks her crew
   Shook their rough heads, and eyed askance,
With doubt and hate that ever grew,
   The captain's brutal countenance,

As slow he paced with frown as black
   As night. At last, with sudden shout,
He turned. " 'Bout ship! We will go back
   And fetch another cargo out!"

They put the ship about again;
   His will was law, they could not choose.
They strove to change her course in vain:
   Down fell the wind, the sails hung loose,

And from the far horizon dim
   An oily calm crept silently
Over the sea from rim to rim;
   Still as if anchored fast lay she.

The sun set red, the moon shone white,
   On idle canvas drooping drear;
Through the vast, solemn hush of night
   What is it that the sailors hear?

Now do they sleep—and do they dream?
   Was that the wind's foreboding moan?

From stem to stern her every beam
    Quivered with one unearthly groan!

Leaped to his feet then every man,
    And shuddered, clinging to his mate;
And sunburned cheeks grew pale and wan,
    Blanched with that thrill of terror great.

The captain waked, and angrily
    Sprang to the deck, and cursing spoke.
"What devil's trick is this?" cried he.
    No answer the scared silence broke.

But quietly the moonlight clear
    Sent o'er the waves its pallid glow:
What stirred the water far and near,
    With stealthy motion swimming slow?

With measured strokes those swimmers dread
    From every side came gathering fast;
The sea was peopled with the dead
    That to its cruel deeps were cast!

And coiling, curling, crawling on,
    The phantom troop pressed nigh and nigher,
And every dusky body shone
    Outlined in phosphorescent fire.

They gained the ship, they climbed the shrouds,
    They swarmed from keel to topmast high;
Now here, now there, like filmy clouds
    Without a sound they flickered by.

And where the captain stood aghast,
    With hollow, mocking eyes they came,
And bound him fast unto the mast
    With ghostly ropes that bit like flame.

Like maniacs shrieked the startled crew!
    They loosed the boats, they leaped within;
Before their oars the water flew;
    They pulled as if some race to win.

With spectral light all gleaming bright
    The Mystery in the distance lay;
Away from that accursed sight
    They fled until the break of day.

And they were rescued, but the ship,
    The awful ship, the Mystery,
Her captain in the dead men's grip,—
    Never to any port came she;

But up and down the roaring seas
    For ever and for aye she sails,
In calm or storm, against the breeze,
    Unshaken by the wildest gales.

And wheresoe'er her form appears
    Come trouble and disaster sore,
And she has sailed a hundred years,
    And she will sail for evermore.

GOOD-BY, SWEET DAY

FOR MUSIC

Good-by, sweet day, good-by!
I have so loved thee, but I cannot hold thee.
Departing like a dream, the shadows fold thee;
Slowly thy perfect beauty fades away:
Good-by, sweet day!

Good-by, sweet day, good-by!
Dear were thy golden hours of tranquil splendor,
Sadly thou yieldest to the evening tender
Who wert so fair from thy first morning ray;
Good-by, sweet day!

Good-bye, sweet day, good-by!
Thy glow and charm, thy smiles and tones and glances,
Vanish at last, and solemn night advances;
Ah, couldst thou yet a little longer stay!
Good-by, sweet day!

Good-by, sweet day, good-by!
All thy rich gifts my grateful heart remembers,
The while I watch thy sunset's smouldering embers
Die in the west beneath the twilight gray.
Good-by, sweet day!

IMPATIENCE

E. L.

Only to follow you, dearest, only to find you!
    Only to feel for one instant the touch of our hand;
Only to tell you once of the love you left behind
        you,—
    To say the world without you is like a desert of
        sand;

That the flowers have lost their perfume, the rose its
        splendor,
    And the charm of nature is lost in a dull eclipse;
That joy went out with the glance of your eyes so
        tender,
    And beauty passed with the lovely smile on your
        lips.

I did not dream it was you who kindled the morning
    And folded the evening purple in peace so sweet;
But you took the whole world's rapture without a
        warning.
    And left me naught save the print of your patient
        feet.

I count the days and the hours that hold us asunder:
    I long for Death's friendly hand which shall rend in
        twain,
With the glorious lightning flash and the golden
        thunder,
    These clouds of the earth, and give me my own
        again!

Love, dost thou wait for me in some rich land
　　Where the gold orange hangs in odorous calm?
Where the clear waters kiss the flowery strand,
　　Bordered with shining sand and groves of palm?

And while this bitter morning breaks for me,
　　Draws to its close thy warm, delicious day;
Lights, colors, perfumes, music, joy, for thee,
　　For me the cold, wild sea, the cloudy gray!

Rises the red moon in thy tranquil sky,
　　Plashes the fountain with its silver talk,
And as the evening wind begins to sigh,
　　Thy sweet girl's shape steals down the garden walk.

And through the scented dusk a white robe gleams,
　　Lingering beneath the starry jasmine sprays,
Till where thy clustered roses breathe in dreams,
　　A sudden gush of song thy light step stays.

That was the nightingale! O Love of mine,
　　Hear'st thou my voice in that pathetic song,
Throbbing in passionate cadences divine,
　　Sinking to silence with its rapture strong?

I stretch my arms to thee through all the cold,
　　Through all the dark, across the weary space
Between us, and thy slender form I fold,
　　And gaze into the wonder of thy face.

Pure brow the moonbeam touches, tender eyes
　　Splendid with feeling, delicate smiling mouth,
And heavy silken hair that darkly lies
　　Soft as the twilight clouds in thy sweet South,—

O beautiful my Love! In vain I seek
　　To hold the heavenly dream that fades from me.
I needs must wake with salt spray on my cheek,
　　Flung from the fury of this northern sea.

OH TELL ME NOT OF
HEAVENLY HALLS

Oh tell me not of heavenly halls,
    Of streets of pearl and gates of gold,
Where angel unto angel calls
    'Mid splendors of the sky untold;

My homesick heart would backward turn
    To find this dear, familiar earth,
To watch its sacred hearth-fires burn,
    To catch its songs of joy or mirth.

I'd lean from out the heavenly choir
    To hear once more the red cock crow,
What time the morning's rosy fire
    O'er hill and field began to glow.

To hear the ripple of the rain,
    The summer waves at ocean's brim,
To hear the sparrow sing again
    I'd quit the wide-eyed cherubim!

I care not what heaven's glories are;
    Content am I. More joy it brings
To watch the dandelion's star
    Than mystic Saturn's golden rings.

And yet—and yet, O dearest one!
    My comfort from life's earliest breath—
To follow thee where thou art gone
    Through those dim, awful gates of Death,

To find thee, feel thy smile again,
    To have eternity's long day
To tell my grateful love,—why, then,
    Both heaven and earth might pass away!

QUESTIONS

The steadfast planet spins through space,
   And into darkness, into light
Swiftly it wheels its living face:
   " 'T is day," we say, or "It is night."

And we who cling and with it turn,
   Till spent is our brief span of years,
Watching our sister stars that burn
   Through the dim trouble of our tears,

We question of the silence vast,
   Of souls that people distant spheres;
What of their future and their past?
   Have they our sorrows, joys, and fears?

Do the same flowers make glad their sight?
   The same birds sing? On their great seas
Do ships like ours, with canvas white,
   Move stately, answering to the breeze?

Have they their Christ, their Christmas Day?
   Know they Mahomet? Buddha? One,
Or all or none? And do they pray?
   And have they wrought as we have done?

We cannot guess; 't is hard indeed,
   Our own orb's tale of its dim past
Through centuries untold to read,
   And who its future shall forecast?

We only know it keeps its place,
   An atom in the universe,
As through the awful realms of space
   The mighty hosts of stars disperse.

We know the hand that holds in check
   The whirling worlds, each in its course,
And saves the universe from wreck
   And peril, this tremendous Force

Holds likewise all our little lives;
   The suns and stars do all obey
His bidding, never planet strives
   To swerve from its appointed way.

The dangerous boon alone to us
   Is given, to choose 'twixt ill and well,
Rebellion or obedience,—thus
   To build our heaven, or dig our hell.

But one great thought our strength upholds:
   Nothing shall perish! Though his rod
Smites sore, his mercy still enfolds
   His own; God's souls are safe with God.

THE HEAVENLY GUEST

The winter night shuts swiftly down. Within his little
   humble room
Martin, the good old shoemaker, sits musing in the
   gathering gloom.
His tiny lamp from off its hook he takes, and lights its
   friendly beam,
Reaches for his beloved book and reads it by the
   flickering gleam.

Long pores he o'er the sacred page. At last he lifts his
   shaggy head.
"If unto me the Master came, how should I welcome
   Him?" he said;
"Should I be like the Pharisee, with selfish thoughts
   filled to the brim,
Or like the sorrowing sinner,—she who weeping
   ministered to Him?"

He laid his head upon his arms, and while he thought,
    upon him crept
Slumber so gentle and so soft he did not realize he slept
"Martin!" he heard a low voice call. He started, looked
    toward the door:
No one was there. He dozed again. "Martin!" he heard
    it call once more.

"Martin, to-morrow I will come. Look out upon the
    street for me."
He rose, and slowly rubbed his eyes, and gazed about
    him drowsily.
"I dreamed," he said, and went to rest. Waking
    betimes with morning light,
He wondered, "Were they but a dream, the words I
    seemed to hear last night?"

Then, working by his window low, he watched the
    passers to and fro.
Poor Stephen, feeble, bent and old, was shoveling away
    the snow;
Martin at last laughed at himself for watching all so
    eagerly.
"What fool am I! What look I for? Think I the
    Master's face to see?

"I must be going daft, indeed!" He turned him to his
    work once more,
And stitched awhile, but presently found he was
    watching as before.
Old Stephen leaned against the wall; weary and out of
    breath was he.
"Come in, friend," Martin cried, "come, rest, and warm
    yourself, and have some tea."

"May Christ reward you!" Stephen said, rejoicing in
    the welcome heat;
"I was so tired!" "Sit," Martin begged, "be comforted
    and drink and eat."

But even while his grateful guest refreshed his chilled
    and toil-worn frame
Did Martin's eyes still strive to scan each passing form
    that went and came.

"Are you expecting somebody?" old Stephen asked.
    And Martin told,
Though half ashamed, his last night's dream. "Truly, I
    am not quite so bold
As to expect a thing like that," he said, "yet, somehow,
    still I look!"
With that from off its shelf he took his worn and
    precious Holy Book.

"Yesterday I was reading here, how among simple folk
    He walked
Of old, and taught them. Do you know about it? No?"
    So then he talked.
With joy to Stephen. " 'Jesus said, 'The kind, the
    generous, the poor,
Blessed are they, the humble souls, to be exalted
    evermore.' "

With tears of gladness in his eyes poor Stephen rose
    and went his way.
His soul and body comforted; and quietly passed on
    the day,
Till Martin from his window saw a woman shivering in
    the cold,
Trying to shield her little babe with her thin garment
    worn and old.

He called her in and fed her, too, and while she ate he
    did his best
To make the tiny baby smile, that she might have a
    little rest;
"Now may Christ bless you, sir!" she cried, when
    warmed and cheered she would have gone;
He took his old cloak from the wall. " 'Twill keep the
    cold out. Put it on."

She wept. "Christ led you to look out and pity
wretched me," said she.
Martin replied, "Indeed He did!" and told his story
earnestly,
How the low voice said, "I will come," and he had
watched the livelong day.
"All things are possible," she said, and then she, also,
went her way.

Once more he sat him down to work, and on the
passers-by to look.
Till the night fell, and then again he lit his lamp and
took his book.
Another happy hour was spent, when all at once he
seemed to hear
A rustling sound behind his chair; he listened, without
thought of fear.

He peered about. Did something move in yonder corner
dim and dark?
Was that a voice that spoke his name? "Did you not
know me, Martin?" "Hark!
Who spoke?" cried Martin. "It is I," replied the Voice,
and Stephen stepped
Forth from the dusk and smiled at him, and Martin's
heart within him leapt!

Then like a cloud was Stephen gone, and once again
did Martin hear
That heavenly Voice. "And this is I," sounded in tones
divinely clear.
From out the darkness softly came the woman with
the little child,
Gazing at him with gentle eyes, and, as she vanished,
sweetly smiled.

Then Martin thrilled with solemn joy. Upon the sacred
page read he:
"Hungry was I, ye gave me meat; thirsty, and ye gave
drink to me;

A stranger I, ye took me in, and as unto the lowliest
    one
Of these my brethren, even the least, ye did it, unto
    Me 'twas done.''

And Martin understood at last it was no vision born of
    sleep,
And all his soul in prayer and praise filled with a
    rapture still and deep.
He had not been deceived, it was no fancy of the
    twilight dim,
But glorious truth! The Master came, and he had
    ministered to Him.

SONG

Lift up thy light, O Soul, arise and shine!
    Steadfast though all the storms of life assail,
Immortal spark of the great Light Divine!
    Against whose power no tempest shall prevail—

Hold high thy light above earth's restless tides,
    Scatter thy messages of light afar!
Falsehood and folly pass, but truth abides,
    Be thine the splendor of her deathless star—

When the world sins and sorrows round thee rave
    Pierce thou the darkness with thy dauntless ray,
Send out thy happy beams to help and save
    "More and more shining to the perfect day."

SONNET

If God speaks anywhere in any voice
To us, his children, surely here and now
We hear him, while the great chords seem to bow
Our heads, and all the symphony's breathless noise
Breaks over us with challenge to our souls!
Beethoven's music! From the mountain peaks
The strong, divine, compelling thunder rolls,
And "Come up higher, come!" the music speaks,
"Out of your darkest valleys of despair
Behold I lift you up on mighty wings
Into Hope's living, reconciling air—
Breathe and forget your life's perpetual stings,
Dream,—folded on the breast of patience sweet,
Some glimpse of pitying love for you may beat!"

ON THE BEACH

The slow, cool, emerald breakers cruising clear
Along the sparkling edge of level sand,
Shatters its crystal arch, and far and near
Its broken splendor spills upon the land.
With rush and whisper, siren sweet and soft
Gently salutes the children of the earth,
And catches every sunbeam from aloft,
Flashes it back in summer mood of mirth:
And with its flood of strong refreshment pours
Health and delight along the sounding shores.

Amid its frolic foam and scattered spray
Tossed lightly, like some dreaming lion's mane,
The tired dwellers of the city play.
Forgetful for a while of care and pain,

While peace broods over all, nor does it seem
As if the sleeping lion could awake;
And yet, when past is this sweet summer dream,
What roar of thunder on the coast will break
When winter's tempests rage in sullen wrath,
Death and disaster in their cruel path,
And hurl against the sandy margin gray
Devouring fury, tumult and dismay!

LOST

Low burns the sunset and the dark is near:
   O where is home! O where is my mother's face!
The long night is before me, full of fear;
   Of the familiar path there is no trace.
The evening wind blows damp upon my cheek,
   The stars begin to twinkle high and clear.
In vain for sign of hope or help I seek,
   For all is strange and lone and sad and drear.

No human sound comes to my anxious ear,
   No cattle low, no dog barks far away,
Only the ripple of the frogs I hear,
   And the thrush singing to the dying day.
Under my feet the sweet fern sprays I crush
   With tangled vines and dead leaves brown and sere,
Faint spicy odors rise—a dewy hush
   Steals o'er the dusky landscape far and near.

Will never more the lights of home appear?
   The blessed lights of home! Where shall I turn,
East, west, north, south to find a ray of cheer?
   Where, in the darkness, do those tapers burn?
Weary, despairing, sorrowful I stray.
   How must your heart be aching, mother dear!
O friends who surely seek me, come this way!
   O that my cry might reach you! I am *here!*

THE DREAM PEDLER

Lo, I come from dreamland dim,
Down the drowsy air I swim,
Ringing soft a pleasant tune,
Through the sharp horns of the moon;
All that fancy fine can paint
Of fair or sweet or wild or quaint,
Through your brain I'll set adrift,
When my slender wand I lift.

Hark, what fairy breezes flow!
Tinkles ices and flutters snow,
Mingled with the summer dreams
Of lilies white on placid streams;
You shall woo a mermaid fair,
You shall fright the imp of care,
'Twixt a dove's wings you shall ride,
Down a cloud-bank you shall slide!

You shall fill a wind-rocked nest,
In a witch's palace rest,
You shall gather flowers afield,
You shall wear a turtle's shield,
By a butterfly be snared,
By a tiny kobold scared;
You shall soar in a balloon,
You shall dance in magic shoon;
    Which will suit you? Pause and choose
    Ere my visions I unloose.

ON QUIET WATERS

O lightly moored the lilies lie.
And look up to the golden sky.
Softly they breathe into the air
Their holy fragrance everywhere:
Delicate, dewy-fresh and sweet.
It steals our charmed sense to greet.
In each pure chalice, dazzling white,
Sits throned a spirit of delight
Our grateful souls with joy to fill,
A pleasure sacred, deep and still,
O lightly moored the lilies lie
Afloat beneath the flowing sky!

From shadow cool to sunshine clear
Safe past the changing shores we steer,
And watch the swallow dip his wing,
And hear the hidden thrushes sing
Each to his mate within the wood,
Safe in their happy solitude.
O perfect morn! O peaceful time!
O life that blossoms at its prime!
We dream in Eden, thou and I
Afloat beneath the golden sky.

THE BURGOMASTER GULL

The old-wives sit on the heaving brine,
    White-breasted in the sun,
Preening and smoothing their feathers fine,
    And scolding, every one.

The snowy kittiwakes overhead,
    With beautiful beaks of gold,

And wings of delicate gray outspread,
　　Float, listening while they scold.

And a foolish guillemot, swimming by,
　　Though heavy and clumsy and dull,
Joins in with a will when he hears their cry
　　'Gainst the Burgomaster Gull.

For every sea-bird, far and near,
　　With an atom of brains in its skull,
Knows plenty of reasons for hate and fear
　　Of the Burgomaster Gull.

The black ducks gather, with plumes so rich,
　　And the coots in twinkling lines;
And the swift and slender water-witch,
　　Whose neck like silver shines;

Big eider-ducks, with their caps pale green
　　And their salmon-colored vests;
And gay mergansers sailing between,
　　With their long and glittering crests.

But the loon aloof on the outer edge
　　Of the noisy meeting keeps,
And laughs to watch them behind the ledge
　　Where the lazy breaker sweeps.

They scream and wheel, and dive and fret,
　　And flutter in the foam;
And fish and mussels blue they get
　　To feed their young at home:

Till hurrying in, the little auk
　　Brings tidings that benumbs,
And stops at once their clamorous talk,—
　　"The Burgomaster comes!"

And up he sails, a splendid sight!
　　With "wings like banners" wide,

And eager eyes both big and bright,
   That peer on every side.

A lovely kittiwake flying past
   With a slippery pollock fine,—
Quoth the Burgomaster, "Not so fast,
   My beauty! This is mine!"

His strong wing strikes with a dizzying shock;
   Poor kittiwake, shrieking, flees;
His booty he takes to the nearest rock,
   To eat it at his ease.

The scared birds scatter to left and right,
   But the bold buccaneer, in his glee,
Cares little enough for their woe and their fright,—
   " 'T will be *your* turn next!" cries he.

He sees not, hidden behind the rock,
   In the sea-weed, a small boat's hull,
Nor dreams he the gunners have spared the flock
   For the Burgomaster Gull.

So proudly his dusky wings are spread,
   And he launches out on the breeze,—
When lo! what thunder of wrath and dread!
   What deadly pangs are these!

The red blood drips and the feathers fly,
   Down drop the pinions wide;
The robber-chief, with a bitter cry,
   Falls headlong in the tide!

They bear him off with laugh and shout;
   The wary birds return,—
From the clove-brown feathers that float about
   The glorious news they learn.

Then such a tumult fills the place
    As never was sung or said;
And all cry, wild with joy, "The base,
    Bad Burgomaster's dead!"

And the old-wives sit with their caps so white,
    And their pretty beaks so red,
And swing on the billows, and scream with delight,
    For the Burgomaster's dead!

THE BUTCHER-BIRD

I'll tell you a story, children,
    The saddest you ever heard,
About Rupert, the pet canary,
    And a terrible butcher-bird.

There was such a blinding snow-storm
    One could not see at all.
And all day long the children
    Had watched the white flakes fall;

And when the eldest brothers
    Had kissed mamma good-night,
And up the stairs together
    Had gone with their bedroom light,

Of a sudden their two fresh voices
    Rang out in a quick surprise,
Mamma! papa! come quickly
    And catch him before he flies!"

On a picture-frame perched lightly,
    With his head beneath his wing,

They had found a gray bird sitting;
   That was a curious thing!

Down stairs to the cosy parlor
   They brought him, glad to find
For the storm-tossed wanderer shelter;
   Not knowing his cruel mind!

And full of joy were the children
   To think he was safe and warm,
And had chosen their house for safety
   To hide from the raging storm!

"He shall stay with the pretty Rupert,
   And live among mother's flowers,
And he'll sing with our robin and sparrow;"
   And they talked about it for hours.

Alas, in the early morning
   There rose a wail and a cry,
And a fluttering wild in the cages,
   And Rupert's voice rang high.

We rushed to the rescue swiftly;
   Too late! On the shining cage,
The home of the happy Rupert,
   All rough with fury and rage,

Stood the handsome, horrible stranger,
   With black and flashing eye,
And torn almost to pieces
   Did poor dead Rupert lie!

Oh, sad was all the household,
   And we mourned for Rupert long.
The fierce wild shrike was prisoned
   In a cage both dark and strong;

And would you like, O children,
His final fate to know?
To Agassiz's Museum
That pirate bird did go!

JACK FROST

Rustily creak the crickets: Jack Frost came down
    last night,
He slid to the earth on a starbeam, keen and sparkling
    and bright;
He sought in the grass for the crickets with delicate icy
    spear,
So sharp and fine and fatal, and he stabbed them far
    and near.
Only a few stout fellows, thawed by the morning sun,
Chirrup a mournful echo of by-gone frolic and fun.
But yesterday such a rippling chorus ran all over the
    land,
Over the hills and the valleys, down to the gray sea-
    sand.
Millions of merry harlequins, skipping and dancing in
    glee,
Cricket and locust and grasshopper, happy as happy
    could be:
Scooping rich caves in ripe apples, and feeding on
    honey and spice,
Drunk with the mellow sunshine, nor dreaming of
    spears of ice!
Was it not enough that the crickets your weapon of
    power should pierce?
Pray what have you done to the flowers? Jack Frost,
    you are cruel and fierce.
With never a sign or a whisper, you kissed them and lo,
    they exhale

Their beautiful lives; they are drooping, their
    sweet colors ebbs, they are pale,
They fade and they die! See the pansies, yet striving
    so hard to unfold
Their garments of velvety splendor, all Tyrian purple
    and gold.
But how weary they look, and how withered, like
    handsome court dames, who all night
Have danced at the ball till the sunrise struck chill to
    their hearts with its light.
Where hides the wood-aster? She vanished as snow
    wreaths dissolve in the sun
The moment you touched her. Look yonder, where
    sober and gray as a nun,
The maple-tree stands that at sunset was blushing and
    red as the sky;
At its foot, glowing scarlet as fire, its robes of
    magnificence lie.
Despoiler! stripping the world as you strip the
    shivering tree
Of color and sound and perfume, scaring the bird and
    the bee,
Turning beauty to ashes—oh to join the swift swallows
    and fly
Far away out of sight of your mischief! I give you no
    welcome, not I!

THE KINGFISHER

Could you have heard the kingfisher scream and
    scold at me
When I went this morning early down to the smiling
    sea!
He clamored so loud and harshly, I laughed at him for
    his pains,
And off he flew with a shattered note, like the sound
    of falling chains

He perched on the rock above me, and kept up such a
   din,
He looked so fine with his collar snow-white beneath
   his chin,
And his cap of velvet, black and bright, and his jacket
   of lovely blue,
I looked, admired, and called to him, "Good morning!
   How do you do?"
But his kingship was *so* offended! He hadn't a
   pleasant word,
Only the crossest jargon ever screamed by a bird.
The gray sandpiper on one leg stood still in sheer
   surprise,
And gazed at me, and gazed at him, with shining
   bead-black eyes,

And pensively sent up so sweet and delicate a note,
Ringing so high and clear from out her dainty,
   mottled throat,
That echo round the silent shore caught up the clear
   refrain,
And sent the charming music back again, and yet
   again.

Then the brown song-sparrow on the wall made haste
   with such a song,
To try and drown that jarring din! but it was all too
   strong.
And the swallows, like a steel-blue flash, swept past
   and cried aloud,
"Be civil, my dear kingfisher, you're far too grand and
   proud."

But it wasn't of any use at all, he was too much
   displeased,
For only by my absence could his anger be appeased.
So I wandered off, and as I went I saw him flutter
   down,
And take his place once more upon the seaweed wet
   and brown.

And there he watched for his breakfast, all
    undisturbed at last,
And many a little fish he caught as it was swimming
    past.
And I forgot his harsh abuse, for, up in the tall
    elm-tree,
A purple finch sat high and sang a heavenly song
    for me.

INHOSPITALITY

Down on the north wind sweeping
    Comes the storm with roaring din;
Sadly, with dreary tumult,
    The twilight gathers in.

The snow-covered little island
    Is white as a frosted cake;
And round and round it the billows
    Bellow, and thunder, and break.

Within doors the blazing drift-wood
    Is glowing, ruddy and warm,
And happiness sits at the fire-side,
    Watching the raging storm.

What fluttered past the window,
    All weary and wet and weak,
With the heavily drooping pinions,
    And the wicked, crooked beak?

Cries the little sister, watching,
    "Whither now can he flee?
Black through the whirling snow-flakes
    Glooms the awful face of the sea,

"And tossed and torn by the tempest,
    He must sink in the bitter brine!
Why could n't we pity and save him
    Till the sun again should shine?"

They drew her back to the fireside,
    And laughed at her cloudy eyes,—
"What, mourn for that robber-fellow,
    The cruelest bird that flies!

"Your song-sparrow hardly would thank you,
    And which is the dearest, pray?"
But she heard at the doors and windows
    The lashing of the spray;

And as ever the shock of the breakers
    The heart of their quiet stirred,
She thought, "Oh would we had sheltered him,
    The poor, unhappy bird!"

Where the boats before the house-door
    Are drawn up from the tide,
On the tallest prow he settles,
    And furls his wings so wide.

Uprises the elder brother,
    Uprises the sister too;
"Nay, brother, he comes for shelter!
    Spare him! What would you do?"

He laughs and is gone for his rifle,
    And steadily takes his aim;
But the wild wind seizes his yellow beard,
    And blows it about like flame.

Into his eyes the snow sifts,
    Till he cannot see aright:
Ah, the cruel gun is baffled!
    And the weary hawk takes flight;

And slowly up he circles,
  Higher and higher still;
The fierce wind catches and bears him away
  O'er the bleak crest of the hill.

A Memorable Murder

A MEMORABLE MURDER

At the Isles of Shoals, on the 5th of March in the year 1873, occurred one of the most monstrous tragedies ever enacted on this planet. The sickening details of the double murder are well known; the newspapers teemed with them for months: but the pathos of the story is not realized; the world does not know how gentle a life these poor people led, how innocently happy were their quiet days. They were all Norwegians. The more I see of the natives of this far-off land, the more I admire the fine qualities which seem to characterize them as a race. Gentle, faithful, intelligent, God-fearing human beings, they daily use such courtesy toward each other and all who come in contact with them, as puts our ruder Yankee manners to shame. The men and women living on this lonely island were like the sweet, honest, simple folk we read of in Björnson's charming Norwegian stories, full of kindly thoughts and ways. The murdered Anethe might have been the Eli of Björnson's beautiful Arne or the Ragnhild of Boyesen's lovely romance. They rejoiced to find a home just such as they desired in this peaceful place; the women took such pleasure in the little house which they kept so neat and bright, in their flock of hens, their little dog Ringe, and all their humble belongings! The Norwegians are an exceptionally affectionate people; family ties are very strong and precious among them. Let me tell the story of their sorrow as simply as may be.

Louis Wagner murdered Anethe and Karen Christensen at midnight on the 5th of March, two years ago this spring. The whole affair shows the calmness of a practiced hand; *there was no malice in the deed*, no heat; it was one of the coolest instances of deliberation ever chronicled in the annals of crime. He admits that these people had shown him nothing but kindness. He says in so many words, "They were my best friends." They looked upon him as a brother. Yet he did not hesitate to murder them. The island called Smutty-Nose by human perversity (since in old times it bore the pleasanter title of Haley's Island) was selected to be the scene of this disaster. Long ago I lived two years upon it, and know well its whitened ledges and grassy slopes, its low thickets of wild-rose and bayberry, its sea-wall still intact, connecting it with the small island Malaga, opposite Appledore, and the ruined break-water which links it with Cedar Island on the other side. A lonely cairn, erected by some long ago forgotten fishermen or sailors, stands upon the highest rock at the southeastern extremity; at its western end a few houses are scattered, small, rude dwellings, with the square old Haley house near; two or three fish-houses are falling into decay about the water-side, and the ancient wharf drops stone by stone into the little cove, where every day the tide ebbs and flows and ebbs again with pleasant sound and freshness. Near the houses is a small grave-yard, where a few of the natives sleep, and not far, the graves of the fourteen Spaniards lost in the wreck of the ship Sagunto in the year 1813. I used to think it was a pleasant place, that low, rocky, and grassy island, though so wild and lonely.

From the little town of Laurvig, near Christiania, in Norway, came John and Maren Hontvet to this country, and five years ago took up their abode in this desolate spot, in one of the cottages facing the cove and Appledore. And there they lived through the long winters and the lovely summers, John making a comfortable living by fishing, Maren, his wife, keeping as bright and tidy and sweet a little home for him as man could desire. The bit of garden they cultivated in the summer was a pleasure to them; they made their house as pretty as they could with paint and paper and gay pictures, and Maren had a shelf for her plants at the window; and John was always so good to her, so kind and thoughtful of her comfort and of what would please her, she was entirely happy. Sometimes she was a little lonely, perhaps, when he was tossing afar off on the sea, setting or hauling his trawls, or had sailed to Portsmouth to sell his fish. So that she was doubly glad when the news came that some of her people were coming over from Norway to live with her. And first, in the month of May, 1871, came her sister Karen, who stayed only a short time with Maren, and then came to Appledore, where she lived at service two years, till within a fortnight of her death. The first time I saw Maren, she brought her sister to us, and I was charmed with the little woman's beautiful behavior; she was so gentle, courteous, decorous, she left on my mind a most delightful impression. Her face struck me as remarkably good and intelligent, and her gray eyes were full of light.

Karen was a rather sad-looking woman, about twenty-nine years old; she had lost a lover in Norway long since, and in her heart she fretted and mourned for this continually: she could not speak a word of English at first, but went patiently about her work and soon learned enough, and proved herself an excellent servant, doing faithfully and thoroughly everything she undertook, as is the way of her people generally. Her personal neatness was most attractive. She wore gowns made of cloth woven by herself in Norway, a coarse blue stuff, always neat and clean, and often I used to watch her as she sat by the fire spinning at a spinning-wheel brought from her own country; she made such a pretty picture, with her blue gown and fresh white apron, and the nice, clear white muslin bow with which she was in the habit of fastening her linen collar, that she was very agreeable to look upon. She had a pensive way of letting her head droop a little sideways as she spun, and while the low wheel hummed monotonously, she would sit crooning sweet, sad old Norwegian airs by the hour together, perfectly unconscious that she was affording such pleasure to a pair of appreciative eyes. On the 12th of October, 1872, in the second year of her stay with us, her brother, Ivan Christensen, and his wife, Anethe Mathea, came over from their Norseland in an evil day, and joined Maren and John at their island, living in the same house with them.

Ivan and Anethe had been married only since Christmas of the preceding year. Ivan was tall, light-haired, rather quiet and grave. Anethe was young, fair, and merry, with thick, bright sunny hair, which was so long it reached, when unbraided, nearly to her knees; blue-eyed, with brilliant teeth and clear, fresh complexion, beautiful, and beloved beyond expression by her young husband, Ivan. Mathew Hontvet, John's brother, had also joined the little circle a year before, and now Maren's happiness was complete. Delighted to welcome them all, she made all things pleasant for them, and she told me only a few days ago, "I never was so happy in my life as when we were all living there together." So they abode in peace and quiet, with not an evil thought in their minds, kind and considerate toward each other, the men devoted to their women and the women repaying them with interest, till out of the perfectly cloudless sky one day a blot descended, without a whisper of warning, and brought ruin and desolation into that peaceful home.

Louis Wagner, who had been in this country seven years, appeared at the Shoals two years before the date of the murder. He lived about the islands during that time. He was born in Ueckermünde, a small town of lower Pomeranie, in Northern Prussia. Very little is known about him, though there were vague rumors that his past life had not been without difficulties, and he had boasted foolishly among his mates that "not many had done what he had done and got off in safety;" but people did not trouble themselves about him or his past, all having enough to do to earn their bread and keep the wolf from the door. Maren describes him as tall, powerful, dark, with a peculiarly quiet manner. She says she never saw him drunk—he seemed always anxious to keep his wits about him: he would linger on the outskirts of a drunken brawl, listening to and absorbing everything, but never mixing himself up in any disturbance. He was always lurking in corners, lingering, looking, listening, and he would look no man straight in the eyes. She spoke, however, of having once heard him disputing with

some sailors, at table, about some point of navigation;
she did not understand it, but all were against Louis,
and, waxing warm, all strove to show him he was in the
wrong. As he rose and left the table she heard him mut-
ter to himself with an oath, "I know I'm wrong, but I'll
never give in!" During the winter preceding the one in
which his hideous deed was committed, he lived at Star
Island and fished alone, in a wherry; but he made very
little money, and came often over to the Hontvets, where
Maren gave him food when he was suffering from want,
and where he received always a welcome and the utmost
kindness. In the following June he joined Hontvet in his
business of fishing, and took up his abode as one of the
family at Smutty-Nose. During the summer he was
"crippled," as he said, by the rheumatism, and they were
all very good to him, and sheltered, fed, nursed, and
waited upon him the greater part of the season. He re-
mained with them five weeks after Ivan and Anethe ar-
rived, so that he grew to know Anethe as well as Maren,
and was looked upon as a brother by all of them, as I
have said before. Nothing occurred to show his true
character, and in November he left the island and the
kind people whose hospitality he was to repay so fearful-
ly, and going to Portsmouth he took passage in another
fishing schooner, the Addison Gilbert, which was
presently wrecked off the coast, and he was again
thrown out of employment. Very recklessly he said to
Waldemar Ingebertsen, to Charles Jonsen, and even to
John Hontvet himself, at different times, that "he must
have money if he murdered for it." He loafed about
Portsmouth eight weeks, doing nothing. Meanwhile
Karen left our service in February, intending to go to
Boston and work at a sewing machine, for she was not
strong and thought she should like it better than
housework, but before going she lingered awhile with her
sister Maren—fatal delay for her! Maren told me that
during this time Karen went to Portsmouth and had her
teeth removed, meaning to provide herself with a new
set. At the Jonsens', where Louis was staying, one day

she spoke to Mrs. Jonsen of her mouth, that it was so sensitive since the teeth had been taken out; and Mrs. Jonsen asked her how long she must wait before the new set could be put in. Karen replied that it would be three months. Louis Wagner was walking up and down at the other end of the room with his arms folded, his favorite attitude. Mrs. Jonsen's daughter passed near him and heard him mutter, "Three months! What is the use! In three months you will be dead!" He did not know the girl was so near, and turning, he confronted her. He knew she must have heard what he said, and he glared at her like a wild man.

On the fifth day of March, 1873, John Hontvet, his brother Mathew, and Ivan Christensen set sail in John's little schooner, the Clara Bella, to draw their trawls. At that time four of the islands were inhabited: one family on White Island, at the light-house; the workmen who were building the new hotel on Star Island, and one or two households beside; the Hontvet family at Smutty-Nose; and on Appledore, the household at the large house, and on the southern side, opposite Smutty-Nose, a little cottage, where lived Jörge Edvardt Ingebertsen, his wife and children, and several men who fished with him. Smutty-Nose is not in sight of the large house at Appledore, so we were in ignorance of all that happened on that dreadful night, longer than the other inhabitants of the Shoals.

John, Ivan, and Mathew went to draw their trawls, which had been set some miles to the eastward of the islands. They intended to be back to dinner, and then to go on to Portsmouth with their fish, and bait the trawls afresh, ready to bring back to set again next day. But the wind was strong and fair for Portsmouth and ahead for the island; it would have been a long beat home against it; so they went on to Portsmouth, without touching at the island to leave one man to guard the women, as had been their custom. This was the first night in all the years Maren had lived there that the house was without a man to protect it. But John, always thoughtful for her, asked Emil Ingebertsen, whom he met on the fishing-grounds, to go over from Appledore and tell her that they had gone on to Portsmouth with the favoring wind, but that they hoped to be back that night. And he would have been back had the bait he expected from Boston arrived on the train in which it was due. How curiously everything adjusted itself to favor the bringing about of this horrible catastrophe! The bait did not arrive till the half past twelve train, and they were obliged to work the whole night getting their trawls ready, thus leaving the way perfectly clear for Louis Wagner's awful work.

The three women left alone watched and waited in vain for the schooner to return, and kept the dinner hot for the men, and patiently wondered why they did not come. In vain they searched the wide horizon for that returning sail. Ah me, what pathos is in that longing look of women's eyes for far-off sails! that gaze so eager, so steadfast, that it would almost seem as if it must conjure up the ghostly shape of glimmering canvas from the mysterious distances of sea and sky, and draw it unerringly home by the mere force of intense wistfulness! And those gentle eyes, that were never to see the light of another sun, looked anxiously across the heaving sea till twilight fell, and then John's messenger, Emil, arrived—Emil Ingebertsen, courteous and gentle as a youthful knight—and reassured them with his explanation, which having given, he departed, leaving them in a much more cheerful state of mind. So the three sisters, with only the little dog Ringe for a protector, sat by the fire chatting together cheerfully. They fully expected the schooner back again that night from Portsmouth, but they were not ill at ease while they waited. Of what should they be afraid? They had not an enemy in the world! No shadow crept to the fireside to warn them what was at hand, no portent of death chilled the air as they talked their pleasant talk and made their little plans in utter unconsciousness. Karen was to have gone to Portsmouth with the fishermen that day; she was all ready dressed to go. Various little commissions were given her, errands to do for the two sisters she was to leave behind. Maren wanted some buttons, and "I'll give you one for a pattern; I'll put it in your purse," she said to Karen, "and then when you open your purse you'll be sure to remember it." (That little button, of a peculiar pattern, was found in Wagner's possession afterward.) They sat up till ten o'clock, talking together. The night was bright and calm; it was a comfort to miss the bitter winds that had raved about the little dwelling all the long, rough winter. Already it was spring; this calm was the first token of its coming. It was the 5th of March; in a few weeks the weather would soften, the grass grow green, and Anethe would see the first flowers in this strange country, so far from her home where she had left father and mother, kith and kin, for love of Ivan. The delicious days of summer at hand would transform the work of the toiling fishermen to pleasure, and all things would bloom and smile about the poor people on the lonely rock! Alas, it was not to be.

At ten o'clock they went to bed. It was cold and "lonesome" up-stairs, so Maren put some chairs by the side of the lounge, laid a mattress upon it, and made up a bed for Karen in the kitchen, where she presently fell asleep. Maren and Anethe slept in the next room. So safe they felt themselves, they did not pull down a curtain, nor even try to fasten the house-door. They went to their rest in absolute security and perfect trust. It was the first still night of the new year; a young moon stole softly down toward the west, a gentle wind breathed through the quiet dark, and the waves whispered gently about the island, helping to lull those innocent souls to yet more peaceful slumber. Ah, where were the gales of March that night have plowed that tranquil sea to foam, and cut off the fatal path of Louis Wagner to that happy home! But nature seemed to pause and wait for him. I remember looking abroad over the waves that night and rejoicing over "the first calm night of the year!" It was so still, so bright! The hope of all the light and beauty a

few weeks would bring forth stirred me to sudden joy.
There should be spring again after the long winter-
weariness.

"Can trouble live in April days,
Or sadness in the summer moons?"

I thought, as I watched the clear sky, grown less hard
than it had been for weeks, and sparkling with stars. But
before another sunset it seemed to me that beauty had
fled out of the world, and that goodness, innocence,
mercy, gentleness, were a mere mockery of empty words.

Here let us leave the poor women, asleep on the
lonely rock, with no help near them in heaven or upon
earth, and follow the fishermen to Portsmouth, where
they arrived about four o'clock that afternoon. One of
the first men whom they saw as they neared the town
was Louis Wagner; to him they threw the rope from the
schooner, and he helped draw her in to the wharf.
Greetings passed between them; he spoke to Mathew
Hontvet, and as he looked at Ivan Christensen, the men
noticed a flush pass over Louis's face. He asked were
they going out again that night? Three times before they
parted he asked that question; he saw that all the three
men belonging to the island had come away together; he
began to realize his opportunity. They answered him
that if their bait came by the train in which they ex-
pected it, they hoped to get back that night, but if it was
late they should be obliged to stay till morning, baiting
their trawls; and they asked him to come and help them.
It is a long and tedious business, the baiting of trawls;
often more than a thousand hooks are to be manipulated,
and lines and hooks coiled, clear of tangles, into tubs, all
ready for throwing overboard when the fishing-grounds
are reached. Louis gave them a half promise that he
would help them, but they did not see him again after
leaving the wharf. The three fishermen were hungry, not
having touched at their island, where Maren always pro-
vided them with a supply of food to take with them; they
asked each other if either had brought any money with

which to buy bread, and it came out that every one had left his pocketbook at home. Louis, standing by, heard all this. He asked John, then, if he had made fishing pay. John answered that he had cleared about six hundred dollars.

The men parted, the honest three about their business; but Louis, what became of him with his evil thoughts? At about half past seven he went into a liquor shop and had a glass of something; not enough to make him unsteady,—he was too wise for that. He was not seen again in Portsmouth by any human creature that night. He must have gone, after that, directly down to the river, that beautiful, broad river, the Piscataqua, upon whose southern bank the quaint old city of Portsmouth dreams its quiet days away; and there he found a boat ready to his hand, a dory belonging to a man by the name of David Burke, who had that day furnished it with new thole-pins. When it was picked up afterward off the mouth of the river, Louis's anxious oars had eaten half-way through the substance of these pins, which are always made of the hardest, toughest wood that can be found. A terrible piece of rowing must that have been, in one night! Twelve miles from the city to the Shoals,— three to the light-houses, where the river meets the open sea, nine more to the islands; nine back again to Newcastle next morning! He took that boat, and with the favoring tide dropped down the rapid river where the swift current is so strong that oars are scarcely needed, except to keep the boat steady. Truly all nature seemed to play into his hands; this first relenting night of earliest spring favored him with its stillness, the tide was fair, the wind was fair, the little moon gave him just enough light, without betraying him to any curious eyes, as he glided down the three miles between the river banks, in haste to reach the sea. Doubtless the light west wind played about him as delicately as if he had been the most human of God's creatures; nothing breathed remonstrance in his ear, nothing whispered in the whispering water that rippled about his inexorable keel, steering straight for

the Shoals through the quiet darkness. The snow lay
thick and white upon the land in the moonlight; lamps
twinkled here and there from dwellings on either side; in
Eliot and Newcastle, in Portsmouth and Kittery, roofs,
chimneys, and gables showed faintly in the vague light;
the leafless trees clustered dark in hollows or lifted their
tracery of bare boughs in higher spaces against the
wintry sky. His eyes must have looked on it all, whether
he saw the peaceful picture or not. Beneath many a hum-
ble roof honest folk were settling into their untroubled
rest, as "this planned piece of deliberate wickedness"
was stealing silently by with his heart full of darkness,
blacker than the black tide that swirled beneath his boat
and bore him fiercely on. At the river's mouth stood the
sentinel light-houses, sending their great spokes of light
afar into the night, like the arms of a wide humanity
stretching into the darkness helping hands to bring all
who needed succor safely home. He passed them, first
the tower at Fort Point, then the taller one at Whale's
Back, steadfastly holding aloft their warning fires.
There was no signal from the warning bell as he rowed
by, though a danger more subtle, more deadly, than fog,
or hurricane, or pelting storm was passing swift beneath
it. Unchallenged by anything in earth or heaven, he kept
on his way and gained the great outer ocean, doubtless
pulling strong and steadily, for he had no time to lose,
and the longest night was all too short for an under-
taking such as this. Nine miles from the light-houses to
the islands! Slowly he makes his way; it seems to take an
eternity of time. And now he is midway between the
islands and the coast. That little toy of a boat with its
one occupant in the midst of the awful, black, heaving
sea! The vast dim ocean whispers with a thousand
waves; against the boat's side the ripples lightly tap, and
pass and are lost; the air is full of fine, mysterious voices
of winds and waters. Has he no fear, alone there on the
midnight sea with such a purpose in his heart? The
moonlight sends a long, golden track across the waves; it
touches his dark face and figure, it glitters on his drip-

ping oars. On his right hand Boone Island light shows like a setting star on the horizon, low on his left the two beacons twinkle off Newburyport, at the mouth of the Merrimack River; all the light-houses stand watching along the coast, wheeling their long, slender shafts of radiance as if pointing at this black atom creeping over the face of the planet with such colossal evil in his heart. Before him glitters the Shoals' light at White Island, and helps to guide him to his prey. Alas, my friendly light-house, that you should serve so terrible a purpose! Steadily the oars click in the rowlocks; stroke after stroke of the broad blades draws him away from the lessening line of land, over the wavering floor of the ocean, nearer the lonely rocks. Slowly the coast-lights fade, and now the rote of the sea among the lonely ledges of the Shoals salutes his attentive ear. A little longer and he nears Appledore, the first island, and now he passes by the snow-covered, ice-bound rock, with the long buildings showing clear in the moonlight. He must have looked at them as he went past. I wonder we who slept beneath the roofs that glimmered to his eyes in the uncertain light did not feel, through the thick veil of sleep, what fearful thing passed by! But we slumbered peacefully as the unhappy women whose doom every click of those oars in the rowlocks, like the ticking of some dreadful clock, was bringing nearer and nearer. Between the islands he passes; they are full of chilly gleams and glooms. There is no scene more weird than these snow-covered rocks in winter, more shudderful and strange: the moonlight touching them with mystic glimmer, the black water breaking about them and the vast shadowy spaces of the sea stretching to the horizon on every side, full of vague sounds, of half lights and shadows, of fear, and of mystery. The island he seeks lies before him, lone and still; there is no gleam in any window, there is no help near, nothing upon which the women can call for succor. He does not land in the cove where all boats put in, he rows round to the south side and draws his boat up on the rocks. His red returning footsteps are found here next day, staining the snow. He makes his way to the house he knows so well.

All is silent: nothing moves, nothing sounds but the hushed voices of the sea. His hand is on the latch, he enters stealthily, there is nothing to resist him. The little dog, Ringe, begins to bark sharp and loud, and Karen rouses, crying, "John, is that you?" thinking the expected fishermen had returned. Louis seizes a chair and strikes at her in the dark; the clock on a shelf above her head falls down with the jarring of the blow, and stops at exactly seven minutes to one. Maren in the next room, waked suddenly from her sound sleep, trying in vain to make out the meaning of it all, cries, "What's the matter?" Karen answers, "John scared me!" Maren springs from her bed and tries to open her chamber door; Louis has fastened it on the other side by pushing a stick through the latch. With her heart leaping with terror the poor child shakes the door with all her might, in vain. Utterly confounded and bewildered, she hears Karen screaming, "John kills me! John kills me!" She hears the sound of repeated blows and shrieks, till at last her sister falls heavily against the door, which gives way, and Maren rushes out. She catches dimly a glimpse of a tall figure outlined against the southern window; she seizes poor Karen and drags her with the strength of frenzy within the bedroom. This unknown terror, this fierce, dumb monster who never utters a sound to betray himself through the whole, pursues her with blows, strikes her three times with a chair, either blow with fury sufficient to kill her, had it been light enough for him to see how to direct it; but she gets her sister inside and the door shut, and holds it against him with all her might and Karen's failing strength. What a little heroine was this poor child, struggling with the force of desperation to save herself and her sisters!

All this time Anethe lay dumb, not daring to move or breathe, roused from the deep sleep of youth and health by this nameless, formless terror. Maren, while she strives to hold the door at which Louis rattles again and again, calls to her in anguish, "Anethe, Anethe! Get out of the window! run! hide!" The poor girl, almost paralyzed with fear, tries to obey, puts her bare feet out of the low window, and stands outside in the freezing snow, with one light garment over her cowering figure, shrinking in the cold winter wind, the clear moonlight touching her white face and bright hair and fair young shoulders. "Scream! scream!" shouts frantic Maren. "Somebody at Star Island may hear!" but Anethe answers with the calmness of despair, "I cannot make a sound," Maren screams, herself, but the feeble sound avails nothing. "Run! run!" she cries to Anethe; but again Anethe answers, "I cannot move."

Louis has left off trying to force the door; he listens. Are the women trying to escape? He goes out-of-doors. Maren flies to the window; he comes round the corner of the house and confronts Anethe where she stands in the snow. The moonlight shines full in his face; she shrieks loudly and distinctly, "Louis, Louis!" Ah, he is discovered, he is recognized! Quick as thought he goes back to the front door, at the side of which stands an ax, left there by Maren, who had used it the day before to cut the ice from the well. He returns to Anethe standing shuddering there. It is no matter that she is beautiful, young, and helpless to resist, that she has been kind to him, that she never did a human creature harm, that she stretches her gentle hands out to him in agonized entreaty, crying piteously, "Oh, Louis, Louis, Louis!" He raises the ax and brings it down on her bright head in one tremendous blow, and she sinks without a sound and lies in a heap, with her warm blood reddening the snow. Then he deals her blow after blow, almost within reach of Maren's hands, as she stands at the window. Distracted, Maren strives to rouse poor Karen, who kneels with her head on the side of the bed; with desperate entreaty she tries to get her up and away, but Karen moans, "I cannot, I cannot." She is too far gone; and then Maren knows she cannot save her, and that she must flee herself or die. So, while Louis again enters the house, she

seizes a skirt and wraps round her shoulders, and makes
her way out of the open window, over Anethe's murdered
body, barefooted, flying away, anywhere, breathless,
shaking with terror.

Where can she go? Her little dog, frightened into
silence, follows her,—pressing so close to her feet that
she falls over him more than once. Looking back she sees
Louis has lit a lamp and is seeking for her. She flies to
the cove; if she can but find his boat and row away in it
and get help! It is not there; there is no boat in which she
can get away. She hears Karen's wild screams,—he is
killing her! Oh where can she go? Is there any place on
that little island where he will not find her? She thinks
she will creep into one of the empty old houses by the
water; but no, she reflects, if I hide there, Ringe will bark
and betray me the moment Louis comes to look for me.
And Ringe saved her life, for next day Louis's bloody
tracks were found all about those old buildings where he
had sought her. She flies, with Karen's awful cries in her
ears, away over rocks and snow to the farthest limit she
can gain. The moon has set; it is about two o'clock in the
morning, and oh, so cold! She shivers and shudders from
head to feet, but her agony of terror is so great she is
hardly conscious of bodily sensation. And welcome is the
freezing snow, the jagged ice and iron rocks that tear her
unprotected feet, the bitter brine that beats against the
shore, the winter winds that make her shrink and trem-
ble; "they are not so unkind as man's ingratitude!" Fall-
ing often, rising, struggling on with feverish haste, she
makes her way to the very edge of the water; down
almost into the sea she creeps, between two rocks, upon
her hands and knees, and crouches, face downward, with
Ringe nestled close beneath her breast, not daring to
move through the long hours that must pass before the
sun will rise again. She is so near the ocean she can
almost reach the water with her hand. Had the wind
breathed the least roughly the waves must have washed
over her. There let us leave her and go back to Louis
Wagner. Maren heard her sister Karen's shrieks as she

fled. The poor girl had crept into an unoccupied room in a distant part of the house, striving to hide herself. He could not kill her with blows, blundering in the darkness, so he wound a handkerchief about her throat and strangled her. But now he seeks anxiously for Maren. *Has* she escaped? What terror is in the thought! Escaped, to tell the tale, to accuse him as the murderer of her sisters. Hurriedly, with desperate anxiety, he seeks for her. His time was growing short; it was not in his programme that this brave little creature should give him so much trouble; he had not calculated on resistance from these weak and helpless women. Already it was morning, soon it would be daylight. He could not find her in or near the house; he went down to the empty and dilapidated houses about the cove, and sought her everywhere. What a picture! That blood-stained butcher, with his dark face, crawling about those cellars, peering for that woman! He dared not spend any more time; he must go back for the money he hoped to find, his reward for this! All about the house he searches, in bureau drawers, in trunks and boxes: he finds fifteen dollars for his night's work! Several hundreds were lying between some sheets folded at the bottom of a drawer in which he looked. But he cannot stop for more thorough investigation; a dreadful haste pursues him like a thousand fiends. He drags Anethe's stiffening body into the house, and leaves it on the kitchen floor. If the thought crosses his mind to set fire to the house and burn up his two victims, he dares not do it: it will make a fatal bonfire to light his homeward way; besides, it is useless, for Maren has escaped to accuse him, and the time presses so horribly! But how cool a monster is he! After all this hard work he must have refreshment to support him in the long row back to the land; knife and fork, cup and plate, were found next morning on the table near where Anethe lay; fragments of food which was not cooked in the house, but brought from Portsmouth, were scattered about. Tidy Maren had left neither dishes nor food when they went to bed. The handle of the tea-pot which she had left on the stove was stained and smeared with blood. Can the human mind conceive of such hideous *nonchalance?* Wagner sat down in that room and ate and drank! It is almost beyond belief! Then he went to the well with a basin and towels, tried to wash off the blood, and left towels and basin in the well. He knows he must be gone! It is certain death to linger. He takes his boat and rows away toward the dark coast and the twinkling lights; it is for dear life, now! What powerful strokes send the small skiff rushing over the water!

There is no longer any moon, the night is far spent; already the east changes, the stars fade; he rows like a madman to reach the land, but a blush of morning is stealing up the sky and sunrise is rosy over shore and sea, when panting, trembling, weary, a creature accursed, a blot on the face of the day, he lands at Newcastle—too late! Too late! In vain he casts the dory adrift; she will not float away; the flood tide bears her back to give her testimony against him, and afterward she is found at Jaffrey's Point, near the "Devil's Den," and the fact of her worn thole-pins noted. Wet, covered with ice from the spray which has flown from his eager oars, utterly exhausted, he creeps to a knoll and reconnoitres; he thinks he is unobserved, and crawls on towards Portsmouth. But he is seen and recognized by many persons, and his identity established beyond a doubt. He goes to the house of Mathew Jonsen, where he has been living, steals up-stairs, changes his clothes, and appears before the family, anxious, frightened, agitated, telling Jonsen he never felt so badly in his life; that he has got into trouble and is afraid he shall be taken. He cannot eat at breakfast, says "farewell forever," goes away and is shaved, and takes the train to Boston, where he provides himself with new clothes, shoes, a complete outfit, but lingering, held by fate, he cannot fly, and before night the officer's hand is on his shoulder and he is arrested.

Meanwhile poor shuddering Maren on the lonely island, by the water-side, waits till the sun is high in heaven before she dares come forth. She thinks he may be still on the island. She said to me, "I thought he must be there, dead or alive. I thought he might go crazy and kill himself after having done all that." At last she steals out. The little dog frisks before her; it is so cold her feet cling to the rocks and snow at every step, till the skin is fairly torn off. Still and frosty is the bright morning, the water lies smiling and sparkling, the hammers of the workmen building the new hotel on Star Island sound through the quiet air. Being on the side of Smutty-Nose opposite Star, she waves her skirt, and screams to attract their attention; they hear her, turn and look, see a woman waving a signal of distress, and, surprising to relate, turn tranquilly to their work again. She realizes at last there is no hope in that direction; she must go round toward Appledore in sight of the dreadful house. Passing it afar off she gives one swift glance toward it, terrified lest in the broad sunshine she may see some horrid token of last night's work; but all is still and peaceful. She notices the curtains the three had left up when they went to bed; they are now drawn down; she knows whose hand has done this, and what it hides from the light of day. Sick at heart, she makes her painful way to the northern edge of Malaga, which is connected with Smutty-Nose by the old sea-wall. She is directly opposite Appledore and the little cottage where abide her friend and countryman, Jorge Edvardt Ingebertsen, and his wife and children. Only a quarter of a mile of the still ocean separates her from safety and comfort. She sees the children playing about the door; she calls and calls. Will no one ever hear her? Her torn feet torment her, she is sore with blows and perishing with cold. At last her voice reaches the ears of the children, who run and tell their father that some one is crying and calling; looking across, he sees the poor little figure waving her arms, takes his dory and paddles over, and with amazement recognizes Maren in her night-dress, with bare feet and streaming hair, with a cruel bruise upon her face, with wild eyes, distracted, half senseless with cold and terror.

He cries, "Maren, Maren, who has done this? what is it?
who is it?" and her only answer is "Louis, Louis, Louis!"
as he takes her on board his boat and rows home with her
as fast as he can. From her incoherent statement he
learns what has happened. Leaving her in the care of his
family, he comes over across the hill to the great house
on Appledore. As I sit at my desk I see him pass the win-
dow, and wonder why the old man comes so fast and anx-
iously through the heavy snow.

Presently I see him going back again, accompanied
by several of his own countrymen and others of our
workmen, carrying guns. They are going to Smutty-
Nose, and take arms, thinking it possible Wagner may
yet be there. I call down-stairs, "What has happened?"
and am answered, "Some trouble at Smutty-Nose; we
hardly understand." "Probably a drunken brawl of the
reckless fishermen who may have landed there," I say to
myself, and go on with my work. In another half-hour I
see the men returning, reinforced by others, coming fast,
confusedly; and suddenly a wail of anguish comes up
from the women below. I cannot believe it when I hear
them crying, "Karen is dead! Anethe is dead! Louis
Wagner has murdered them both!" I run out into the
servants' quarters; there are all the men assembled, an
awe-stricken crowd. Old Ingebertsen comes forward and
tells me the bare facts and how Maren lies at his house,
half crazy, suffering with her torn and frozen feet. Then
the men are dispatched to search Appledore, to find if by
any chance the murderer might be concealed about the
place, and I go over to Maren to see if I can do anything
for her. I find the women and children with frightened
faces at the little cottage; as I go into the room where
Maren lies, she catches my hands, crying, "Oh, I so glad
to see you! I so glad I save my life!" and with her dry
lips she tells me all the story as I have told it here. Poor
little creature, holding me with those wild, glittering,
dilated eyes, she cannot tell me rapidly enough the whole
horrible tale. Upon her cheek is yet the blood-stain from
the blow he struck her with a chair, and she shows me

two more upon her shoulder, and her torn feet. I go back for arnica with which to bathe them. What a mockery seems to me the "jocund day" as I emerge into the sunshine, and looking across the space of blue, sparkling water, see the house wherein all that horror lies!

Oh brightly shines the morning sun and glitters on the white sails of the little vessel that comes dancing back from Portsmouth before the favoring wind, with the two husbands on board! How glad they are for the sweet morning and the fair wind that brings them home again! And Ivan sees in fancy Anethe's face all beautiful with welcoming smiles, and John knows how happy his good and faithful Maren will be to see him back again. Alas, how little they dream what lies before them! From Appledore they are signaled to come ashore, and Ivan and Mathew, landing, hear a confused rumor of trouble from tongues that hardly can frame the words that must tell the dreadful truth. Ivan only understands that something is wrong. His one thought is for Anethe; he flies to Ingebertsen's cottage, she may be there; he rushes in like a maniac, crying, "Anethe, Anethe! Where is Anethe?" and broken-hearted Maren answers her brother, "Anethe is—at home." He does not wait for another word, but seizes the little boat and lands at the same time with John on Smutty-Nose; with headlong haste they reach the house, other men accompanying them; ah, there are blood-stains all about the snow! Ivan is the first to burst open the door and enter. What words can tell it! There upon the floor, naked, stiff, and stark, is the woman he idolizes, for whose dear feet he could not make life's ways smooth and pleasant enough—stone dead! Dead—horribly butchered! her bright hair stiff with blood, the fair head that had so often rested on his breast crushed! cloven, mangled with the brutal ax! Their eyes are blasted by the intolerable sight: both John and Ivan stagger out and fall, senseless, in the snow. Poor Ivan! his wife a thousand times adored, the dear girl he had brought from Norway, the good, sweet girl who loved him so, whom he could not cherish tender-

ly enough! And he was not there to protect her! There
was no one there to save her!

"Did Heaven look on
And would not take their part!"

Poor fellow, what had he done that fate should deal him
such a blow as this! Dumb, blind with anguish, he made
no sign.

"What says the body when they spring
Some monstrous torture-engine's whole
Strength on it? No more says the soul."

Some of his pitying comrades lead him away, like one
stupefied, and take him back to Appledore. John knows
his wife is safe. Though stricken with horror and con-
sumed with wrath, he is not paralyzed like poor Ivan,
who has been smitten with worse than death. They find
Karen's body in another part of the house, covered with
blows and black in the face, strangled. They find Louis's
tracks,—all the tokens of his disastrous presence,—the
contents of trunks and drawers scattered about in his
hasty search for the money, and, all within the house and
without, blood, blood everywhere.

When I reach the cottage with the arnica for Maren,
they have returned from Smutty-Nose. John, her hus-
band, is there. He is a young man of the true Norse type,
blue-eyed, fair-haired, tall and well-made, with handsome
teeth and bronzed beard. Perhaps he is a little quiet and
undemonstrative generally, but at this moment he is
superb, kindled from head to feet, a fire-brand of woe and
wrath, with eyes that flash and cheeks that burn. I speak
a few words to him,—what words can meet such an occa-
sion as this!—and having given directions about the use
of the arnica, for Maren, I go away, for nothing more can
be done for her, and every comfort she needs is hers. The
outer room is full of men; they make way for me, and as I
pass through I catch a glimpse of Ivan crouched with his
arms thrown round his knees and his head bowed down
between them, motionless, his attitude expressing such

abandonment of despair as cannot be described. His whole person seems to shrink, as if deprecating the blow that has fallen upon him.

All day the slaughtered women lie as they were found, for nothing can be touched till the officers of the law have seen the whole. And John goes back to Portsmouth to tell his tale to the proper authorities. What a different voyage from the one he had just taken, when happy and careless he was returning to the home he had left so full of peace and comfort! What a load he bears back with him, as he makes his tedious way across the miles that separate him from the means of vengeance he burns to reach! But at last he arrives, tells his story, the police at other cities are at once telegraphed, and the city marshal follows Wagner to Boston. At eight o'clock that evening comes the steamer Mayflower to the Shoals, with all the officers on board. They land and make investigations at Smutty-Nose, then come here to Appledore and examine Maren, and, when everything is done, steam back to Portsmouth, which they reach at three o'clock in the morning. After all are gone and his awful day's work is finished at last, poor John comes back to Maren, and kneeling by the side of her bed, he is utterly overpowered with what he has passed through; he is shaken with sobs as he cries, "Oh, Maren, Maren, it is too much, too much! I cannot bear it!" And Maren throws her arms about his neck, crying, "Oh, John, John, don't! I shall be crazy, I shall die, if you go on like that." Poor innocent, unhappy people, who never wronged a fellow-creature in their lives!

But Ivan—what is their anguish to his! They dare not leave him alone lest he do himself an injury. He is perfectly mute and listless; he cannot weep, he can neither eat nor sleep. He sits like one in a horrid dream. "Oh, my poor, poor brother!" Maren cries in tones of deepest grief, when I speak his name to her next day. She herself cannot rest a moment till she hears that Louis is taken; at every sound her crazed imagination fancies he is coming back for her; she is fairly beside

herself with terror and anxiety; but the night following
that of the catastrophe brings us news that he is
arrested, and there is stern rejoicing at the Shoals; but
no vengeance taken on him can bring back those un-
offending lives, or restore that gentle home. The dead are
properly cared for; the blood is washed from Anethe's
beautiful bright hair; she is clothed in her wedding-dress,
the blue dress in which she was married, poor child, that
happy Christmas time in Norway, a little more than a
year ago. They are carried across the sea to Portsmouth,
the burial service is read over them, and they are hidden
in the earth. After poor Ivan has seen the faces of his
wife and sister still and pale in their coffins, their ghastly
wounds concealed as much as possible, flowers upon
them and the priest praying over them, his trance of
misery is broken, the grasp of despair is loosened a little
about his heart. Yet hardly does he notice whether the
sun shines or no, or care whether he lives or dies. Slowly
his senses steady themselves from the effects of a shock
that nearly destroyed him, and merciful time, with im-
perceptible touch, softens day by day the outlines of
that picture at the memory of which he will never cease
to shudder while he lives.

Louis Wagner was captured in Boston on the eve-
ning of the next day after his atrocious deed, and Friday
morning, followed by a hooting mob, he was taken to the
Eastern depot. At every station along the route crowds
were assembled, and there were fierce cries for ven-
geance. At the depot in Portsmouth a dense crowd of
thousands of both sexes had gathered, who assailed him
with yells and curses and cries of "Tear him to pieces!"
It was with difficulty he was at last safely imprisoned.
Poor Maren was taken to Portsmouth from Appledore
on that day. The story of Wagner's day in Boston, like
every other detail of the affair, has been told by every
newspaper in the country: his agitation and restlessness,
noted by all who saw him; his curious, reckless talk. To
one he says, "I have just killed two sailors;" to another,
Jacob Toldtman, into whose shop he goes to buy shoes,

"I have seen a woman lie as still as that boot," and so on. When he is caught he puts on a bold face and determines to brave it out; denies everything with tears and virtuous indignation. The men whom he has so fearfully wronged are confronted with him; his attitude is one of injured innocence; he surveys them more in sorrow than in anger, while John is on fire with wrath and indignation, and hurls maledictions at him; but Ivan, poor Ivan, hurt beyond all hope or help, is utterly mute; he does not utter one word. Of what use is it to curse the murderer of his wife? It will not bring her back; he has no heart for cursing, he is too completely broken. Maren told me the first time she was brought into Louis's presence, her heart leaped so fast she could hardly breathe. She entered the room softly with her husband and Mathew Jonsen's daughter. Louis was whittling a stick. He looked up and saw her face, and the color ebbed out of his, and rushed back and stood in one burning spot in his cheek, as he looked at her and she looked at him for a space, in silence. Then he drew about his evil mind the detestable garment of sanctimoniousness, and in sentimental accents he murmured, "I'm glad Jesus loves me!" "The devil loves you!" cried John, with uncompromising veracity. "I know it wasn't nice," said decorous Maren, "but John couldn't help it; it was too much to bear!"

The next Saturday afternoon, when he was to be taken to Saco, hundreds of fishermen came to Portsmouth from all parts of the coast, determined on his destruction, and there was a fearful scene in the quiet streets of that peaceful city when he was being escorted to the train by the police and various officers of justice. Two thousand people had assembled, and such a furious, yelling crowd was never seen or heard in Portsmouth. The air was rent with cries for vengeance; showers of bricks and stones were thrown from all directions, and wounded several of the officers who surrounded Wagner. His knees trembled under him, he shook like an aspen, and the officers found it necessary to drag him along, telling him he must keep up if he would save his life. Except that they feared to injure the innocent as well as the guilty, those men would have literally torn him to pieces. But at last he was put on board the cars in safety, and carried away to prison. His demeanor throughout the term of his confinement, and during his trial and subsequent imprisonment, was a wonderful piece of acting. He really inspired people with doubt as to his guilt. I make an extract from The Portsmouth Chronicle, dated March 13, 1873: "Wagner still retains his amazing *sang froid*, which is wonderful, even in a strong-nerved German. The sympathy of most of the visitors at his jail has certainly been won by his calmness and his general appearance, which is quite prepossessing." This little instance of his method of proceeding I must subjoin: A lady who had come to converse with him on the subject of his eternal salvation said, as she left him, "I hope you put your trust in the Lord," to which he sweetly answered, "I always did, ma'am, and I always shall."

A few weeks after all this had happened, I sat by the window one afternoon, and, looking up from my work, I saw some one passing slowly,—a young man who seemed so thin, so pale, so bent and ill, that I said, "Here is some stranger who is so very sick, he is probably come to try the effect of the air, even thus early." It was Ivan Christensen. I did not recognize him. He dragged one foot after the other wearily, and walked with the feeble motion of an old man. He entered the house; his errand was to ask for work. He could not bear to go away from the neighborhood of the place were Anethe had lived and where they had been so happy, and he could not bear to work at fishing on the south side of the island, within sight of that house. There was work enough for him here; a kind voice told him so, a kind hand was laid on his shoulder, and he was bidden come and welcome. The tears rushed into the poor fellow's eyes, he went hastily away, and that night sent over his chest of tools,—he was a carpenter by trade. Next day he took up his abode here and worked all summer. Every day I carefully observed him as I passed him by, regarding him with an inexpressible pity, of which he was perfectly unconscious, as he seemed to be of everything and everybody. He never raised his head when he answered my "Good morning," or "Good evening, Ivan." Though I often wished to speak, I never said more to him, for he seemed to me to be hurt too sorely to be touched by human hand. With his head sunk on his breast, and wearily dragging his limbs, he pushed the plane or drove the saw to and fro with a kind of dogged persistence, looking neither to the left nor right. Well might the weight of woe he carried bow him to the earth! By and by he spoke, himself, to other members of the household, saying, with a patient sorrow, he believed it was to have been, it had been so ordered, else why did all things so play into Louis's hands? All things were furnished him: the knowledge of the unprotected state of the women, a perfectly clear field in which to carry out his plans, just the right boat he wanted in which to make his voyage, fair tide, fair wind, calm sea, just moonlight enough; even the ax with which to kill Anethe stood ready to his hand at the house door. Alas, it was to have been! Last summer Ivan went back again to Norway—alone. Hardly is it probable that he will ever return to a land whose welcome to him fate made so horrible. His sister Maren and her husband still live blameless lives, with the little dog Ringe, in a new home they have made for themselves in Portsmouth, not far from the river-side; the merciful lapse of days and years takes them gently but surely away from the thought of that season of anguish; and though they can never forget it all, they have grown resigned and quiet again. And on the island other Norwegians have settled, voices of charming children sound sweetly in the solitude that echoed so awfully to the shrieks of Karen and Maren. But to the weirdness of the winter midnight something is added, a vision of two dim, reproachful shades who watch while an agonized ghost prowls eternally about the dilapidated houses at the beach's edge, close by the black, whispering water,

seeking for the woman who has escaped him—escaped to
bring upon him the death he deserves, whom he never,
never, never can find, though his distracted spirit may
search till man shall vanish from off the face of the earth,
and time shall be no more.

Celia Thaxter

Chapter Notes

Introduction

1. Robert E. Spiller. *The Cycle of American Literature: An Essay in Historical Criticism.* (New York: The Free Press, 1955) p. 124.
2. Sandra M. Gilbert and Susan Gubar. *The Madwoman in the Attic: The Woman Writer and the Nineteenth-Century Literary Imagination.* (New Haven: Yale University Press, 1979).
3. Anna Mary Wells. *Dear Preceptor: The Life and Times of Thomas Wentworth Higginson.* (Boston, Houghton Mifflin Co., 1963) p. 116.
4. Nathaniel Hawthorne. *The American Notebooks.* (Columbus: Ohio State University Press, 1974) vol. 8, p. 537.
5. Margaret Fuller. *Women in the Nineteenth Century.* (Originally published in Boston, Roberts Brother, 1874; Reprinted in Westport, Conn. by Greenwood Press, 1968) p. 38.
6. Hawthorne, *op. cit.*, p. 516.
7. See letter from Levi Lincoln Thaxter to Thomas Wentworth Higginson, April 20, 1842, Houghton Library, Harvard University, Cambridge, Mass.
8. Margaret Fuller, *op. cit.*, p. 40.
9. Margaret Fuller, *op. cit.*, p. 38.
10. Celia Thaxter. *Among the Isles of Shoals.* (Boston: The Houghton Mifflin Co., 1873) p. 143.
11. Margaret Fuller, *op. cit.*, p. 39.
12. Mary Thacher Higginson. *Letters and Journals of Thomas Wentworth Higginson, 1846–1906.* (New York: Da Capo Press, 1956) p. 25.
13. Margaret Fuller, *op. cit.*, p. 39.
14. Margaret Fuller, *op. cit.*, p. 120.
15. Rosamond Thaxter. *Sandpiper: The Life and Letters of Celia Thaxter.* (Francestown, NH: The Golden Quill Press, 1963) p. 131.
16. Virginia Woolf. *A Room of One's Own.* (New York: Harcourt, Brace & World, 1929) p. 51.
17. Margaret Fuller, *op. cit.*, p. 127.

18. Margaret Fuller, *op. cit.*, p. 109.
19. Annie Fields and Rose Lamb. *Letters of Celia Thaxter.* (Boston: Houghton and Mifflin and Co., 1895) p. 71.
20. Margaret Fuller, *op. cit.*, p. 159.
21. Margaret Fuller, *op. cit.*, p. 43.
22. *Ibid.*, p. 104.
23. Paula Blanchard. *Margaret Fuller: From Transcendentalism to Revolution.* (New York: Delta-Seymore-Lawrence, 1979) p. 62.
24. *Ibid.*, p. 149.
25. Annie Fields and Rose Lamb, *op. cit.*, p. 5.
26. Nathaniel Hawthorne, *op. cit.*, vol. 8, p. 517.
27. Celia Thaxter. *The Heavenly Guest: With Other Unpublished Writings*, ed. Oscar Laighton. (Andover, Mass: Smith & Coutts Co. Printers, 1935) p. 17.
28. W. S. Tryon. *Parnassus Corner: A Life of James T. Fields, Publisher to the Victorians.* (Boston: Houghton Mifflin Co., 1963) p. 382.
29. *Ibid.*, p. 367.
30. Annie Fields and Rose Lamb, *op. cit.*, p. 88.
31. Walter Barnes. *The Children's Poets.* (Younker-on-Hudson, New York: World Book Co., 1925) p. 234.
32. Ann Douglas. *The Feminization of American Culture.* (New York: Avon Books, 1978) pp. 6-9.
33. Albert Gelpi. "Emily Dickinson and the Deerslayer," *Shakespeare's Sisters*, ed. Sandra Gilbert and Susan Gubar, (Bloomington, Indiana: University Press, 1979) pp. 123-134.
34. John Albee. "Memories of Celia Thaxter," *The Heavenly Guest: With Other Unpublished Writings*. Ed. Oscar Laighton, (Andover, Mass: Smith & Coutts Co. Printers, 1935) p. 167.
35. Margaret Fuller, *op. cit.*, p. 38.
36. Adrienne Rich. *Snapshots of a Daughter-in-Law. Poems 1964-62.* (New York: W. W. Norton & Co., 1967) p. 36.

Chapter One

1. Rutledge, Lyman. *The Isles of Shoals in Lore and Legend.* (Boston, The Star Island Corporation, 1965) pp. 61-66.
2. Thaxter, Rosamond. *Sandpiper: The Life and Letters of Celia Thaxter.* (Francestown, NH, The Golden Quill Press, 1963) p. 20.
3. McGill, Frederick T., Jr. *Letters to Celia: Written During the Years 1860-1875 to Celia Laighton Thaxter by Her Brother*

Cedric Laighton. (Boston, The Star Island Corporation, 1972) p. 130.

4. *Ibid.*, p. 28.

5. Thaxter, *op. cit.*, p. 23.

6. Unpublished letter, Celia Thaxter to Henry Wadsworth Longfellow, April 3, 1878. Ms. in Houghton Library, Harvard University.

7. Thaxter, *op. cit.*, p. 33.

8. Thaxter, *op. cit.*, p. 34.

9. Autobiographical fragment in the Isles of Shoals Room, Portsmouth, N.H., Public Library.

10. Thaxter, Rosamond. Interview on June 15, 1979 at Kittery Point, Me.

11. Thaxter, *op. cit.*, p. 30.

12. Thaxter, *op. cit.*, p. 29.

13. Hawthorne, Nathaniel. *The American Notebooks*, ed. by Randall Stewart, New Haven, Yale University Press, 1932, pp. 271–272.

14. Fields, Annie and Rose Lamb. *Letters of Celia Thaxter*, (Boston, Houghton and Mifflin and Co., 1895) p. 4.

15. *Ibid.*, p. 9.

16. *Ibid.*, p. 11.

17. Unpublished letters from Celia Thaxter to her son John Thaxter, March 27, 1876–June 22, 1885. Portsmouth, N.H., Public Library.

18. This photograph can be seen in the Thaxter-Laighton Museum in the Henry G. Vaughn Memorial Cottage on Star Island.

19. Fields, *op. cit.*, p. 15.

20. Fields, *op. cit.*, p. 16.

21. Thaxter, *op. cit.*, pp. 177–179. See also Louise Greer. *Browning in America*, (Chapel Hill, The University of North Carolina Press, 1952,(pp. 157–159.

22. Wells, Mary. *Dear Preceptor: The Life and Times of Thomas Wentworth Higginson*. (Boston, Houghton-Mifflin and Co., 1963) p. 70.

Chapter Two

1. Thomas H. Johnson (ed.,) *The Complete Poems of Emily Dickinson*. (Boston, Little, Brown & Co., 1960) p. 333.

2. Annie Fields and Rose Lamb (eds.,) *The Poems of Celia*

Thaxter. (Appledore Edition,) (Boston, Houghton, Mifflin &
Co., 1896) pp. 5-9. Most quotations from Thaxter's poetry will
come from the Appledore Edition unless otherwise stated.
Hereater the notation "AE" will denote the Appledore Edi-
tion.

3. Richard Cary. "The Multi-colored Spirit of Celia Thaxter,"
Colby College Quarterly, Series VI, No. 12, Dec. 1964, p. 518.

4. Adrienne Rich. *Snapshots of a Daughter-In-Law. Poems
1954-62.* (New York, W. W. Norton & Co., 1967) p. 36.

5. AE, *op. cit.*, pp. 1-2.

6. Tillie Olsen. *Silences.* (New York, Delacorte Press/Seymour
Lawrence 1978) p. 6.

7. H. W. Garrod (ed.,) *The Poetical Works of John Keats.* (Lon-
don, Oxford University Press, 1962) p. 208.

8. Johnson, *op. cit.*, p. 249.

9. Maud Bodkin, *Archetypal Patterns in Poetry: Psychological
Studies of Imagination.* (London, Oxford University Press,
1934) p. 13.

10. John Cody. *After Great Pain: The Inner Life of Emily
Dickinson.* (The Belknap Press of Harvard Univ. Press, Cam-
bridge, Mass., 1971) pp. 303-311.

11. *Ibid.*, p. 304.

12. *Ibid.*, p. 304.

13. *Ibid.*, p. 305.

14. AE, *op. cit.*, p. 3.

15. Frederick T. McGill, Jr. *Letters to Celia: Written During
the Years 1860-1875 to Celia Laighton Thaxter by Her Brother
Cedric Laighton.* Boston, The Star Island Corporation, 1972,
p. 52.

16. Mary Wells. *Dear Preceptor: The Life and Times of
Thomas Wentworth Higginson.* (Boston, Houghton-Mifflin
and Co., 1963) p. 298.

17. *Ibid.*, p. 188.

18. Rosamond Thaxter. *Sandpiper: The Life and Letters of
Celia Thaxter.* Francestown, N.H., The Golden Quill Press,
1963, p. 173.

19. Annie Fields and Rose Lamb. *Letters of Celia Thaxter.*
(Boston, Houghton and Mifflin and Co., 1895) p. 23.

20. AE, *op. cit.*, p. 24.

21. Fields, *Letters, op. cit.*, p. 26.

22. AE, *op. cit.*, p. 32.

23. AE, *op. cit.*, pp. 25-27.

24. Johnson, *op. cit.*, p. 252.

25. AE, *op. cit.*, p. 37.

26. Fields, *Letters, op. cit.*, p. 26.

27. Johnson, *op. cit.*, p. 115.

28. AE, *op. cit.*, pp. 6, 177.

29. H. E. Scudder (ed.) *The Complete Poetical Works of James Russell Lowell.* Cambridge, Mass., p. 106.

30. Thaxter to A. Fields. Feb. 7, 1872. Papers of Annie Fields, Boston Public Library, Boston, Mass. Some of the letters in this collection have been edited by Alice Downey, Nottingham, N.H. Mrs. Downey has generously shared her editions of these letters with me. Some of these editions were printed in *A Stern and Lovely Scene: A Visual History of the Isles of Shoals*, a catalogue to an exhibit presented at the University Art Galleries, University of New Hampshire, 1978. The letters of Annie Fields remain, for the most part, unedited.

31. Sandra M. Gilbert and Susan Gubar. *The Madwoman in the Attic: The Woman Writer and the Nineteenth-Century Literary Imagination.* (New Haven, Yale University Press, 1979) p. 60.

32. Elaine Showalter. *A Literature of Their Own.* (Princeton, Princeton University Press, 1977) pp. 73-99.

33. Thaxter, R., *op. cit.*, pp. 204-205.

34. Theodore Roethke. "The Poetry of Louise Bogan," in *Selected Prose of Theodore Roethke.* Ed. Ralph J. Mills, Jr., (Seattle: University of Washington Press, 1965) pp. 133-134.

35. AE, *op. cit.*, p. 41.

36. Fields, *Letters, op. cit.*, p. 44.

37. AE, *op. cit.*, p. 20.

38. Thaxter, R., *op. cit.*, p. 115.

39. Fields, *Letters, op. cit.*, pp. 69-70.

40. *Ibid.*

Chapter Three

1. Thomas H. Johnson (ed.,) *The Complete Poems of Emily Dickinson.* (Boston, Little, Brown & Co., 1960) p. 703.

2. Annie Fields and Rose Lamb. *Letters of Celia Thaxter.* (Boston, Houghton and Mifflin & Co., 1894) p. 26.

3. Frederick T. McGill, Jr. *Letters to Celia: Written During the Years 1860-1875 to Celia Laighton Thaxter by Her Brother Cedric Laighton.* (Boston, The Star Island Corporation, 1972) p. 252.

4. John B. Pickard (ed.) *The Letters of John Greenleaf Whittier: 1861-1892.* Vol. 3, Cambridge, Mass., The Belknap Press, Harvard University Press, 1975, p. 228.

5. Elizabeth Stuart Phelps. *Chapters from a Life.* (Boston, Houghton-Mifflin & Co., 1897) p. 175.

6. William Dean Howells. *Literary Friends and Acquain-*

tances: A Personal Retrospect of American Authorship.
Edited by David F. Hiatt and Edwin H. Cady, (Bloomington
and London, Indiana University Press, 1968) p. 107.

7. Sandra M. Gilbert and Susan Gubar. *The Madwoman in the
Attic: The Woman Writer and the Nineteenth-Century
Literary Imagination.* (New Haven, Yale University Press,
1979) p. 44.

8. Gilbert and Gubar, *op. cit.,* p. 51.

9. Unpublished letter, Celia Thaxter to Annie Fields, Nov. 3,
1872, Boston Public Library, transcribed by Alice Downey.

10. Robert and Seon Manley. *Islands: Their Lives, Legends
and Lore.* (Philadelphia, Chilton Books, 1970) p. 786.

11. B. A. Botkin. *A Treasury of New England Folklore.* (New
York, Crown Publishers, 1947) p. 177–183. Botkin quotes ex-
tensively from Thaxter's *Among the Isles of Shoals,* and
praises Mrs. Thaxter's skill as a folklorist. He finds her work
highly reliable.

12. Fields, *AE, op. cit.,* p. 61.

13. Rosamond Thaxter. *Sandpiper: The Life and Letters of
Celia Thaxter.* (Francestown, N.H. The Golden Quill Press,
1963) p. 284.

14. Fields, *AE, op. cit.,* p. 66.

15. R. Thaxter, *op. cit.,* p. 97.

16. Fields, *Letters, op. cit.,* pp. 49–50.

17. Unpublished letter, Celia Thaxter to Annie Fields, March
7, 1878, Portsmouth Public Library.

18. Unpublished letter, Celia Thaxter to Annie Fields, March
7, 1878, Boston Public Library, transcribed by Alice Downey.

19. Mary Wells. *Dear Preceptor: The Life and Times of
Thomas Wentworth Higginson.* (Boston, Houghton Mifflin &
Co., 1963) p. 276.

20. Unpublished letter, Celia Thaxter to Elizabeth Whittier, no
date, Portsmouth Public Library.

21. Pickard, *op. cit.,* p. 596.

22. *Ibid.,* p. 601.

23. Unpublished letter, Celia Thaxter to John G. Whittier,
Jan. 31, 1874, Portsmouth Public Library.

24. Pickard, *op. cit.,* p. 613.

25. Fields, *AE, op. cit.,* p. 100.

26. Gilbert and Gubar, *op. cit.,* p. 59.

27. Celia Thaxter, autobiographical fragment, Portsmouth
Public Library, pp. 25–26.

28. *Ibid.,* p. 10.

29. *Ibid.,* p. 9.

30. *Ibid.,* pp. 3–4.

31. *Ibid.,* p. 18.

32. *Ibid.*, pp. 15-16.

33. Unpublished letter, Celia Thaxter to John G. Whittier, Jan. 31, 1874, Portsmouth Public Library.

34. R. Thaxter, *op. cit.*, pp. 130-131.

35. Unpublished letter, Celia Thaxter to Annie Fields, Jan. 17, 1877, Boston Public Library, transcribed by Alice Downey.

36. Unpublished letter, Celia Thaxter to Annie Fields, Nov. 30, 1888, Boston Public Library, transcribed by Alice Downey.

37. Unpublished letter, Celia Thaxter to Annie Fields, 1892, Boston Public Library, transcribed by Alice Downey.

38. Ellen B. Ballou. *The Building of the House: Houghton Mifflin's Formative Years.* (Boston, Houghton Mifflin Co., 1970) p. 201.

39. Unpublished letter, Celia Thaxter to Annie Fields, May 1, 1877, Boston Public Library, transcribed by Alice Downey.

Chapter Four

1. Thomas H. Johnson (ed.,) *The Complete Poems of Emily Dickinson.* (Boston, Little, Brown & Co., 1960) p. 460.

2. Mary Wells. *Dear Preceptor: The Life and Times of Thomas Wentworth Higginson.* (Boston, Houghton Mifflin Co., 1963) p. 278.

3. Parnassus Book Service. Yarmouth Port, on Cape Cod Mass.

4. Letters are on file in the Portsmouth Public Library in the Isles of Shoals Room.

5. Daniel R. Addison (ed.). *Lucy Larcom: Life, Letters and Diary.* (Boston, Houghton Mifflin Co., 1895) p. 164.

6. Walter Barnes. *The Children's Poets.* Younkers on Hudson, N.Y., World Book Co., 1955, p. 233.

7. *Ibid.*, p. 234.

8. Celia Thaxter. *Stories and Poems for Children.* (Boston & New York, Houghton Mifflin Co., 1883) p. 137.

9. *Ibid.*, p. 165.

10. Perry D. Westbrook, "Celia Thaxter: Seeker of the Unattainable." *Colby Library Quarterly*, Series VI, No. 12, Dec. 1964, p. 502.

11. Annie Fields and Rose Lamb (eds.,) *The Poems of Celia Thaxter.* (Appledore Edition,) (Boston, Houghton Mifflin Co., 1896) p. 242.

12. Nathaniel Hawthorne. *The American Notebooks.* (Columbus, Ohio State University Press, 1974) vol. 8, p. 516.

13. Annie Fields and Rose Lamb. *Letters of Celia Thaxter.* (Boston, Houghton and Mifflin Co., 1895) p. xxviii.

14. Rosamond Thaxter. *Sandpiper: The Life and Letters of Celia Thaxter*. (Francestown, N.H., The Golden Quill Press, 1963) p. 221.
15. Fields, *AE, op. cit.*, p. 199.
16. *Ibid.*, p. 218.
17. Fields, *Letters, op. cit.*, p. xxv. See also R. Thaxter, *op. cit.*, pp. 163-165.
18. Theodore Roethke. *The Collected Poems of Theodore Roethke*. (New York, Doubleday & Co., Inc., 1966) p. 102.
19. R. Thaxter, *op. cit.*, p. 192.
20. Fields, *AE, op. cit.*, p. 220.
21. Celia Thaxter. *The Heavenly Guest: With Other Unpublished Writings*. Edited by Oscar Laighton, (Andover, Mass., Smith & Coutts Co. Printers, 1935) p. 17.
22. Fields, *AE, op. cit.*, p. 165.
23. R. Thaxter, *op. cit.*, p. 228.
24. *Verses* was found in the Isles of Shoals Room of the Portsmouth Public Library, Portsmouth, N.H.
25. *Ibid.*
26. *Ibid.*
27. *Ibid.*

Chapter Five

1. Annie Fields and Rose Lamb (eds.,) *The Poems of Celia Thaxter*. (Appledore Edition,) (Boston, Houghton Mifflin Co., 1896) p. 19.
2. Thomas H. Johnson (ed.,) *The Complete Poems of Emily Dickinson*. (Boston, Little, Brown & Co., 1960) p. 677.
3. Christoper Ricks. *The Poetry of Tennyson*. (New York, W. W. Norton & Co., 1969) p. 1458.
4. All obituaries and reviews, unless otherwise footnoted, were found in the Thaxter family scrapbook now in the hands of Miss Rosamond Thaxter of Kittery Point, Maine. Miss Thaxter graciously and generously allowed me to read and make copies of all materials in her personal library, a room which contains Celia Thaxter's furniture, books, paintings, and many personal items. These notes were made on June 15, 1979. The scrapbook was assembed by Miss Thaxter's mother, Mary Gertrude Stoddard Thaxter who was an admirer of Celia Thaxter's work long before she married John Thaxter, Celia's second son, on June 1, 1887. Most of the clippings in the scrapbook are not identified either as to date or newspaper. Mary Gertrude Stoddard seemed willing to collect the unfavorable reviews as well as the favorable ones. A complete list of

reviews and obituaries published in the major newspapers of the day has been taken from the P. M. Loving bibliography.

5. Fields, *AE, op. cit.*, p. iii.

6. *Ibid.*, p. 5.

7. *Ibid.*, p. 41.

8. Elizabeth Stuart Phelps. *Chapters from a Life.* (Boston, Houghton Mifflin Co., 1897) p. 175.

9. S. G. W. Benjamin. *The Atlantic Islands—As Resorts of Health and Pleasure.* (New York, Harper and Bros., 1878) p. 213.

10. William Dean Howells. *Literary Friends and Acquaintances: A Personal Retrospect of American Authorship.* Edited by David F. Hiatt and Edwin H. Cady, (Bloomington and London, Indiana University Press, 1968) p. 107.

11. The Isles of Shoals Room, Portsmouth Public Library, Portsmouth, N.H.

12. Celia Thaxter. *The Heavenly Guest: With Other Unpublished Writings.* Edited by Oscar Laighton, (Andover, Mass., Smith & Coutts Co. Printers, 1935) pp. 155-160.

13. Nina Baym. *Women's Fiction: A Guide to Novels by and about Women in America, 1820-1870.* (Ithaca, N.Y., Cornell University Press, 1978) p. 15.

14. Edgar Allan Poe. *Complete Works.* Edited by James A. Harrison, (17 volumes) (New York, Thomas Y. Crowell Co., 1902) vol. XVI, p. 12.

15. Annie Fields and Rose Lamb. *Letters of Celia Thaxter.* (Boston, Houghton and Mifflin and Co., 1895) p. 8.

16. *Ibid.*, p. 5.

17. Ruth Finnegan. *Oral Poetry: Its Nature, Significance, and Social Context.* (New York, The Cambridge University Press, 1977) p. 28.

18. M. A. DeWolfe Howe. *Memories of a Hostess.* (Boston, Atlantic Monthly Press, 1922) p. 98.

19. Fields, *Letters, op. cit.*, p. xxxviii.

20. Finnegan, *op. cit.*, p. 25.

21. Fields, *Letters, op. cit.*, p. 56.

22. Johnson, *op. cit.*, p. 678.

A Bibliography of the Works of Celia Thaxter

Poems. New York, Hurd and Houghton, 1872, 1874, 1876.

Among the Isles of Shoals. Boston, J. R. Osgood & Co., 1873; Houghton Mifflin Co., 1899, 1901. Bowie, Md., Heritage Books, 1978.

Drift-Weed. Boston, Houghton, Osgood & Co., 1879; Houghton Mifflin Co., 1894.

Poems for Children. Boston, Houghton Mifflin Co., 1883, 1884.

The Cruise of the Mystery, and other Poems. Boston, Houghton Mifflin Co., 1886.

Idyls and Pastorals: A Home Gallery of Poetry and Art. Boston, Lothrop & Co., 1886.

Yule Log. New York, Prang, 1889.

My Lighthouse, and Other Poems. Boston, Prang, 1890.

Verses. Boston, Lothrop, 1891.

An Island Garden. Boston, Houghton Mifflin Co., 1894, 1904. Bowie, Md., Heritage Books, 1978.

Stories and Poems for Children. Boston, Houghton Mifflin Co., 1895, 1896, 1906.

Letters of Celia Thaxter. Edited by Annie Fields and Rose Lamb. Boston, Houghton Mifflin Co., 1895, 1897.

The Poems of Celia Thaxter. Edited by Annie Fields and Rose Lamb. Appledore Edition. Boston, Houghton Mifflin Co., 1896, 1899, 1902, 1906.

The Heavenly Guest. Edited by Oscar Laighton, Andover, Mass., Smith & Coutts, 1935.

Sandpiper, and Sandalphon. Taylorville, Ill., Parker Publishing Co., n.d.

Maize, the Nation's Emblem. Taylorville, Ill., Parker Publishing Co., n.d.

A Bibliography of Secondary Sources

Addison, Daniel Dulaney. *Lucy Larcom—Life, Letters, and Diary*. Boston: Houghton Mifflin Company, 1894.

Austin, James C. *Fields of the Atlantic Monthly: Letters to an Editor, 1861-1870*. San Marino, California, Huntington Library, 1953.

Ballou, Ellen B. *The Building of the House: Houghton Mifflin's Formative Years*. Boston, Houghton Mifflin Company, 1970.

Barnes, Walter. *The Children's Poets*. Younker-on-Hudson, N.Y., World Book Company, 1925.

Baym, Nina A. *Women's Fiction: A Guide to Novels by and about Women in America 1820-1870*. Ithaca, New York, Cornell University Press, 1978.

Benjamin, S.G.W. *The Atlantic Islands—As Resorts of Health and Pleasure*. New York, Harper and Brothers, Publishers, 1878.

Blanchard, Paula. *Margaret Fuller: From Transcendentalism to Revolution*. New York, Dell Publishing Company, Inc., 1978.

Bodkin, Maud. *Archetypal Patterns in Poetry: Psychological Studies of Imagination*. London, Oxford University Press, 1934.

Botkin, B.A. *A Treasury of New England Folklore*. New York, Crown Publishers, 1947.

Brooks, Van Wyck. *New England Indian Summer*. New York, E.P. Dutton and Company, 1940.

_____. *The Confident Years 1885-1915*. New York, E.P. Dutton and Company, 1952.

Carter, Everett. *Howells and the Age of Realism*. Hamden, Conn., Archon Books, 1966.

Cary, Richard. "The Multi-Colored Spirit of Celia Thaxter." *Colby College Library Quarterly* vol. 6 (Dec. 1964), pp. 512-536.

Cody, John. *After Great Pain: The Inner Life of Emily Dickinson*. Cambridge, Mass., Harvard University Press, 1971.

"Celia Thaxter's Grave and Garden." *Literary World* 30:265, (August 19, 1899).

De Piza, Mary Dickson. *Celia Thaxter: Poet of the Isles of Shoals.* Unpublished Doctoral Dissertation, University of Pennsylvania, 1955.

Douglas, Ann Wood. *The Feminization of American Culture.* New York, Avon Books, 1978.

Fields, Annie Adams. *Authors and Friends.* Boston, Houghton Mifflin Company, 1897.

_____ (Ed.) *Letters of Sarah Orne Jewett.* Boston, Houghton Mifflin Company, 1911.

_____. *A Shelf of Old Books.* New York, Scribner's Sons, 1894.

Fields, James. *Yesterdays with Authors.* Boston, Houghton Mifflin Company, 1882.

Finnegan, Ruth. *Oral Poetry: Its Nature, Significance and Social Content.* New York, Cambridge University Press, 1977.

Fuller, Margaret. *Woman in the Nineteenth Century.* Originally published in Boston by Roberts Brothers, 1874; Reprinted in Westport, Conn. by Greenwood Press, 1968.

Garrod, H.W., ed. *The Poetical Works of John Keats.* London, Oxford University Press, 1962.

Gilbert, Sandra and Susan Gubar, eds. *Shakespeare's Sisters: Feminist Essays on Women Poets.* Bloomington, University of Indiana Press, 1979.

_____. *Mad Woman in the Attic: The Woman Writer and the Nineteenth Century Literary Imagination.* New Haven and London, Yale University Press, 1979.

Greer, Louise. *Browning and America.* Chapel Hill, North Carolina University Press, 1952.

Hawthorne, Nathaniel. *The American Notebooks.* Columbus, Ohio State University Press, 1974.

Higginson, Mary Thacher. *Letters and Journals of Thomas Wentworth Higginson.* Boston, Houghton Mifflin Company, 1915.

Higginson, Thomas Wentworth. *Cheerful Yesterdays.* Boston, Houghton Mifflin Company, 1898.

Howe, Mark Anthony DeWolfe. *Memories of a Hostess: A Chronicle of Eminent Friendships Drawn Chiefly from the Diaries of Mrs. J. T. Fields.* Boston, St. Martin's Press, 1922.

_____. *the Atlantic Monthly and Its Makers.* Boston, Atlantic Montly Press, Inc., 1919.

Howells, William Dean. *Literary Friends and Acquaintances: A Personal Retrospect of American Authorship.* Edited by David F. Hiatt and Edwin H. Cady, Bloomington, University of Indiana Press, 1968.

Jackson, Helen Hunt. *Poems.* New York, Arno Press, 1972.

Johnson, Thomas (Ed.) *The Complete Poems of Emily Dickinson.* Little, Brown and Company, 1960.

Juhasz, Suzanne. *Naked and Fiery Forms: Modern American Poetry by Women. A New Tradition.* New York, Colophon Books, 1976.

Kaplan, Cora. *Salt and Bitter and Good—Three Centuries of English and American Women Poets.* New York, Paddington Press, Ltd., 1975.

Kuntz, Joseph M. *A Checklist of Interpretations Since 1925 of British and American Poems, Past and Present.* Denver, Swallow Press, 1962.

Laighton, Oscar. "The Heavenly Guest," *New England Quarterly*, 8:518–533, (Dec. 1935).

———. *Ninety Years at the Isles of Shoals.* Boston, The Star Island Corporation, 1971.

Lee, G. S. "Celia Thaxter," *Critic* 28 (ns25), 209–210, (March 28, 1896).

Loving, P.M. *Bio-Bibliography of Celia Laighton Thaxter, 1835–1894.* Unpublished Master's Thesis in Library Science, University of Minnesota, 1966.

Manley, Seon and Robert. *Islands: Their Lives, Legends and Lore.* Philadelphia, Chilton Books, 1970.

Martin, Jay. *Harvests of Change: American Literature 1865–1914.* Englewood Cliffs, N.J., Prentice Hall, 1967.

McGill, Frederick T., ed. *Letters to Celia: Written During the Years 1860-1875 by Her Brother Cedric Laighton.* Boston, The Star Island Corporation, 1972.

McMahon, Helen. *Criticism of Fiction: A Study of Trends in the Atlantic Monthly, 1857-1898.* New York, Bookman Associates, 1952. Reprinted New York, AMS Press, 1973.

Mills, Ralph J., Jr., ed. "The Poetry of Louise Bogan," *Selected Prose of Theodore Roethke.* Seattle, University of Washington Press, 1965.

Moore, Isabel. *Talks in a Library with Laurence Hutton.* New York, G.P. Putnam's Sons, 1905.

Olsen, Tillie. *Silences.* New York, Delacourte Press/Seymour Lawrence, 1978.

Pachter, Mark, ed. *Telling Lives: The Biographer's Art.* Washington D.C.: New Republic/National Portrait Gallery, 1979.

Pattee, F.L. *A History of American Literature Since 1870.* New York, The Century Company, 1915.

_____. *Sidelights on American Literature.* The Century Company, 1922.

Pearce, Roy Harvey. *The Continuity of American Poetry.* Princeton: Princeton University Press, 1961.

Pickard, John, B., ed. *The Letters of John Greenleaf Whittier.* Cambridge, Mass., Belknap Press of Harvard University Press, 1975.

_____. *Memorabilia of John Greenleaf Whittier.* Hartford, Conn., Emerson Society, 1968.

Poe, Edgar Allan. *Complete Works.* Edited by James A. Harrison, 17 volumes, New York, Thomas Y. Crowell Company, vol. XVI, 1902.

Pollard, John A. *John Greenleaf Whittier: Friend of Man.* Boston, Archon Books, 1969.

Rich, Adrienne. *Snapshots of a Daughter-In-Law. Poems 1954-62.* New York, W.W. Norton and Co., 1967.

Ricks, Christopher, ed. *The Poetry of Tennyson.* New York, W.W. Norton and Company, Inc., 1969.

Rutledge, Lyman. *The Isles of Shoals in Lore and Legend.* Boston, The Star Island Corporation, 1965.

Scudder, Horace E., ed. *The Complete Poetical Works of James Russell Lowell.* Boston, Houghton Mifflin Company, 1898.

Segnitz, Barbara and Carol Rainey. *Psyche: The Feminine Poetic Consciousness.* New York, The Dial Press, 1973.

Shaw, John Mackay. *The Poems, Poets and Illustrators of St. Nicholas Magazine, 1873-1943: An Index.* Tallahassee, Florida State University Press, 1965.

Showalter, Elaine. *A Literature of Their Own.* Princeton, N.J., Princeton University Press, 1977.

Spacks, Patricia Meyer. *The Female Imagination.* New York, Avon Books, 1975.

Spiller, Robert E. *The Cycle of American Literature: An Essay in Historical Criticism.* New York, The Free Press, 1955.

_____ et al., eds. *The Literary History of the United States.* Fourth Edition. New York, Macmillan, 1974.

Spofford, Harriet Prescott. *A Little Book of Friends.* Boston, Little, Brown and Company, 1916.

Stearns, F.P. *Sketches from Concord and Appledore.* New York, G.P. Putnam's Sons, 1895.

Stedman, Edmund Clarence. *Poets of America.* Boston, Houghton Mifflin Company, 1913.

A Stern and Lovely Scene: A Visual History of the Isles of Shoals. Durham, N.H., University of New Hampshire Art Galleries, 1978.

Stone, Edward. *Voices of Despair.* Athens, Ohio University Press, 1966.

Stubbs, M. Wilma. "Celia Laighton Thaxter, 1835-1894." *New England Quarterly* 8 (Dec. 1935), pp. 518-533.

_____. "Celia Thaxter, Poet of Nature," *Nature Magazine* 25 (June 1935), pp. 297-298.

Thaxter, Rosamond. *Sandpiper: The Life and Letters of Celia Thaxter.* Francestown, New Hampshire, The Golden Quill Press, 1963.

Thompson, Slason. *The Humbler Poets: A Collection of Newspaper and Periodical Verse 1870-1885.*

Tryon, Warren Stenson. *Parnassus Corner: A Life of J. T. Fields, Publisher to the Victorians.* Boston, Houghton Mifflin Co. 1963.

"Unsigned Letter," *Critic* 19 (ns 16): 72 (August 15, 1891).

Vaughn, Dorothy. "Celia Thaxter's Library," *Colby College Quarterly* 6 (Dec. 1964), pp. 536-550.

Von Frank, Albert J. *Whittier: A Comprehensive Annotated Bibliography.* New York, Garland Publishers, 1976.

Walker, Robert H. *The Poet and the Gilded Age: Social Themes in Late Nineteenth Century American Verse.* New York, Octagon Books, 1969.

Ward, Elizabeth Stuart Phelps. *Chapters from a Life.* Boston, Houghton Mifflin Co., 1897.

Warren, Robert Penn. *John Greenleaf Whittier's Poetry: An Appraisal and a Selection.* Minneapolis, University of Minnesota Press, 1971.

Wells, Anna Mary. *Dear Preceptor: The Life and Times of Thomas Wentworth Higginson.* Boston, Houghton Mifflin Co., 1963.

Welter, Barbara. *Dimity Convictions: The American Woman in Nineteenth Century.* Athens, Ohio University Press, 1976.

Westbrook, Perry D. *Acres of Flint: Writers of Rural New England, 1870-1900.* Washington, D.C., Scarecrow Press, 1951.

_____. "Celia Thaxter's Controversy with Nature," *New England Quarterly* 20 (Dec. 1947), pp. 492-515.

_____. "Celia Thaxter: Seeker of the Unattainable," *Colby College Quarterly* 6 (Dec. 1964), pp. 500-512.

White, Barbara. *American Women Writers: An Annotated Bibliography of Criticism.* New York, Garland Publishing Co., 1977.
Wood, Ann Douglas. "The Literature of Impoverishment: The Women Local Colorists in America, 1865–1914," Women's Studies, 1972, vol. 1, pp. 3–45.
Ziff, Lazarus. *The America of the 1890's.* New York, Viking Press, 1966.

Index of First Lines

About your window's happy height, 186
Across the narrow beach we flit, 147
And like the lighthouse on the rock you stand, 182
As happy dwellers by the seaside hear, 186
At daybreak in the fresh light, hopefully, 154
Because I hold it sinful to despond, 160
Black lie the hills; swiftly doth daylight flee, 138
Black sea, black sky! A ponderous steamship
    driving, 170
Could you have heard the kingfisher scream and
    scold at me, 212
Crushing the scarlet strawberries in the grass, 167
Down on the north wind sweeping, 214
Fragrant and soft the summer wind doth blow, 161
From out the desolation of the North, 162
Good-by, sweet day, good-by!, 193
If God speaks anywhere, in any voice, 185, 203
I lit the lamps in the lighthouse tower, 141
I'll tell you a story children, 209
In childhood's fair season, 152
In Ipswich town, not far from the sea, 165
Lift up the light, O Soul, arise and shine!, 202
Lightly she lifts the large, pure, luminous shell, 164
Lo, I come from dreamland dim, 205
Low burns the sunset and dark is near, 204
My little granddaughter, who fain would know, 179
Not so! You stand as long ago a king, 181

Oh tell me not of heavenly halls, 196
O lightly moored the lilies lie, 206
Only to follow you, dearest, only to find you, 194
O Pilgrim, comes the night so fast?, 187
O sailors, did sweet eyes look after you, 150
O sovereign Master! stern and splendid power, 174
Rock, little boat, beneath the quiet sky, 139
Rustily creak the crickets: Jack came down, 211
September's slender crescent grows again, 148
So break these shores, wind-swept and all
    the year, 145
"Tell us a story of these isles," they said, 182
That was a curlew calling overhead, 153
The children wandered up and down, 188
The day is bitter. Through the hollow sky, 178
The old-wives sit on the heaving brine, 206
The slow, cool, emerald breakers cruising clear, 203
The steadfast planet spins through space, 197
The swallow twitters about the eaves, 149
The winter night shuts swiftly down. Within
    this little, 198
They called the little schooner the White Rover, 176
They crossed the lonely and lamenting sea, 172
This grassy gorge, as daylight failed last night, 157
Throughout the lonely house the whole day long, 140
Through the wide sky thy north wind's thunder
    roars, 169
Upon my lips she laid her touch divine, 159
Upon the sadness of the sea, 185

Index

A

Albee, John, 24
Among the Isles of Shoals
  (C. Thaxter), 25, 77
Appledore Hotel, 15, 18
Appledore Island, 17
"At the Breaker's Edge,"
  169–170
  discussion of, 77
Autobiography, of Celia
  Thaxter, 35, 90–94

B

"Before Sunrise," 157–159
"Beethoven," 185
  discussion of, 174–175
Blanchard, Paula, 3
Brook Farm, 18
Browning, Robert, 19
"The Butcher-Bird,"
  209–211
  discussion of, 107
"The Burgomaster Gull,"
  206–209

C

Cody, John, 52–53
"Contrast," 178–179
  discussion of, 87
"The Cruise of the
  Mystery," 188–192
  discussion of, 112–113
*The Cruise of the Mystery
  and Other Poems*
  (C. Thaxter), 115

D

Dickinson, Emily, 3, 52
  on sorrow, 64
Double monologue, of
  "Land-Locked," 48–50
"The Dream Peddler," 205
  discussion of, 119
Driftweed (1878, C.
  Thaxter), 82, 85, 87
  women in, 198

E

Education:
  of Celia Thaxter, 9–11
  of women, 5–6
Emerson, Ralph W., 17
"Expectation," 140–141

F

"A Faded Glove," 179–181
  discussion of, 87–88
Fields, Annie, Celia Thaxter
  letters to, 14, 15
Fields, James T., 21
  and Celia Thaxter, 58–60
  and Henry W.
  Longfellow, 22
Fireside poets, 20–23
Fuller, Margaret, 3, 5, 11
  and Celia Thaxter,
  compared, 15–17, 25
  on education of
  women, 5–6
  on Miranda, 6–7, 8
  as Transcendentalist, 13

G

Gilbert, Sandra, 2
"Good-by, Sweet Day," 193
Greely, Adolphus W., 79
Gubar, Susan 2
"Guendolen," discussion
    of, 81

H

Hawthorne, Nathaniel, 5
    at Appledore Island, 18
    on Celia Thaxter, 39, 111
"Heartbreak Hill," 165–167
    discussion of, 77–78
The Heavenly Guest (C.
    Thaxter), 121
"The Heavenly Guest,"
    198–202
"Hiawatha," (H. W.
    Longfellow), 22
Higginson, Thomas W., 17,
    37, 57
    on Celia Thaxter, 8
Hjelma, 35, 90–94
Howells, William D., 20, 75,
    129
Hoxie, Elizabeth C., 40, 69,
    132

I

"Impatience," 194–195
    discussion of, 113
"Imprisoned," 164–165
"Inhospitality," 214–216
"In Kittery Churchyard,"
    167–168
    discussion of, 80–81
"In May," 153–154
An Island Garden (C.
    Thaxter), 15, 25

J

"Jack Frost," 211–212
    discussion of, 107

James, Henry, 21
Jewett, Sarah Orne, 127
Johnson, Thomas, 3

K

Keats, John, 50–51
"The Kingfisher," 212–214

L

Laighton, Cedric, 74
Laighton, Celia, *see*
    Thaxter, Celia
Laighton, Eliza, 77
    death of, 84
Laighton Hotels, 29
Laighton, Thomas, 6, 27–29
"Land-Locked," 138
    death imagery in, 51
    discussion of, 22, 43,
        49–51
    double monologue
        of, 48–50
    publication of in the
        Atlantic, 48
    sexual theme in, 53
    symbol of the sea in,
        52–53
Larcom, Lucy, 23, 105–106
"Lars," 182–184
Letters (1895, C. Thaxter),
    125
Longfellow, Henry W., 22
    influence of on C.
        Thaxter, 31
"Lost," 204
    discussion of, 119
"Love Shall Save Us All,"
    187
Lowell, James R., 20, 48

M

*The Madwoman in the
    Attic: The Woman
    Writer and the*

Nineteenth Century Literary Imagination (Gubar and Gilbert), 2

A Memorable Murder (1875, C. Thaxter), 217–244
discussion of, 82

Miranda, Margaret Fuller on, 6–7, 8–9

Mitchell, S. W., 17

"Mutation," 186–187

N

Newtonville, life in, 38–39, 41, 43, 84–85

O

"Ode to a Nightingale" (Keats), 50–51

"Off Shore," 139–140
discussion of, 54

"Oh Tell Me not of Heavenly Halls," 196

Olsen, Tillie, 50

"On Quiet Waters," 206
discussion of, 120

"On the Beach," 203–204
discussion of, 119–120

"O were I loved as I desire to be," discussion of, 117

P

Pain, in Celia Thaxter's poetry, 63–64

Phelps, Elizabeth S., 22, 23, 75, 128–129

Poe, Edgar A., 131

Poems (1872, C. Thaxter), 76

Poems (1874, C. Thaxter), 76

Poems (Appledore Edition, 1896, C. Thaxter), 125, 127

Poets:
fireside, 20–23
women, 132–133

Q

"Questions," 197–198
discussion of, 109

R

Religion, and Celia Thaxter, 22–24, 69–71, 108–109, 111

"Remembrance," 161

Repression, of female writers, 1–3

Rich, Adrienne, 25

"Rock Little Boat,"
discussion of, 120–121

"Rock Weeds," 145
discussion of, 64–65

S

"The Sandpiper," 147
discussion of, 76, 107

Sea, symbolism of, 52–53

Sexuality
in "Rock Weeds," 64
theme of in poetry, 53–55

Showalter, Elaine, 65

Sigourney, Lydia, 64, 131

Silence, in Celia Thaxter's poetry, 69

"Song," 202

"A Song of Hope,"
discussion of, 114

Sonnets, of Celia Thaxter, 117–118, 181–182, 186, 203

"Sorrow," 159–160
discussion of, 63

Sorrow, in Celia Thaxter's poetry, 63–64

"The Spaniards Graves,"
    150-151
  discussion of, 60-61
Spiller, Robert, 1-2
Star Island, life on, 39
*Stories and Poems for
    Children* (1883, C.
    Thaxter), 105
"A Summer Day," 154-157
"The Sunrise Never Failed
    Us Yet," 185-186
"The Swallow," 149-150
  discussion of, 69
Symbolism, of the sea,
    52-53

T

Thaxter, Celia, 2-3
  adulthood of, 14
  in autobiography, 33, 35,
    37, 90
  and the Brownings, 19
  childhood of, 7, 27-32
  classifying, 24-25
  control of by the Fieldses,
    22
  death of, 124
  education of, 6, 9-11, 29
  female experience of,
    75-76
  financial worries of,
    95-96
  "first story" of, 4
  as freelance writer, 96,
    103
  heart disease in, 119
  and her sons, 41, 84,
    104-105
  as "Island Miranda," 5
  and John G. Whittier, 58
  and James T. Fields,
    58-60
  "Land-Locked" by, 47-54
  letters of to Annie Fields,
    14, 15

  and Levi Thaxter, 32-33,
    38, 43, 47, 55-56, 82-84
  life of in Newtonville,
    38-39, 41, 43, 84-85
  and Margaret Fuller,
    compared, 15-17, 25
  married life of, 38, 39-40
  paintings of, 101
  poetry of:
    appreciation of, 130-131
    children's, 106-107
    on her mother's death,
      113-115
    readings of, 19-20,
      133-134
    silence in, 50, 69
    sorrow in, 63-64
    unsigned, 62
  as popular artist,
    102-103, 111-112
  and the price of success,
    73-74, 86
  and religion, 22-24,
    69-71, 108-109, 111
  romantic life of, 94-95
  "second story" of, 4
  sonnets of, 117-118
  as storyteller, 105-106
  symbol of the sea, 52-53
  on White Island, 29, 31
Thaxter, John, 41, 104-105
Thaxter, Karl, 38, 41
Thaxter, Levi, 5
  on Appledore Island, 18
  attraction to Celia
    Thaxter, 56-58
  and Celia Thaxter's
    education, 13, 32, 43-44
  death of, 101, 103
  engagement of to Celia
    Thaxter, 32-33
  failures of, 12, 38-39, 43
  married life of, 38
  as reader of Browning,
    19, 44
  and Transcendentalism, 9

Ticknor and Fields, 21
Transcendentalism, 11–12
  and Levi Thaxter, 9
  of Margaret Fuller, 13
  and women's rights, 12
"A Tryst," 162–164
  discussion of, 78–81
Twain, Mark, 20
"Twilight," 148
"Two," discussion of,
  116–117

V

Verses (1891, C. Thaxter),
  118–119

W

"Watching," 152–153
  discussion of, 31, 61–62
"The Watch of Boon
  Island," 172–174
Weiss, J., 18
Westbrook, Perry, 108
"Wherefore," 170–171
White Island, life on, 18,
  29, 31
"The White Rover,"
  176–178

Whittier, John G., 17,
  74–75
  and Celia Thaxter, 58,
  86–87
  on "The Faded Glove,"
  87–88
  on "The Wreck of the
  Pocahontas," 66
"Wild Nights" (E.
  Dickinson), 52
Women:
  in Celia Thaxter's
  autobiography, 91–93
  in Driftweed poems, 89
  education and, 5–6
  lack of elegies for, 14
  as poets, 132–133
  rights of, 12–13
  as writers, 1–2, 65, 66–67
Women in the Nineteenth
  Century (M. Fuller), 5, 6,
  14
Woolf, Virginia, 10
"The Wreck of the
  Pocahontas," 141–145
  discussion of, 31, 66–68
Writers, women, 1–2, 65,
  66–67